MARIETTA WETHERILL

REFLECTIONS ON LIFE WITH THE NAVAJOS IN CHACO CANYON

EDITED AND COMPILED BY
KATHRYN GABRIEL

INTRODUCTORY ESSAY BY
ELIZABETH JAMESON

JOHNSON BOOKS: BOULDER

For Lou Blachly,
who interviewed Marietta Wetherill;
for Eloisa Bergère Brown,
on behalf of another pioneer, Eloisa Luna;
and, as always, for my husband,
David Loving.

© 1992 by Kathryn Gabriel

Cover illustration by Molly Gough inspired by a photograph of
Marietta Wetherill taken in 1904.

Library of Congress Cataloging-in-Publication Data

Wetherill, Marietta, 1876-1954.
    Marietta Wetherill: reflections on life with the Navajos in Chaco
Canyon / [edited by] Kathryn Gabriel.
        p.   cm.
    ISBN 1-55566-090-8
    1. Wetherill, Marietta, 1876-1954. 2. Indianists—New Mexico—
Chaco Canyon—Biography. 3. Folklorists—New Mexico—Chaco
Canyon—Biography. 4. Navajo Indians —Social life and customs.
I. Gabriel, Kathryn. II. Title.
E76.45.W47A3   1992   92-9391
978.9'82—dc20   CIP

Printed in the United States of America by
Johnson Printing
1880 South 57th Court
Boulder, Colorado 80301

Contents

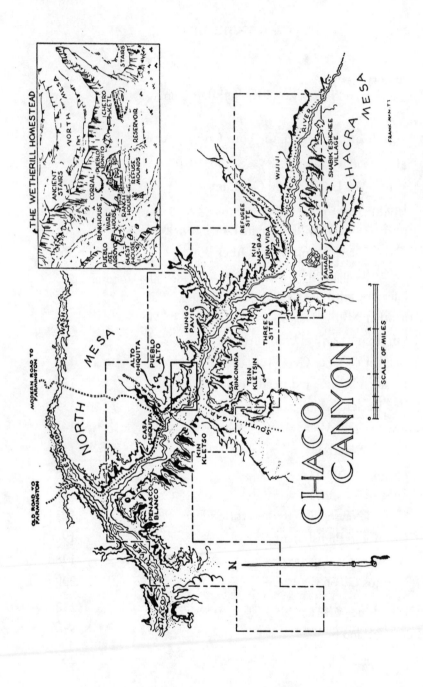

Map of Chaco Canyon and Wetherill homestead by Frank McNitt from his book, *Richard Wetherill: Anasazi*, University of New Mexico Press, 1966. Courtesy University of New Mexico Press.

Introductory Essay

SEX, LIVES, AND HISTORY
BY
ELIZABETH JAMESON
Associate Professor, History
University of New Mexico

What matters is that lives do not serve as models; only stories do that. And it is a hard thing to make up stories to live by. We can only retell and live by the stories we have read or heard. We live our lives through texts. They may be read or chanted, or experienced electronically, or come to us, like the murmurings of our mothers, telling us what conventions demand. Whatever their form or medium, these stories have formed us all; they are what we must use to make new fictions, new narratives.[1]
—Carolyn G. Heilbrun
Writing a Woman's Life

WESTERN HISTORY, like most history, is a story. Told from a particular point of view, it has a beginning and an end, both chosen by the chronicler. As a story that provides a model of our shared past, it is as important for whom and what it omits as for the collective legacy it creates.[2]

History is, in fact, many stories, enacted by many players, told from different vantage points in the drama. Told and retold, it renegotiates our relationships between how we see the present and how we think we got there. Our dialogues with the past are also dialogues with our experience. They allow us to see new possibilities, new actors, new outcomes in the story. Viewed in this way, Marietta Wetherill's spoken narrative is simultaneously her own dialogue with her life, as she gives it shape and meaning and decides what mattered, and a story that pushes us to confront our own scripts of men's and women's lives, our own notions of how history happens.

For the past several decades, many historians have been writing new narratives of the American West. These accounts are more conflicted, include more actors, and are less heroic than the popular West of film and legend.[3] Older western histories provided a stock series of stories, mostly adventure tales, seen and told from the perspectives of white men. The story began when they landed at Jamestown, and launched a heroic quest westward, taming the wilderness to their needs. Part of that "wilderness" included the native peoples, who appeared, in the story, devoid of history or culture, as one more natural obstacle to white mastery of the land.[4] The action focused on the Euro-American frontier, a place where young men came of age exploring, trapping, warring, brawling, prospecting, and cowpunching. The story ended when the new land was tamed. A bit of zest went out of the tale when our heroes fenced their piece of range. We shifted our focus to the next frontier, the next struggle for contested terrain.

Deliberately simplifying the plot in this way, we can begin to see how it distorts the story. It becomes, like all historical narratives, a partial tale ordered through human imaginations. Marietta Wetherill's story forces us to confront some of its omissions and its biases. Her narrative, which Kathryn Gabriel edited from Louis Blachly's oral history interviews, shifts the focus of older western histories. The historical gaze moves from the trail westward to the Southwest, from white men to women and Navajos, from heroic conquest to contested arenas of struggle, from the certainty of European superiority to a complex encounter between peoples. But neither Marietta Wetherill nor her story could entirely escape the relationships of race, gender, and national conquest that brought her to Chaco Canyon. Her story shatters the mold of older western histories without entirely escaping its confines.

It is hard to break new historical ground. Most of us, raised on the western frontier adventure, find it hard to find a new vantage point. We look from the East to the West, not north from Mexico, or south from Canada, or west from Asia, although from many "westerners" these were the directions of the journeys. We view the story as a "coming into the country," not from the perspectives of American Indians buffeted by successive waves of strangers. We expect the frontier success story, not the tales of thousands who failed and left, nor mundane accounts of the thousands of daily tasks it took to build homes, families, and communities. We expect conflict between people of different cultures, not a trading of skills and resources. Sometimes, it is through biography, an individual life that doesn't fit the mold, that we rethink the historical vantage point from which we view the past.

Marietta Wetherill's life breaks a number of conceptual molds. Until the appearance of numerous western women's histories in the past decade, the western historical landscape included few women.[5] The women we did see fit a small number of stereotypes, first identified by the folklorist Beverly Stoeltje.[6] Western women were either good or bad, the good ones either passive civilizers or oppressed helpmates, the bad ones hellraisers or whores. The civilizers tamed the West (and took the fun out of the masculine adventure), not by anything they did, but simply by being. When the good women came to town, the men took baths, built schools and churches, and became respectable community builders. The men, however, were still the actors. The women simply provided their off-stage motivation. Helpmates, the other stereotypical "good women," worked harder, but were no less passive. Unsuited to the land, they were generally dragged west against their better judgment. But their commitment to man and family left them no alternative—once in the West, they built and defended homesteads, raised and processed enormous quantities of food, and kept house in primitive conditions. They "stood by their men," bore their children, and were back in fields by sunrise. Overworked and downtrodden, they remained oppressed victims of masculine desires.

On the other side of the stereotype were the bad women—adventurous hellraisers like Calamity Jane or Poker Alice, who broke the conventional female mold, and who functioned, self-sufficient, on the masculine frontier. But if they embodied qualities considered admirable in western men, the same virtues cast women as historical deviants. Whatever their achievements, in breaking the conventional female narrative, they were "condemned" to live alone. Matt Dillon never kissed Miss Kitty. The lot of truly "bad" women—prostitutes and dance hall workers—was worse. First sanitized to fit the mold of "good women" by being cast as the "whore with a heart of gold," they were then fit into the historical plotline in the only way that allowed for a tidy ending—they died young, and alone.[7]

These one-dimensional women were mostly foils for the men of traditional western adventures. It was hard to see them partly because we inherited stock narratives of women's lives that ended before adult-hood.[8] The traditional female story is a long foreground of waiting for Prince Charming to rescue and awaken her. When the Prince arrives, the maiden marries him, and they ride off, as the sun sinks slowly into the West, to live happily ever after. Her story ends before the real work of relationship, children, and settlement begins. In the older western narrative, the land replaces the woman. It is virgin territory to be won and conquered.[9] In neither saga do we learn what happens after conquest, to the woman or the landscape.

Marietta Wetherill, like most real women in the real West, shatters our visions of women and their land. She refuses to fit their molds. A multidimensional woman, she clearly relished adventure, was strong and capable of self-sufficient action. She refused to stay at home like a good civilizer, or to relinquish home and family like a true hellraiser. We see in her a complex weave of "public" and "private" concerns and competencies. She forces us to confront, not a virgin land, but a land which had been occupied for centuries, to see the ancient Anasazi civilizations which preceded European "discovery," and to appreciate the Navajos who adopted her. Her saga violates the stereotypes and plotlines of traditional history.

Yet neither her life nor her narrative can entirely break its conventions. We encounter her, as Blachly did, not as an independent actor, but as the wife of Richard Wetherill, the "discoverer" of Mesa Verde and Chaco Canyon. Even if she considered herself an anthropologist and sought to understand and to record Navajo customs and ceremonials, she could not act outside a history of conquest and conflict, which was implicated, finally, in her husband's death. She was honest enough to recognize that her friendships with her Navajo neighbors left no one unchanged. Acknowledging their historical agency, and her own, she shifted the creation tale of western lore to an encounter among peoples, including women and people of color. Richard Wetherill's murder could be reduced to the tragic end of a western adventure. But Marietta Wetherill blamed the U.S. government for her husband's death, more than the Navajos who killed him. Her version complicates the saga of how the West was won, and lost.

Yet we, and maybe she as well, lack the tools to imagine her life entirely on its own terms, separate from the stories that have shaped our views of the past, our understanding of who and what was important. We look at her primarily because she was Richard Wetherill's wife. Or at least, that is how this narrative, constructed from her interviews, is framed. Her childhood prepares her to meet and marry Richard Wetherill, to relish his interests, and to share his life in Chaco Canyon. Most of the narrative covers the years of her marriage. It ends shortly after Richard Wetherill's death, when Marietta is still a young woman. His life, rather than hers, establishes the time frame for the story.

This is, nonetheless, in important ways, Marietta Wetherill's story, not Richard's. Even during their marriage, the focus in more often on her own activities, and not on her husband. Most strikingly, it is not a tale of solitary adventure but of relationships. The primary encounters are between Marietta and American Indians. It is those relationships that, in the telling, dignify both her and them. Next in importance is the Wetherill's marriage, despite a sense that her children held her deeply. Only after Richard's death do Marietta's relationships with her children come to the foreground.

These emotional shifts create tension in the narrative. So does Marietta's insistent claim to authority and adventure usually reserved to men—sometimes credited to them in other stories of the same events. Kathryn Gabriel does a meticulous job of documenting differences between Marietta Wetherill's account and those recorded elsewhere. These disagreements demonstrate abundantly that the story depends on the storyteller. Still, it may not matter enormously which version is correct. It may matter less, for instance, whether Marietta Wetherill herself was kidnapped by Paiutes or whether she appropriated someone else's story, than to recognize why she and other people claimed these adventures as their own. Whether Marietta Wetherill or John Doe was kidnapped does not matter so much as the fact that they both considered kidnapping an adventure worth claiming. Public "masculine" adventure was important and engaging. It seemed more important then, for instance, how one made and washed diapers in the desert, a fact of domestic history which might deeply interest some audiences. Certainly we learn some interesting domestic details from Marietta Wetherill. But there is a tension between the mundane details, which remain largely off-stage in this narrative, and more public events, adventures, and encounters with the strange and the unknown.

If that is the story we read, it is probably partly a consequence of the oral history record, of the particular encounter between Lou Blachly and Marietta Wetherill, partly a matter of what each considered important or "newsworthy," and partly the consequence of the narratives of women's lives available to Lou Blachly, Marietta Wetherill, Kathryn Gabriel, and to us.

Could we hear this story differently? Would Marietta Wetherill tell it differently if we asked her different questions? Although these are questions raised most pointedly by oral history, they are in fact questions embedded in all sources, all interpretations, all histories. We can perhaps be most healthily skeptical about the past when we recognize that it is told and recorded by people in particular times and contexts. Thus, we recognize that the oral record is shaped partly by the questions asked, the relationship between the interviewer and the narrator, the filters of time and memory and self-presentation. Women reveal some things more easily to women than to men.[10] Old people share different things with the young and with their peers. Most of us do not remember dates or names with total accuracy. And what we think is important frames both the questions we ask and the information we volunteer. Kathryn Gabriel has been admirably scrupulous in detecting and recording possible inconsistencies and inaccuracies in these interviews. The care involved in such meticulous editing adds depth and dimension to the text.

These tensions and nuances are important not just because they reveal mysteries in the historical record, but because they are common to all our sources. People who write also have partial memories, respond to questions of importance and meaning which are often unstated, sometimes get names and dates wrong, and write in particular times and contexts, to a particular audience. Because our culture values the written word over the oral account, because the spoken word is different from the written word, and because spoken language loses some of its authenticity and authority when it is transcribed, it is important to suspend disbelief when we encounter disagreements between Marietta Wetherill's spoken narrative and other texts. We need to recognize this narrative for the rich document it is—a work of triple authorship, reflecting the preoccupations and inherited frameworks of the interviewer, Lou Blachly; the narrator, Marietta Wetherill; and the compiler and editor, Kathryn Gabriel. In this historical trialogue perhaps there were things Marietta Wetherill would have emphasized more than the questions Lou Blachly chose to pursue. Perhaps on another day, at another time in her life, she would have told it differently. And other historians may return to the interviews and edit from them different narratives, choosing different beginnings, different ends, different stories, different relationships.

This is not to say historians simply write fictions. We rely on the words in our sources. But we return to them with new questions and new frameworks through which we see women, history, and the West. That is how we write and rewrite and reinterrogate and re-envision the past. If future historians find new frameworks for Marietta Wetherill's life, and the lives of other women, it will be partly because this narrative forces us in particular ways outside the older boundaries of how we have viewed women and viewed the West. We form new histories, like new fictions, from the stories we have heard. It is a particular gift of this story that it asks us to stretch those boundaries, to see through the eyes of a particular woman, and through her eyes to envision a new story, with more players, and less glory in the struggle. Her life enables us to envision a new script for a game of cowboys and Indians, one with parts that Navajo children and little girls might comfortably play. It helps us hear the voices of new actors in western history, to let their words reverberate against our memories, and through their stories to invent ourselves, our pasts, anew.

NOTES

[1]Carolyn G. Heilbrun, *Writing a Woman's Life* (New York: Ballantine Books, 1988), p. 37.

[2]For a stimulating discussion of narrative in environmental histories, see William Cronon, "A Place for Stories: Nature, History, and Narrative," *Journal of American History* 78, no. 4 (March 1992): 1347-76.

[3]The themes and stories of the new western history vary, and its practitioners are by no means in agreement with one another. Most share one or more of the following concerns: they abandon the frontier framework; they emphasize conflict and conquest; they include the perspectives of race, ethnicity, class, and/or gender; and they do not see European "civilization" as an unmixed blessing, either for people or the land. Some examples include William Cronon, *Changes in the Land: Indians, Colonists, and the Ecology of New*

England (New York: Hill and Wang, 1983); Patricia Nelson Limerick, *The Legacy of Conquest: The Unbroken Past of the American West* (New York: W. W. Norton & Company, 1987); Donald Worster, *Rivers of Empire: Water, Aridity, and the Growth of the American West* (New York: Pantheon, 1985); Rodolfo Acuna, *Occupied America: A History of Chicanos*, 3rd ed. (New York: Harper and Row, 1988); Sarah Deutsch, *No Separate Refuge: Culture, Class, and Gender on an Anglo-Hispanic Frontier in the American Southwest, 1880-1940* (New York: Oxford University Press, 1987); Richard White, *The Roots of Dependency: Subsistence, Environment, and Social Change among the Choctaws, Pawnees, and Navajos* (Lincoln: University of Nebraska Press, 1983). White's textbook, *It's Your Misfortune and None of My Own* (Norman: University of Oklahoma Press, 1991), provides a good overview from many of these perspectives.

⁴This is not to suggest that the works cited above were the first to break this mold. Indeed, they built upon challenges to the frontier framework of a previous generation of historians who stressed regional development, cultural continuities, the Spanish borderlands, and the twentieth century West, to name but a few themes that violated narratives based on the Euro-American frontier. See for instance Earl Pomeroy, "Toward a Reorientation of Western History: Continuity and Environment," *Mississippi Valley Historical Review* 41 (March 1955): 579-600; Gerald D. Nash, *The American West in the Twentieth Century: A Short History of an Urban Oasis* (Englewood Cliffs, N.J.: Prentice-Hall, 1973); John Francis Bannon, *The Spanish Borderlands Frontier, 1513-1821* (New York: Holt, Reinhart, and Winston, 1970). I am here talking partially about histories based on Frederick Jackson Turner's frontier thesis, "The Significance of the Frontier in American History," in *Annual Report of the American Historical Association for the Year 1893* (Washington, D.C.: U.S. Government Printing Office, 1894). I am concerned mostly with narratives, some conscious fictions, some not, that shaped our collective imagination of "how the West was won." See for instance, Henry Nash Smith, *The Virgin Land: The American West as Symbol and Myth* (Cambridge: Harvard University Press, 1950); Richard Slotkin, *Regeneration Through Violence* (Middletown, Conn.: Wesleyan University Press, 1973); and John G. Cawelti, *The Six-Gun Mystique*, 2nd ed. (Bowling Green, Ohio: Bowling Green University Press, 1984).

⁵See Susan Armitage and Elizabeth Jameson, eds., *The Women's West* (Norman: University of Oklahoma Press, 1987); Lillian Schlissel, Vicki Ruiz, and Janice Monk, eds., *Western Women: Their Land, Their Lives* (Albuquerque, University of New Mexico Press, 1988); Sheryll Patterson-Black, "Women Homesteaders on the Great Plains Frontier," *Frontiers* 1, no. 2 (Spring 1976): 67-88; Glenda Riley, *Frontierswomen: The Iowa Experience* (Ames: Iowa State University Press, 1981); Julie Roy Jeffrey, *Frontier Women: The Trans-Mississippi West, 1840-1880* (New York: Hill & Wang, 1979); Sandra L. Myres, *Westering Women and the Frontier Experience, 1800-1915* (Albuquerque: University of New Mexico Press, 1982).

For works on women in the West, see Joan M. Jensen and Darlis A. Miller, "The Gentle Tamers Revisited: New Approaches to the History of Women in the American West, *Pacific Historical Review* 49, no. 2 (May 1980): 173-213; Rayna Green, "Native American Women," *Signs: Journal of Women in Culture and Society* 6, no. 2 (Winter 1980): 248-67; Lyle Koehler, "Native Women of the Americas: A Bibliography," *Frontiers* 6, no. 3 (Fall 1981): 73-101; Catherine Loeb, "La Chicana: A Bibliographic Survey," *Frontiers* 5, no. 2 (Summer 1980): 59-74; Lenwood G. Davis, *The Black Woman in American Society: A Selected Annotated Bibliography* (Boston: Hall, 1975); Lawrence B. DeGraef, "Race, Sex, and Region: Black Women in the American West, 1850-1920," *Pacific Historical Review* 49, no. 2 (May 1980): 285-314; Elizabeth Jameson, "Toward a Multicultural History of Women in the Western United States," *Signs* 13, no. 4 (Summer 1988): 761-791.

For treatments of encounters between Euro-American and Native American women, see Susan Armitage, "Everyday Encounters: Indians and White Women in the Palouse," *Pacific Northwest Forum* 7, no. 3-4 (Summer/Fall 1982): 27-30; and "Women's Literature and the American Frontier: A New Perspective on the Frontier Myth," in *Women, Women Writers, and the West*, ed. L. L. Lee and Merrill Lewis (Troy, N.Y.: Whitson, 1979), pp. 5-11; and Glenda Riley, *Women and Indians on the Frontier, 1825-1915* (Albuquerque: University of New Mexico Press, 1984). For references on American Indian women, see Beatrice Medicine, "The Role of Women in Native American Societies; A Bibliography," *Indian Historian* 8, (1975): 50-54; Rayna Green, "Native American Women: *Signs: Journal of Women in Culture and Society* 6, no. 2 (Winter 1980), 248-67; Lyle Koehler, "Native Women of the Americas: A Bibliography," *Frontiers* 6, no. 3 (Fall 1981): 73-101; and Rayna Green, *Native American Women: A Bibliography* (Wichita Falls, Texas: OHOYO Research Center, 1981). Some of the most useful work on Native American women and the record of their lives has been written by anthropologists. For one particularly fine example, see Patricia Albers and Beatrice Medicine, *The Hidden Half: Studies of Plains Indian Women* (Lanham, Maryland: University Press of America, 1983). A recent interesting collection which discusses women anthropologists in the Southwest is Barbara A. Babcock, *Daughters of the Desert: The Women Anthropologists and the Native American Southwest, 1880-1980* (Albuquerque: University of New Mexico Press, 1988). For work on American Indian Women's narratives, see Gretchen M. Bataille and Kathleen Mullen Sands, *American Indian Women: Telling Their Lives* (Lincoln: University of Nebraska Press, 1984).

[6]Beverly Stoeltje, "A Helpmate for Man Indeed: The Image of the Frontier Woman," *Journal of American Folklore* 88, no. 347 (January-March 1975): 27-31. For work that challenged the grip of these stereotypes on historical narratives, see Susan Armitage, "Through Women's Eyes: A New View of the West," in Armitage and Jameson (n. 5 above), pp. 9-18; and Elizabeth Jame-

son, "Women as Workers, Women as Civilizers: True Womanhood in the American West," in Armitage and Jameson (n. 5 above), pp. 145-64.

[7]See Stoeltje (n. 7 above) and Armitage (n. 7 above).

[8]See Heilbrun (n. 1 above), especially pp. 60-75.

[9]See Smith (n. 4 above) for this vision of the land itself as virgin.

[10]*Frontiers: A Journal of Women Studies* published two special issues on women's oral history, vol. 2, no. 2 (Summer 1977) and vol. 7, no. 1 (1983), which contain oral histories of western women, accounts of oral history projects in western states, and lists of oral history collections in western states.

Introduction: Checkerboard History of the Four Corners Area

ORAL HISTORIAN STUDS TERKEL once asked, "When the Chinese wall was built, where did the masons go for lunch? When the Spanish Armada sank, King Philip of Spain wept, but were there no other tears?" Through oral interpretations, Terkel searched for other tears, other lives to augment historical events. The exhuming of ancient cities doesn't exactly rank with the building of great walls or the sinking of armadas. Yet on the cusp of the twentieth century, Chaco Canyon, a thousand-year-old buried city in the northwestern corner of the Territory of New Mexico, became a cul-de-sac of history where three ethnic groups converged on one grave robber, Richard Wetherill. Through the reflections of one eyewitness, Marietta Wetherill, we learn there were many tears.

It was the end of a gilded era, a time of robust national economic expansion, industrial escalation, and government corruption. In the West, Indian fighters, cattlemen, and homesteaders embraced Darwin's theory of evolution as a code of ethics. Native Americans, particularly the Navajos who lived around Chaco Canyon, were perceived as a force to be reckoned with, despite the thirty years that had passed since their internment at Fort Sumner, New Mexico.

Richard Wetherill was a product of his times. He was the rancher who discovered the cliff cities of Mesa Verde in Colorado in 1888, among several other important Anasazi sites. In 1896, he organized the first excavation of the Anasazi ruins at Pueblo Bonito at Chaco Canyon, which was occupied between 900 A.D. and 1130 A.D. He moved his bride, Marietta, into the canyon in 1897, and in subsequent years tried to homestead the acreage containing Pueblo Bonito. After he removed boxcars full of artifacts (he wanted to lay railroad track through Chaco), his archaeological practices and homestead motives came under fire. His efforts to hang on to his stake led to his being shot to death by a Navajo in 1910.

Authors Frank McNitt and David Brugge have already researched the life and times of Richard Wetherill, but the details of his daily life comes from Marietta. Although McNitt was able to interview her before she died, the bulk of material was saved through the foresightedness of one newspaperman of Silver City, New Mexico, Lou Blachly, and the Pioneers Foundation. When Marietta was seventy-seven, he recorded her stories, about an hour of audio tape for every year of her life. The last tape was completed in October 1953, nine months before her death.

From Marietta we learn where the masons—in this case the archaeologists, scholars, cowboys, traders, and Navajos—went for lunch. Because of her particular duties on this armada, they came to Marietta's dining room table. Marietta shows us the details of the workaday lives of both the Anglo Americans and the Navajos. Her reminiscences fill in the background and give texture to the times so focused on that arid hotbed of antiquity.

Just how a refined young girl like Marietta came to marry a rugged man like Richard, eighteen years her senior, makes sense considering her upbringing. Born to Quaker parents in Serena, Illinois, on October 5, 1876, Marietta was raised with a keen interest in music, travel, and indigenous people. Before Marietta's parents married, her father, Sidney LaVern Palmer, played for John Philip Sousa, and her mother, Elizabeth Ann Hoag, studied with the New England Conservatory of Music in Boston and once played the piano for the Queen's tea in London. The family moved to Burdette, Kansas, when Marietta was six or seven and she, her brother, Sidney LaVern Jr., and her sister, Edna, learned to play musical instruments.

The restless Sidney Palmer frequently loaded his family in the horse-drawn Studebaker wagon he outfitted for musicians and hauled them around the country "giving entertainments." The Palmers made their first trip to the Southwest in the mid 1880s, just before Richard Wetherill discovered Mesa Verde. Over the course of several trips, the Palmers visited most of the Pueblo Indians along the Rio Grande, working their way into the Indians' trust with their music, not unlike the Pueblo mythological character, Kokopelli the flute player.

On the Palmers' third trip to the Southwest, they finally met Richard Wetherill at his parents' home in Mancos, Colorado. The Wetherill family was the lure out west for the Palmers, as for so many other tourists. Richard was the oldest of five brothers and a sister (Benjamin Alfred, John, Winslow, Clayton, and Louisa Wade), and they all stuck close to their filial home, helping with the ranch and searching for lost cities. Alfred claimed to have discovered Cliff Palace at Mesa Verde the year prior to Richard's discovery, but was too busy to do anything about it. The Wetherill ranch became a bulging museum for all the artifacts they found.

The Wetherills had been as peripatetic as the Palmers. They moved to the Four Corners area in 1880 via Iowa, Kansas, Missouri, Utah, and Colorado. As a Quaker, the patriarch, Benjamin Kite Wetherill, was involved in Indian mediation and at Mancos struck a friendship with the raiding Utes and Paiutes, who were feared by most of the other settlers. When the Palmers arrived on the Wetherill doorstep, the two families formed an instant bond.

The Palmers soon became interested in Chaco Canyon, and Richard guided them there in 1895. The Palmers had tried to reach Chaco Canyon on other trips, but failed, and Richard had never gone before. It was there that Richard realized he wanted the young Marietta for his wife. They were married the next year and immediately launched another expedition into Chaco Canyon.

Richard Wetherill's excavations were funded by the Hyde Exploring Expedition (HEE). His two benefactors, whom he had met in 1893, were Talbot and Fred Hyde, sons of a New York physician and heirs to the BaBo soap fortune built by their grandfather, Benjamin Babbit. The American Museum of Natural History in New York received the bulk of the artifacts the HEE exhumed. The Hydes continued to fund the expedition and the trading post network until Richard became a political embarrassment beginning in 1901. Richard's infatuation with Chaco Canyon outlasted the Hyde investment and it contributed to his death.

The romantic pitch of the day is noteworthy because the Wetherills, and everyone who sought them or fought them, were thoroughly steeped in it. Willa Cather captured the fever in the character, Tom Outland, in *The Professor's House (1925)*. Outland, who was based on Richard Wetherill, was a haunted, misunderstood character who discovered a "superior people . . . who when compared to the roving Navajo must have been quite complex." Outland experienced the mesa where he discovered the Cliff

3

Dwellers as a "religious emotion." Richard's emotions come through in Marietta's stories, but whereas he fixed on the past, she turned her attention to the Navajos of the present. She didn't see them as a commodity as Richard saw them, but as objects of art.

Savages Never Reared These Structures

That the Hydes would throw their money into that dry hole in the Southwest with few dividends is not too difficult to understand considering that the search for antiquity was in vogue, and the romantic association certainly leant intrigue to the brothers' lives. Richard Wetherill was not the first amateur to embark feverishly on an expedition to exotic places and to capitalize on it.

In 1839, John L. Stephens, a New York lawyer-journalist, got himself appointed to President Martin Van Buren's Special Mission to the Central American Federation. The assignment gained for Stephens diplomatic immunity while he explored the Maya ruins. When he visited Copán, the first of forty sites he was to explore, Stephens described that expectancy of discovery Richard Wetherill must have felt when digging in the ruins at Pueblo Bonito: "I leaned over with breathless anxiety while the Indians worked, and an eye, an ear, a foot, or a hand was disentombed . . . the mystery [of the rain forest] that hung over it, all created an interest higher, if possible, than I had ever felt among the ruins of the Old World."

Stephens was acutely aware that the temples he surveyed were erected "before the Europeans knew of the existence of this continent" and that "savages never reared these structures, savages never carved these stones." As Richard tried to do with the ruins at Pueblo Bonito, Stephens hoped to purchase, refit, and repeople the palace of Palenque. The price was right, but he could not under law become a landowner unless he married into citizenship, which proved to be "embarrassing and complicated."

Another to arouse the romantic fever of the day was William H. Prescott (1796-1859), who wrote *History of the Conquest of Mexico* and *History of the Conquest of Peru* with dim eyesight, his left eye having been struck by a piece of hard bread. The Palmers and the Wetherills were avid readers, and it isn't inconceivable that they read Prescott. The woman who lent me a tattered copy of these two combined volumes considered it her bible when she lived in

4

South America and Mexico in the late 1950s. Prescott, who relied mainly on the reports of the Spanish scholars and priests during the Conquest, impressed the American public with descriptions of great buildings and scientific sensibilities. He himself was not quite as awe-struck: "An acquaintance with some of the more obvious principles of astronomy is within the reach of the rudest people . . . [and] could be the result only of a long series of nice and patient observations, evincing no slight progress in civilization."

Scoring the sophistication of the ancient cultures was the order of the day. When scholars first began dissecting the Anasazi ruins at Chaco Canyon and Mesa Verde, they echoed Stephens's sentiment that "savages never reared these structures." Because of Stephens and Prescott, the Anasazi scholars began searching for the connection to the high civilizations of Mesoamerica, for surely these structures were not the work of the Navajo or Pueblo ancestors. The buildings at Chaco did not resemble the mud and stick huts of the Navajos or the relatively less than magnificent apartment complexes of the Pueblos. Chaco archaeologist Neil Judd was to observe in 1925, "No other apartment house of comparable size was known in America or in the Old World until the Spanish Flats were erected in 1882 at 59th and Seventh Avenue, New York City." This notion even influenced the work of ethnohistorians Adolf F. Bandelier, who scoured the Southwest and northern Mexico, and Frank H. Cushing, who lived with and studied the Zuñis. When First Lieutenant James H. Simpson surveyed Chaco Canyon in 1849, just after the United States acquired New Mexico from Mexico as a result of the Mexican War, he said he could not say with certainty that the ruins of Chaco were Aztec, but, then again, he couldn't say they weren't. As it turns out, the Aztecs founded Tenochtitlán a hundred years after roaming the countryside to the north and a hundred years after Chaco Canyon was abandoned.

After the Mexican War, settlers had difficulty warding off raiding Navajos, Apaches, Utes, and Comanches. It was a curious paradox of history that while Americans stood in awe of the great monuments of stone in the Four Corners area, the federal government was systematically removing the living, breathing Indians who roamed the very canyons where the monuments stood. A string of forts was built across the Southwest, and Secretary Richard

McCormick named one of the military settlements in Arizona, and its first capital, after Prescott, whom he had read and admired. But the United States was a newcomer to the three-hundred-year-old war between the Navajos and the Europeans.

When Marietta and Richard entered the scene toward the end of the nineteenth century, they caught the aftermath of that war. They made friends with, and, yes, exploited the Navajos who lived right on the rimrock of the Chaco Canyon, where their families had lived for generations. To her credit, Marietta quickly cultivated an empathy for the Navajos and their bout with the various governments. Since the main topic of Marietta's oral history concerns the Chaco Navajos, it is important to understand who they were and what that three-century-long war was all about.

Enforced Enlightenment at Bayonet Point

Chaco Canyon is in the heart of Navajo country, or Dinétah, "among the Navajo." The Navajos are not the natural descendants of the Anasazi of Chaco Canyon. They arrived well after the Anasazi abandoned the canyon for good in the middle of the thirteenth century. When the Chaco Anasazi left the canyon, they splintered off into different tribes, as did the Kayenta and Mesa Verde Anasazi, and migrated to places like Pecos and Pajarito Plateau in New Mexico, and splintered off again to settle in places like Taos and Cochiti. With a few exceptions, it is difficult to trace specific pueblos to ancient ruins since only twenty pueblos now exist out of the hundred that were occupied at the time of the Spanish Conquest. We suspect that at least Zia, Acoma, and Zuñi are descendants of Chaco.

The Navajos are a different group altogether. They are categorized as Athapascan people who migrated from Canada and Alaska and are linked with other Na-Dene language groups that also embrace the Apaches and the Kiowas. The Diné (People), as they call themselves, didn't enter the archaeological record in northwestern New Mexico until the late 1400s or early 1500s, in a Navajo-Pueblo refugee site in Gobernador Canyon near Chaco Canyon. The next phase of Navajo occupation appears in the 1600s on Black Mesa in northern Arizona. Spanish scholars didn't begin documenting the Navajos until around 1630. The first archaeological evidence that the Navajos lived in Chaco Canyon dates to 1720, although the National Park Service recently found a site that dates much earlier.

If the Navajos came any earlier, they were so stealthy, they left no footprints. As it turns out, they probably became detectable when they formed alliances with the Pueblos against other groups and later the Spanish. From the Pueblos, they learned such things as housing construction, weaving, and socialization, which is recordable by archaeologists. The Navajos have a reputation for being enemies of the Pueblos, probably because of their long dispute with the Hopis over land. In truth, the Navajos conspired with the Pueblos against the Spanish at least once and were on hand for the great revolt in 1680 that drove the Spaniards back to Mexico for twelve years.

New Mexico was first explored in 1540 by Francisco Vásquez de Coronado in search of the "Seven Cities of Cibola." He found only the villages of the Hopis and Zuñis. On his second trip in 1542, he pushed up the Rio Grande and enslaved Indians he found there. Spanish explorer Juan de Oñate invaded New Mexico in 1598 on a gold and missionary expedition. The Pueblos who resisted Spanish rule were tortured and enslaved. Unwilling to give up their ancient rites, a Tewa Pueblo Indian named Popé led the 1680 revolt.

As a result of the Spanish invasion, the Navajos acquired the knowledge of silverwork, clothing, ovens, and horses. Over the next century the Navajos grew in number and organization and became a formidable opponent for the Spanish. Mobile now, the Navajos began raiding Spanish settlements during the last half of the eighteenth century, and the Spanish reciprocated. The Navajos told Marietta their ancestors killed for the metal bands around barrels that served as anvils for silversmithing and the red bayeta lining of the soldiers' capes that became useful in weaving. The Navajos retreated to "Casa Fuerte," probably the ruins of Chaco Canyon, and Spanish campaigns were launched to dig them out. (Marietta said the Navajos told her they used Pueblo Pintado, a Chacoan outlier, as a stronghold.) The Spaniards held young Navajo boys as slaves, as spoils of war. Turning the captured into slaves was practiced by all parties.

Mexico negotiated a treaty with the Navajos in 1786, but early in the 1800s the settlers again started expanding into Navajoland, and the cycle resumed. More treaties were made and broken through 1846, but no one treaty was enough to hold the divided Navajos.

Although the outcome of the Mexican War changed the players, it did not change the game. The United States government inherited the Mexican government's Indian problems, although it saw itself as the savior of the Navajos for having just defeated their enemy. Alas, the Navajos did not see it that way, and a series of conflicts and treaties followed with little impact. In 1860, the ancient war came to a head when Manuelito and Barboncito led a thousand Navajos in attack on Fort Defiance.

The Civil War between 1861 and 1865 did more to step up the campaign against the Navajos by the U.S. Army than to delay it. A volunteer army led by Indian fighter Kit Carson lost a battle on February 21, 1862, to the Confederates at Valverde in New Mexico, and for a brief period the Confederate flag flew over Santa Fe until General Henry Hopkins Sibley realized that victory was unsupportable. Union General James H. Carleton was dispatched to Santa Fe shortly thereafter. He saw it as his job to curtail the activities of Confederate soldiers as well as Indian hostilities, and he enlisted Kit Carson to help him.

Christopher "Kit" Carson came to New Mexico from Missouri as a youth in 1826 on a Santa Fe wagon train and became an independent trapper. Such men as he spearheaded the economic conquest of New Mexico. He later became involved in land speculation, New Mexico's third big business. Between 1842 and 1846, he opened up Wyoming, the Oregon Trail, and the California territory. He distinguished himself as a scout in the Mexican War. In 1851, he hooked up with the territory of New Mexico's first governor, James S. Calhoun, to command volunteer companies to guard the northern frontier against Indian attack.

Two years before becoming governor, Calhoun served as Superintendent of Indian Affairs, when he put together a tough policy of taming the "wild" Indians, according to Howard Roberts Lamar in *The Far Southwest*. He considered Pueblos to be the tamed Indians and wished to grant property and voting rights to them, but he wanted to transform the Navajos, Utes, Comanches, and Apaches into peaceful agriculturalists. This he would do by "enforced enlightenment . . . at the point of a bayonet," if necessary. Calhoun's major agenda was in making New Mexico a state, which didn't happen until 1912.

Under Carleton's orders, Carson rounded up thousands of Navajos, beginning in 1864, marched them on the Long Walk to Fort Sumner in the Bosque Redondo area in eastern New Mexico (known as *Hweeldi*, the Navajo way of pronouncing *fuerte* or fort), where they spent the next four years cooped up with their enemy and linguistic cousins, the Mescalero Apaches. Here Carleton hoped to replace the old hunting and raiding instincts with literacy and Christianity, but their own ancient beliefs were reinforced when a Navajo ceremony seemed to divine their release. Many died on the walk either at the hands of the soldiers or by exhaustion, and many more died in the camp of hunger, illness, or exposure to the cold during an especially bad winter. Carleton had to admit defeat and released the Indians in 1868, but he considered it a successful failure. At the camp, the Navajos observed the routine of daily white life, he said, and more importantly, they were treated as a unified group, and one hoped they would see themselves this way. An outgrowth of the incarceration was witchcraft, which proved to stymie their growth, as Marietta reveals.

The Treaty of 1868 created a reservation for the Navajos of about three and a half million acres in their original homeland, straddling what was to become the state line of Arizona and New Mexico. The reservation fell eighteen miles short of Chaco Canyon. Under this treaty, education was promised, though it was to come slowly. Ruth Underhill, author of *Here Come the Navaho!*, said Manuelito, the Navajo war chief, made this plea to Chee Dodge, a young interpreter at Fort Sumner:

> My Grandchild, the whites have many things which we Navajos need. But we cannot get them. It is as though the whites were in a grassy canyon and there they have wagons, plows, and plenty of food. We Navajos are up on the dry mesa. We can hear them talking but we cannot get to them. My Grandchild, education is the ladder. Tell our people to take it.

9

The Great Gambler of Pueblo Bonito

To a Navajo living on the mesa, the sight of Richard and Marietta Wetherill driving their wagons full of food and equipment into Chaco Canyon might have seemed like a prophecy come true. The relationship between the Wetherills and the Navajos was established relatively quickly considering all that had gone on before that moment. Marietta's oral history demonstrates that the ladder from the rimrock to the canyon bottom was used by both the Navajos and the Wetherills.

Richard Wetherill's success—and demise—was due largely to the Native Americans. Richard didn't actually discover Mesa Verde in the true meaning of the word. A Ute allowed him to see the old cities on their sacred land. Likewise, the ruins at Chaco Canyon were in the sacred province of the Navajos. The Navajos considered the Anasazi ruins to be remnants of the previous world, the Fourth World, and they were to be respected, if not feared. The Navajos did nothing to hamper Richard's digging. In fact, they did the digging themselves at fifty cents a day against tribal taboo and personal fear of death.

Richard was an opportunist and had a gift for turning adversity into asset. In an effort to "protect" the ruins from academic interlopers and other pot looters, Richard filed a homestead claim on the acres containing Pueblo Bonito in 1900, which triggered criticism of vandalism (by Edgar Hewett, then of the New Mexico Normal University) and a federal investigation. Richard was ordered to stop excavating until investigation brought in a verdict. Richard was never again able to resume his excavations, but he stayed in the canyon to develop the homestead. He built a rug factory for the Navajo weavers at Pueblo Bonito, and he traded their silver and turquoise jewelry for groceries. He built a trading post empire that brought the rugs to Times Square. When he was squeezed out of that business, he stepped up his livestock business on the range around Chaco Canyon. When servants of the Commission of Indian Affairs blockaded him by giving land allotments to the Navajos, he employed the Navajos to herd his sheep on shares for him. When Chaco Canyon was made a national park in 1907, he gave up his claim to Pueblo Bonito proper but held the rest of the land until his death in 1910. In 1912, the patent to the land was granted.

10

INTRODUCTION

A Quaker, Richard thought he was good to his Indians. Where else could they buy such traditional Navajo foods as coffee beans, cane sugar, and canned asparagus other than at Richard's convenient trading post? He and other traders in the area like Lorenzo Hubbell are accused by modern scholars of having encouraged dependency, but I think it worked both ways. Peter Iverson said the Navajos survived with the largest reservation in the country, perhaps due to such diverse exposure to so many different elements. Had the government known about the rich resources of minerals on the Navajo reservation today, however, it might not have been so liberal with the land.

David Brugge, author of the National Park Service report, *History of the Chaco Navajos*, speculated that Richard reminded the Chaco Navajos of the mythological Noqoìlpi, the Great Gambler who moves into Chaco Canyon and wins all the riches and great houses and people through gambling. This seems a likely analogy when weighed against their natural tendency toward irony. The Navajo called Richard "Anasazi" after the "ancient ones" he so relentlessly pursued. It's a dubious distinction, because the name, depending on how it is pronounced, means ancient enemy. In the legend, the people who lose to the Gambler prevail in the end by using their supernatural resources to beat him at his own game and shoot him into the sky. The Gambler then becomes the god of the Mexicans. This story may have been adapted to explain an earlier time when the Indians came into contact with the Spanish Conquistadors. The Navajos took care of the Spanish, and they took care of Richard, too. The Navajo who finally shot Richard with a .33 caliber Winchester had enough motives of his own to dismiss most implications of conspiracy, but not all of them.

Marietta believed that the agents of the Commission of Indian Affairs were responsible for Richard's murder, the circumstances of which were thoroughly investigated in Brugge's book, and Frank McNitt's *Richard Wetherill: Anasazi* published in 1957. (The authors each offer opposing perspectives.) It is clear that the Indian agents perceived Richard as a threat and collected sworn affidavits that he handcuffed Navajos, locked them in the ruins, and helped himself to their horses and sheep to pay their debts. Suspiciously, most of the data was taken posthumously. Thus the commission is another key component in the background for Marietta's oral history.

The Commission of Indian Affairs (later to become the Bureau of Indian Affairs) was first established in 1832. It controlled trade with the tribes, supervised their removal to the West, administered the reservations, and doled out rations. It was to keep Indians on their reservations and squatters off. During the closing decades of the nineteenth century, the commission was riddled with scandal as unscrupulous Indian agents, contractors, and politicians made millions selling out the interests of their charges. The commission used its powers under the Dawes Severalty Act of 1887 and the Burke Act of 1906 to encourage the sale of some ninety million acres of Indian lands to white investors while rewarding individual Indians with land grants and citizenship if they would renounce tribal allegiance.

That these practices continued in the Four Corners area is not clear, but it would certainly explain the compromise in which the Indian agents may have found themselves. They saw traders and cattlemen as personal competition as well as a threat to those they protected. Richard posed a double threat.

Under the Allotment Act of 1887, Chaco Navajos were granted patents to off-reservation land for which they could claim long-term residency. The allotment plan was compounded by the Navajo tendency to change addresses according to the seasons, railroad easements, ruins, traders, and the legal obstacles the white ranchers cast in the commission's way. One maneuver cattlemen used was to purchase or lease railroad lands and to apply for a permit to cross Indian lands to get to it, a tactic Richard may have employed. In this way, stockowners could hop their cattle or sheep across the Navajo reservation like pieces on a checkerboard, or they could squat on Indian lands. The Four Corners area is known as a checkerboard because the grid of ownership is divided among public, private, and Navajo interests. The Wetherills had railroad entitlement in Marietta's name, as well as in the name of an alleged adopted Navajo son, and the Indian agents suspected fraud.

Telling a Good Story

These were the circumstances of Marietta's life, but not the main subject of her oral history. She didn't dwell on the politics surrounding Richard's murder. Although she did hire attorneys to see that the man who killed Richard, Chis-chilling-begay, was convicted, she didn't blame the Navajo people as a whole. The Navajos charged Marietta with a mission to tell their story. That story, for better or worse, was the crux of her history, possibly even her life.

Marietta endeared herself to many Navajo men, women, and children. She formed a special affinity with several singers (whom she calls medicine men) because they gave her the most information, including Hosteen Bí'al, who adopted her into the Chee clan. At their side, she learned the secrets of sand painting and the curing dances, observed the harsh code of Navajo ethics, doctored their illnesses, midwifed their babies, and witnessed the execution of a bewitched singer. Perhaps it was because of their confinement at Fort Sumner that the Navajos thought she would help them gain understanding and respect from the dominant culture. "Her head is round, not flat like ours," they said of her. "Her tongue is thin enough to speak the tongue of the Diné. She will remember and tell our story to the white man."

Marietta claimed a genius for remembering detail. Even Lou Blachly said she had a phenomenal, exceptional memory. As a child, she could recite an entire civil government textbook or play any song on almost any instrument after hearing it just once, and she could pick up the language of most tribes in just a short time. Memory was an attribute of the Victorian Age, especially for a woman. Marietta was not really involved in Richard's politics, and this may have had as much to do with the discrepancy in their ages as it had to do with gender roles. Memory was her contribution, her purpose in life.

Marietta's recollections, which (transcribed) amount to more than two thousand single-spaced typed pages, are suffused with exhaustive detail that a woman would traditionally remember: the daily lives and relationships of all those who lived near Pueblo Bonito.

Sharon Niederman, author of *A Quilt of Words: Women's Diaries, Letters & Original Accounts of Life in the Southwest, 1860-1960*, said Marietta was similar to other southwestern pioneer women who left a legacy of history. "Unlike their husbands and brothers, for the most part they did not subdue or tame the land and the native people; rather, they lived with conditions as they found them or could improve them, and their fascination led them to observe and to report their experiences." Niederman says a pioneer woman's history is similar to a quilt, "the sum of many small, random-seeming puzzle pieces that, with patience, fit together into a whole picture." Marietta is no exception. Her stories were random, but by the end, you know Chaco Canyon down to the beating drums, the suffocating heat, blue smoke incense, and lice itch. She doesn't simply tell about cleaning and cooking and birthing babies; if a person bled, she describes it—with a practiced tone.

However, by the time she came to record her recollections, Marietta's memory, in some ways, was actually pretty bad. She confuses dates, events, and people, and didn't experience some of the episodes she claims as her own. One of her favorite stories is about being kidnapped by the Paiutes. This is a true story, but she wasn't the one who was kidnapped. Perhaps her advanced age lowered the shades on her faculty of recall. This would explain the lapses in memory and the confusion. She admits to having no memory for dates or sequence of events, and her concept of reality is sometimes elastic. In 1932, one of her incredible stories was published in *Scribners Magazine*, and when it was criticized, she changed the story.

Excuses are readily available. Marietta's husband, Richard, received all the attention for their work at Chaco, though not all of it positive. Marietta rode shotgun on Richard's wagon. Maybe she was told more than once that she was incapable of grasping the scientific detail Richard sifted from the dirt. Not that she complained. She herself said she was an anthropologist, not an archaeologist. She complains about not getting credit for the assistance she lent the ethnologists when they came to Chaco. She had no ambition or support to pursue an academic career and get the credit she said she deserved.

Richard died when she was only thirty-three. She carried on the family business of ranching, perhaps because of the influence of Richard's gangster cowboy, Will Finn, who remained with her as foreman until he died. The point being, Marietta's life didn't end with Richard's death. When Richard was buried, however, he took with him the richest part of Marietta's life.

Richard appears in Marietta's oral history as one of the characters, but not the main one. If there was romantic love between them, she didn't reveal much of it. She called him Mr. Wetherill from the time she married him until the time she died. He called her Asdzání, or Woman. The Navajo called her Asdzání Anasazi, or the old enemy's woman.

Marietta's romance was with the Indians, and through Richard she pursued her avocation of learning all about them, doing so where few women could live alone. Richard replaced her father in that sense, someone who could create adventure for her.

Marietta had an ego. She is the compassionate yet feisty heroine of her stories, which gives her a way of sharing her husband's halo and to validate her life. Perhaps it is no accident that she died within nine months of telling her story. Her life's purpose was done.

Marietta closely identified with the Navajos, and she was often mistaken for one, so she says. She was five feet, one-and-a-half inches tall, round to heavy at times, with dark hair. Even Geronimo thought she was an Apache, if that story is to be believed. Marietta took her adoption seriously, although the Navajos actually wanted to adopt Richard as a gesture of goodwill. She tried to behave like a Navajo and was accepted as one in return. The behavior may have spared her life when Richard was killed, for they told her they would not kill one of their own. She may have also picked up her propensity for storytelling from the Navajos in the process. She may be guilty of what she accuses the Navajos of doing, and that is of taking advantage of the truth. "They love to fool the white man," she says. The late artist, David Chethlahe Paladin, himself half Navajo, once told me, "Among the Navajo, it isn't important that you tell the truth, only that you tell a good story."

Some of the blame for Marietta's storytelling flaws could be laid at the feet of Lou Blachly, who recorded the stories of more than a hundred pioneers during the 1950s. "Social historians looking for an accurate picture of the times in which the narrators lived are likely to be disappointed by the Pioneers Foundation tapes," wrote oral historian Douglas M. Dinwiddie. "The major reason for this is Lou Blachly's fascination with violence, outlaws, Indian raids, and the generally sensational aspect of the New Mexico west."

Louis Bradley Blachly was born in 1889 on the Western Slope of the Rocky Mountains near Delta, Colorado. In 1893, Blachly's father was shot to death during a robbery where he worked as a cashier in the Farmer and Merchants Bank in Delta he helped create. Blachly had a degree in economics, served in the army as an artillery instructor, and later as a civil servant in the Lend-Lease program which took him to North Africa and Berlin. In 1949, he went to work for the weekly New Mexican newspaper, the *Silver City Enterprise* as advertising manager and columnist. The old-timers of Silver City inspired him to write a column called, "I'll Never Forget." Over the years he interviewed such people as Caesar Brock, a pioneer rancher in the Burro Mountains; Wayne Whitehill, the son of the sheriff who arrested Billy the Kid; and Jack Stockbridge, who was a Rough Rider in Cuba, a forest ranger, and a miner and prospector.

Blachly soon saw the value of his interviews as books and screenplays. In 1952, he became secretary and sole interviewer for the newly formed Pioneers Foundation, which was incorporated, and in which he sold stock shares. Through the foundation, he would be able to copyright his interviews and sell the rights. He then went to work full-time on the project. Blachly first employed a stenographer until a theatre owner lent him the newfangled, yet bulky, tape recorder. He recorded the stories of more than a hundred pioneers.

Blachly hoped to earn a living as an interviewer for the foundation but failed. He promised big profits for the membership, and when they didn't materialize, many became frustrated, as he himself did. He turned toward major corporations and universities for funding, finally resorting to circulating a paper titled, "Death and the Tape Recorder," in which he divided pioneers into three categories: those who had been interviewed and died, those who died before they could be interviewed, and those on the threshold of death "waiting for the return of the man with his tape recorder."

In May of 1953, the University of New Mexico agreed to catalog and transcribe the more than six hundred tapes. Some tapes, however, remained in a library vault at what is now Western New Mexico University and in the basement of the American National Bank in Silver City. By 1955, UNM had paid Blachly mileage and per diem up to two thousand dollars so that he could continue his work, but he quit within two years and moved to Tucson, Arizona, to pursue other interests. He died there in 1965.

Blachly developed a system whereby he gave a narrator a stack of note cards for the purpose of noting stories they would like to tell. He then collected the cards, classified them into categories such as early childhood memories, marriage, etc. He numbered the cards according to category and, with the narrator's assistance, he resorted the cards chronologically and blended in whatever corroborative material he had. He turned to experts for advice, including famed western historians Bernard DeVoto and Myra Ellen Jenkins, then a UNM graduate student. Although Dinwiddie believed Blachly's interviews to be invaluable and the project admirable, he was "less than an ideal interviewer." He didn't follow up on dates, he paid little attention to redundancy, and he inserted stories about himself that had little to do with the narrator's recollections. The narrators described old photographs and artifacts that have never been recovered, including most of the photographs Marietta described.

Because of the wordiness and redundancy of Marietta's narration, it is heavily edited, although I strived to retain her voice. I blended several versions of the same story and sometimes removed them from the original context to present some form of story. When I caught mistakes, I corrected them in the footnotes, which I hope do not intrude too much on the story.

But Marietta told a good story and a valid one. I don't believe she purposely misrepresented the Navajos, although she places them in a light that might draw criticism. Marietta may have inserted herself into a story where she didn't belong, but that doesn't mean the story didn't happen, with or without her. Ironically, Marietta had much to say about the integrity of journalists who tended to misquote her.

Marietta was an adventurer, but she was pragmatic in her observations. When she described a Navajo ceremony, she may have confused the details, but she didn't shroud it in mysticism. She didn't judge their code of ethics no matter how repugnant it might have been to a Victorianesque lady. She once witnessed a mother club her delinquent son to death, and although Marietta didn't condone it, she understood it to be a tactic of survival. She also understood that this behavior was the exception and not the norm. Marietta's empathy for the Navajos, and her desire to become their friend were not invented, even if she and Richard saw themselves as rescuers of the primitive tribe.

I do not offer Marietta's taped recollections as pure ethnohistory, because she even misses the basic rudiments of Navajo religion, but then perhaps the religion was not as formalized as it is now in textbooks. Instead, I offer this as a story about intercultural relations, the ladders from the mesa top to the grassy canyons. Despite the blemishes in Marietta's storytelling, despite the Wetherills' soured good intentions, the wish to learn all about the Native Americans' past and present cannot be dismissed.

An archaeologist once told me that to analyze an artifact, one must sometimes destroy it. This is why archaeologists are disliked by museum curators, she said. Indigenous people cannot be treated like museum pieces, marked with accession numbers, and preserved in a box. To learn of a people one has to become involved with them. Something is always given, and something is taken away and sometimes even destroyed. This is true for the one being observed and for the one observing. The drama the Wetherills encountered with the Navajos symbolizes the cultural conflict and curiosity between the Native Americans and the Euroamericans through history, and the curiosity may have led to Richard Wetherill's death.

The tears of delight and pain, even fifty years later, are still evident in Marietta Wetherill's spoken word.

|| ▲ ||

1

Her Head is Round

I WAS ADOPTED INTO the Navajo tribe when I was twenty-two and living in Chaco Canyon with Mr. Wetherill. The Chee clan, one of the sixteen original clans[1] to have climbed out of the earth into this world, was chosen for me on account of the white blood in my veins and the fact that I would want to eat fish and eggs and pork and other food denied all the other clans. There were many things that the Chee clan were allowed that the others were denied. The Chee clan was more worldly.

The clan adopted me through blood transfusion and it was the most excellent opportunity to get blood poisoning.[2] Yei Tsosi, the medicine man[3] performing the ceremony, scratched me on the top of my arm back of my thumb, just a little scratch about a quarter-inch long, and it showed a little blood. Then he scratched the inside of the arm of the medicine man that was adopting me, old Hosteen Bí'al. Our scratches were bound together with a buckskin string. Our hands held little bags of cornmeal and little bags of pollen. Yei Tsosi touched our feet, our knees, our hands, our mouths, and the top of our heads with an ear of corn and then sprinkled those places with corn pollen. It took about a half hour.

And so went that ceremony of the blood transfusion the first day, and the second day another little scratch was made, and the third day another little scratch was made. Our arms were bound together those three days, and then I was a Navajo, and I have those scratches on my arm now. One shows pretty good, on account I kept peeling off the scab, but the others don't show so well.

Hosteen Bí'al's family was there, his five wives and their children, who didn't pay much attention to me. They hummed a little anthem. They hoped that this child would grow up to be a good child, would grow up to be thought of highly by the People, as they called themselves, would help the Diné in any way she could, and that they would help her in any way they could. They would tell her many things that other people didn't know about the Navajo so that when she was among white people, she could tell them how the Navajo lived. They weren't bad people, they weren't thieves, they didn't go on the warpath and try to hurt the white men.

Actually, the Navajo wanted to adopt Mr. Wetherill because he was giving a sick man a *yeibichai*[4] at our house. Mr. Wetherill was too busy in the ruins to be adopted, so I volunteered. I became the daughter of Hosteen Bí'al; to all intents and purposes I belonged to him. I was his child and he was always good to me and did many things for me and told me many things that I've always appreciated. I think that probably having the blood transfusion was one of the reasons I felt I wanted to do something for the Navajo tribe. And since I'm an old lady now, I find that so much has been written about them that hasn't been intelligently done. The real Navajo had a reason for everything and no one has ever written about that.

I tried to live up to them. One time I rode up the canyon and an old squaw stopped me and asked me where I was going and what I was carrying on the back of my saddle. "I'm taking a twenty-five pound sack of flour and some coffee and sugar to Old Mother Cats," I said. "Nobody seems to take care of her and she belongs to my clan."

She put her arms around me. "You're a real Navajo." Of course, they never would have said Navajo. They called themselves Diné, the People.

How many times had I seen Tomacito riding on his horse over the mesa, whip in one hand, singing at the top of his voice. I don't think in all the things I've seen in my life I ever saw anything that impressed me quite the way it did to see a Navajo sing. Tomacito, he could be a half a mile off and I'd still hear him. He'd sing low, then come up high, and then come down low again. "My grandmother is getting old and she's not very well but the children are all right and the sheep are fat and the grass is growing and the Great Spirit[5] is sending the rain." I'd see Hosteen Hataalii Nez Begay come over the mesa and go down into the canyon, and I'd know then that Mocking Bird Canyon was going to have a little sing.

The *hogans*, or houses, were scattered throughout the Penestuja country south of the Chaco. Here's one in the canyon, there's one up on the rimrock, and another one over here four or five miles away. A runner would spread the news that Hosteen Hataalii Nez Begay or some other medicine man was going to stay all night and have a little *biji*, a one-day ceremony. The neighbors would come and have coffee and a bite to eat and a visit, and the medicine man would tell them what was going on in the community.

If I took the notion, I'd go to the ceremonies my clan had. If the babies were asleep and I had a good girl looking after them, why I'd get on my horse and go singing up the canyon, too. I was welcome because I was part of them.

One time thirty or forty children were there and I sat down with them. The squaws came out and sat by me. Then the medicine man came along and asked each child, "What did I sing at your hogan?" The kids were scared to death and they cuddled up to their mothers and cried. The clowns, dressed ridiculously, switched them a little bit and the medicine man said, "Next year you remember what I told you. If you ever want to sing in the big yeibichai you've got to remember what I teach you."[6] It was like kindergarten.

Then he asked me what he sang at Mocking Bird's biji and I hummed it to him and he rewarded me with a silver concha for remembering the song. The squaws laughed and hugged and patted me. "See how the white people remember?" the medicine man would say. "Her head's round and she remembers and she's going to tell all these things some day to the white people. As soon as she gets back to the house she's going to write to it all down."[7] Which I never did.

Father sent me to the Chicago School of Dramatic Art to study elocution when I was a child. The man there said he never saw anything like my memory. He said, "I only gave you that piece yesterday and you have all twenty-odd verses. How do you do that?" I couldn't solve a simple problem in mental arithmetic if my life depended on it. I never studied much; it was hard work. Anything I could commit to memory was easy for me. I had civil government letter perfect, but arithmetic and deportment kept me back. If we were on a trip in the Southwest or someplace like that, my parents would put us in school for a couple weeks just to see if we were progressing in our studies at the right pace. They told us if we weren't, they'd send us to school back in Kansas. I'd memorize the textbooks so that wouldn't happen.

The medicine men wanted me to see and learn everything so that I could tell the white people. One of the things I learned was that the Navajo were superstitious. When we first went to Chaco Canyon there wasn't a Navajo living there, not a one. They herded their sheep in there but they didn't live in the canyon. They lived up on the mesa tops and the rimrocks. They did camp at the end of the canyon where it opened out into that great vast country and also in the canyon that went straight south out of Chaco. We always called that the [South] Gap because we could look straight south for miles. But they never lived in the canyon and when I asked them why they said it was crowded with the souls of too many dead people there.

I was riding home one time with Jessie, an Indian girl, very intelligent. We heard an owl hoot up on the cliff and she said, "Stop," and got off her horse. "What's the matter?" "Shhh, be quiet." She took a little stick and drew a little round circle there in the sand, with round circles all around it. Then she took her hand and built up a little mound of dirt in the center and she said, "Now the evil spirit[8] in that owl will come over here to see what we were doing and he'll stay here until we get home."

Can you imagine living in fear like that? If a duck flew over their hogan in a certain direction they'd think it prophesied a death in the family. It seemed to me that they lived in a sort of constant terror of the evil spirit. "Why do you fear the evil spirit?" I'd ask. "I'm not afraid of any evil spirit. I've never done anything."

"I've never done anything, either, but the evil spirit will get you," they'd say. The first time we came to Chaco Canyon the Navajo advised us to leave, because it was such a dangerous place to live. After Mr. Wetherill was killed they said to me, "We told you, but you wouldn't listen."

Those ruins were on Mr. Wetherill's homestead claim and the agreement was that when they made Chaco Canyon a national monument, he would turn over to the government all the land on which the ruins were and they could give him land someplace else around there. At least they made Chaco Canyon a national monument [in 1907], which was exactly what Mr. Wetherill wanted, but he never lived to settle the claim.

Mr. Wetherill was known all over the world for his work. He had his work in every museum in the United States and in foreign countries. He was not only an explorer but an adventurer, too. He had discovered the Mesa Verde cliff dwellings. He had developed Chaco Canyon a hundred and fifty miles from Albuquerque and there hadn't been two people here that had ever seen it. He put it on the map. His name is in all the scientific books written on Chaco Canyon.

When Mr. Wetherill was killed, we put the body on the back porch and the Indians came and sang and danced around him. He was later buried up the canyon from Pueblo Bonito and there are as many as twenty graves there now because so many Indians wanted to be near him. They didn't want to kill him. They went to their hogans that day and talked all through the night about how they could have done it differently, but the Navajo didn't kill Mr. Wetherill. Those Indian agents, both white men, killed him. They wanted control of Chaco Canyon. They promised the Navajo they would build a school there and dam up the canyon for enough water for all their cattle and horses if only they made Mr. Wetherill go away.

But I'm not bitter.

I've had people question my sanity for loving the Navajo after what they done. I can't condemn them all for one accident of wrath. I never blamed the Navajo for what happened to my family.

I've lived among the Indians all my life and I always wanted to know all about them. That was the thing . . . my life. I always said that was what I was going to do, I was going to study Indians all my life, and I came very near doing it.

Now that I'm old, I'm going to tell you the story of the Navajo, as intelligently as I can.

NOTES

[1]One version of the Navajo legends is that when Changing Woman, a mythological deity, made human beings, she created six groups who formed the original clans. Marietta mentions the sixteen original clans often and once drew pictures of them. The number four, or multiples of four, carries great significance in Navajo numerology, and a reference to the sixteen original clans hasn't turned up in published ethnology, nor has reference to the Chee clan and eating restrictions.

[2]When the story of her adoption was first published in *Scribners Magazine* in May 1932, Navajos wrote letters denying that they adopted non-Indians in this type of ceremonial, but she insisted it was true.

[3]Those who perform curing ceremonials are called *hataalii*, or singers, or chanters. "Medicine man" is a title imposed on the position by whites. A sing is usually done in conjunction with sandpainting and dancing in costume.

[4]Yeibichai, also ye'i bichei, is a dance in the Night Chant or Night Way in which dancers wear masks of the *Yeis*, or gods, the male and female figures who represent the forces of nature.

[5]Marietta refers to the Great Spirit often and translates it, to *Nataani Soto*, in Navajo. But the Navajo do not traditionally have a supreme being. Perhaps the Navajo invented the term in response to the Christian God. The closest to omniscience are Changing Woman, Sun, and the Twin War Gods, with the Sun possibly being the most powerful, although not as important today. Lesser deities include the Yeis.

[6]Some whipping does occur in initiation into certain rites.

[7]The Navajo, had flat heads because they kept their babies strapped to cedar bark cradleboards. Aleš Hrdlička, a physical anthropologist noted in 1908 that questions pertaining to intentional deformation met with laughter. An older woman said the Navajo doesn't like a head that protrudes behind, illustrating the words with her hands.

[8]The dead are considered the source of *chindee*, or malevolent ghosts. The ruins are called *kits'iil*, and are the *Anaasázi Bighan*, Home of the Ancient Enemy, who contributed to the destruction of the Fourth World. These sacred places figure prominently by name in their origin legends, or *Diné Bahane'*, and are considered to be *báábázid*, literally "for it there is fear and reverence," because of the supernatural forces still lingering around them. Only specialized persons can approach these ruins. But not all Navajos believed this way, hence the looting of the ruins.

2

When My Trail Crossed Geronimo's

WE READ ABOUT RICHARD WETHERILL discovering those ruins at Mesa Verde, but we didn't meet the Wetherills until after several trips west. We got the idea to be a traveling musical family on our first trip to Colorado. We went home and practiced a whole year and returned to Colorado the following summer. Father bought a stereopticon and I lectured about travel in Europe, though I'd never been there and couldn't pronounce all the names correctly.

The song "Irish Washerwoman" reminds me of the time we played in Crippled Creek. "On a three-legged stool sits Paddy so free; no king in his palace so happy as he." I haven't thought of that song in fifty years. We stopped for a number of days. There were so many miners there. After we gave one entertainment they insisted on our staying and giving more and then we played at night for dances.

The first night I was dressed in a little dotted-Swiss dress with the little ruffled skirts and underskirts that stood all out, red stockings and red slippers and a red ribbon in my dark hair. We played "Irish Washerwoman" on our string instruments and the miners threw thirty-one silver dollars on the stage. It was all silver and it just rang and rang and I thought we were getting so much.

My father, Sidney LaVern Palmer, could play any instrument, just like my son, Dick. He was a marvel with the violin, never took a lesson in his life. His flute playing intrigued the Indians. Sent for the flute in Europe someplace. Now Father, during his early life, played the E-flat cornet in John Philip Sousa's band. He used to travel seventy-six miles to Chicago to play in that band.

Father was an inventor. He invented the player piano and sold the model for five dollars. Never had it patented. The man who bought it made a million dollars on it. When he was a telegraph operator, Father invented a set of mirrors so that the operator could see the train coming both ways. This thing was in every telegraph office in the United States and Europe, too. My father built a trailer for his automobile chassis and sold it to Henry Ford.

After sitting in the same chair as a telegraph operator for seventeen years, he moved our family to Kansas where he became involved in land development. We did most of our traveling out of Kansas after he made a little money. Father made a lovely camping wagon, a Studebaker with a cedar roof which he kept polished. It extended out over the wheels, a good looking affair and well made. It was so arranged that we could all sleep inside if necessary. The door was in the back and the seats opened up like piano stools. Mother and Father slept in the bottom of the wagon, my brother slept on one side, and I on the other, and my sister had a hammock that stretched across the wagon. Our instruments were kept in built-in cabinets covered with glass; there was even a place for dishes fixed very much like on a steamship. Everything had hooks over them so they would stay in their places and there was a place in the back for clothing.

My brother, Vern, who was six years younger than me, turned out to be a little like Father. Made himself a world authority on mineralogy. He's passed on now. Worked for the Guggenheims for thirty-three years and they carried him around on a gold plate. When the Guggenheims sold to Federated Metals in New Jersey, Vern went right along. Made discoveries in the amalgamation of ores and in mining and he made some machinery. The models cost $75,000 to make. They gave him any money he needed for inventions. Sidney LaVern Palmer, Jr. I'm like him.

I was a little like my father, too. I could play anything and I thought about inventions, too. When I was a little girl and Mother told me to clean under the stove, I wondered why the stove didn't have an apron around the legs to keep the dirt from getting under there or why the bathtub didn't go all the way to the floor so that you wouldn't have to crawl under to get the soap and socks. Somebody eventually thought of those things. But you see I was a woman. I didn't use my inventing. It isn't that it wasn't there. It isn't that I didn't have those thoughts. I did have.

My mother, Elizabeth Ann Palmer, was a graduate from the New England Conservatory of Music in Boston and then Grandfather sent her to Italy to study music. She told me the nicest thing she ever did was to play for a tea for Queen Victoria in London. She sang two little pieces: "I Dreamt I Dwelt in Marble Halls," and

"The Last Rose of Summer." She had a wonderful voice. We didn't pay much attention to what our mother did outside of cooking and seeing that we were properly clothed. She spent hours inserting lace in my little aprons, such an artist at everything she did. I remember standing at the side of the piano and she would say, "Get a little chair and sit by Mother."

The grand piano had teeth marks all around those grapes and things on the legs. Mother would tie me there because I wouldn't stay and practice. She'd tie me there and then I chewed. I guess that's why I eventually learned to play.

I disgusted my sister, Edna, once. She was eight years younger than I. I visited her in Kansas after I was married. She'd been practicing hard on a piano piece, "Tripping Through the Meadow." Practiced for months getting ready for a recital. I sat down and played it after hearing her play it for a couple days. She said, "Why didn't you tell me you could play it?" I said, "I've never heard it before." She got sick and I ended up playing in the concert. She taught music in a government conservatory in Panama. Her husband was Goethal's private secretary when the Panama Canal was being built and she taught piano and took cornet lessons because she wanted me to excel in cornet. To me it was as natural as breathing. If I hear a piece twice, I can play it, even now with these old stiff hands that look like I'd found them in an alley some place.

With parents like mine, I ought to have made something of myself, but I didn't. Three girls and a boy in my family. The last sister didn't come until I was twenty, well after I married Mr. Wetherill. She is the most talented, but I hardly know her. I was so crazy about the outdoors and so crazy about the Indians. I've never done anything but crawl. Always been looking for something.

I was only a little girl when Grandfather [Mark] Hoag held me on his knee and told me stories about crossing the plains. He told me about how they had to circle their wagons and fight off the Indians and how the Indians would go around the wagons yelling and whooping and shooting arrows at them.

Grandfather Hoag had a hunger for traveling. When he was a young man, he left New York, where he was born, and built a little cottage on a piece of land near Chicago, now Hyde Park. But he got dissatisfied and a man came along and told him all about the wonders of the West. He traded land for a team of oxen and a yoke and a wagon with bows and canvas to cover it and started south through southern Illinois. He bought land and lived there for ten years. He grew vegetables and cut hay with a butcherknife and baled it. He traded his hay and vegetables for gold to the pioneers who passed by his property during the Gold Rush of 1849. Sold his onions for a dollar apiece.

He put his best gold nuggets around his waist in a buckskin belt he made, then he packed the rest into a rawhide trunk and he went to San Francisco. After a while he thought it would be interesting to sail to New York on a chartered ship.

The ship got down past South America and got too close to the coast. A terrific wind came up and his boat was wrecked on the rocks. Grandfather and his pals made a raft out of the doors from the ship and set the raft out onto the water. They were thrashed around and one of the men got frightened and jumped off the raft. The four men left hung on the best they could. Grandfather lost his little trunk when everything was washed off the raft.

Their raft was torn to pieces and they were thrown against the rock and one of the men's legs were broken. They couldn't hang on to the rocks for long. They crawled toward the shore and a wave came along and took them back into the sea. My grandfather was a large, vigorous man, and he and two of the other men finally got off the rocks and got to shore.

They lay there all day. They were so bruised and battered they didn't know whether they were going to live or not and this man with the broken legs was suffering terrible. Their clothes were torn off them and they didn't know what to do.

They laid there through the night naked, and the next morning some Indians came and carried them to their camp. They laid the man out with the broken legs and took care of him and he recovered. They all did.

Grandfather stayed there with those Indians three years, always looking for a ship, always looking for a way to get away. They learned to talk the language pretty well and the Indians finally told them if they would walk straight south for one moon, they would come to the Point of Land. They knew then that they must have shipwrecked on the coast of Chile. The Indians told them to build

28

a big fire and someday a ship would come by and get them. But, they warned, be careful of the other Indians who might not like you as much as we do.

Grandfather and the other men started out and they walked and walked. They had learned to trap birds and fish and live just the same as the Indians. They finally got down to the horn and built a big fire and fed it day and night. Finally a ship came by and took them around to New York.

Grandfather made so much money in hogs that he built a lovely home for us. We traveled some from Illinois. Visited the Seminoles in Florida and the Sioux in the Dakotas. But we did most of our traveling after Grandfather died and we moved to Kansas.

Sometimes we'd be gone for two or three months. Other times until the snow run us off. We were such tramps. Mother and Father would put a ruler on the map and figure the miles as the crow flies, but that was never accurate. Sometimes we didn't make much mileage in a day because we'd have to stop and look at things. Other days we could travel twenty-five miles. That was a big, good day.

We'd start out early in the morning and then we always stopped at noon to let the mules roll. Tender and True, from a biblical song, were the names of two of our mules. The one had a lovely disposition and was always willing to work but if I slapped the other with the reins, she was liable to kick back because her ears were tender. When we went to New Mexico, we bought two lead mules who took to the whip better. They were called Canyon and Mesa. Father said, "They've got the stuff to pull us where we want to go and just keep away from them," which I did.

Every morning we'd have to get up and hunt our stock. Sometimes we didn't find it or somebody'd run it off, so that they'd get a little bounty to help find it. We learned that always the fella [often a Navajo] that came in the morning and offered to go get them was the one that hid them behind some hill. It never worried us any because we knew they'd bring them in. They could tell we had money to pay for it.

On one trip we traveled from Albuquerque, New Mexico, clear to Taos and back and we visited every Indian village on the Rio Grande, both sides. The Indians who lived along the Rio Grande are named for their adobe apartment house villages called *pueblos* by the Spaniards. Sometimes we were on the wrong side of the river from the pueblo, so we waded into water up to our waists, and the Indians would come out and take our hands, us children.

The Indians were as offish as wild rabbits the first day of the visit. Father showed them the money he would pay for a piece of pottery or corn fodder for the mules. They took it and got whatever it was we wanted, very business-like. But after we played for them once, they jumped at the chance to do things for us. They followed us around like the pied piper.

The Pueblo people were the smartest people in the world. They never quarreled about accepting other denominational efforts to civilize them. For centuries the Jesuits built missionary churches right at the pueblos, and the Indians always let them in. But they continued their ceremonies in secret before or after church services or before the big public ceremonies. The Navajos would come by the hundreds the same as we did to get food and to trade and to see the dances so that they could copy them or improve their own. They all used one another's ideas.

Father and Mother were Quakers, not particularly religious. Father was an atheist. He said we evolved from bugs and worms and fish. I didn't know what he was talking about until I was much older. On the other hand, Mother and Father were great temperance workers in Kansas; they couldn't believe the overindulgence of liquor. They drove forty miles to a temperance meeting and they once entertained Carrie Nation when she was on one of her raids.

Father read *The Age of Reason: An Investigation of True and Fabulous Theology* by Thomas Paine, an author of revolutionary times. He dared say what he thought was right. So many people have those feelings but they don't dare share them. They're afraid. I once read about a Mr. So and So who was put in jail for building a telescope because someone thought he would interfere with the heavenly bodies. They sometimes say that you never get to the age of reason, they're all such fools, but that isn't the way they mean.

Both Grandmother Palmer and Grandmother Hoag were religious, the two I was named for, Mary and Etta. Grandmother Hoag was a wonderful woman and housekeeper and was good to everybody. She wanted the words, "I have no enemies," chiseled on her tombstone. All the people she knew were her friends and she hoped to meet them in the hereafter and she was sure she would.

I remember sitting by Grandmother Palmer's bed when she was dying. I was only twelve then. I told her God had been good to her and he was going to take her right to heaven. "That's what makes me feel so bad," she said. "I've been a good Congregationalist all my life and I will go to heaven, I know that, but I'll be so lonesome there." "What do you mean?" I asked. She said, "Your father's a wicked man, he don't believe in God at all, and your grandfather [William Palmer], he's wicked, too. They would never have him in heaven the way he is. And look at Jess and Corey, they belong to the Episcopal Church, they would never go to heaven; and I won't have anybody there." I've thought of that a lot. I wouldn't want to be there in heaven, either. Of course, I got my idea of religion from the Indians. The Navajo didn't believe in a heaven after death.

The first time we went to Jemez Pueblo we found the priest locked in stocks because he'd interfered with their ceremonials. Mother and Father put logs under him so he could sit and they wrapped him with a sheepskin they found on a fence. Mother fed him coffee and breakfast. Father gave the governor of the pueblo a silver dollar, which was a tremendous amount of money in those days, and they unlocked him. But Father had to sponsor him and say that he wouldn't let him go into the *estufas* or interfere with any ceremonials again.

When evening came we could hear singing coming from the estufa. An *estufa* [or kiva] is an underground chamber where they do all their secret work. "Estufa" is a Spanish word meaning stove, because believe you me it gets hot down there with fifty or sixty big husky Indians adancin' and the perspiration just rollin' off of them. You'd sweat too, I'll tell you, and it doesn't smell too good, either.

The men have their own estufas and the women have theirs. Sometimes they weave and make baskets and other ceremonial items in there. The Pueblos can take a month getting ready for the ceremonials. They have to catch birds and select feathers for the different costume pieces, such as the pompon that's on the head, and paint them and tie horse hair to the ends of them. They have to go to the mountains and the valley for certain medicines, then dry and grind them up. The houses all have to be replastered inside and out.

31

And then there is the food—just think what those hungry Navajos ate when they came. Hundreds of pounds of corn has to be ground for the bread and to sprinkle on the dancers. Everybody in the community from the smallest child has to work in the preparations.

All that had been done before we got there. We didn't know anything about it but we did want to see inside the estufa. We went up to the top of the estufa and Father told the guard at the tip of the ladder in the opening that we'd like to go down in and see what they were doing. He refused to let us. Father asked where the governor was and the Pueblo pointed below. "Bring him up," Father said. So he brought the governor up and Father gave him two dollars in silver, which was a fortune. "My daughter and I want to go down in to the estufa," he said all in hand motions because we didn't speak much Spanish [which most Pueblo Indians could speak] and we didn't speak [Towa, the language of Jemez Pueblo]. They consulted awhile and then one Indian said we were crazy in the head anyway and let us go down, it wouldn't do any harm.

Of course we didn't understand at the time what it was all about because we never had been among these Indians before, but we did learn a lot. We saw that they believed in it, and that it was a sacred ceremony and deserved anybody's respect. We watched for a little while and then Father gave each man there ten cents. He always kept his pockets full of change. And we left.

The next morning the governor and an interpreter who spoke as much English as we spoke Spanish said they would like to have us lead the parade to the church. We played a Sousa's march and walked deliberately to the church—Father and I played the B-flat cornet, Brother the alto, Mother the tuba, Sister the triangle. Can you imagine how absolutely funny?

The priest waited for the procession at the door. He just put up a hand to end the parade and motioned us inside. We walked in and laid our instruments on a bench and then we sat on the floor—there were no pews—while he did whatever he did. I didn't understand it but he anointed some of them and put his hands out like he was blessing the dancers, and then everybody walked out and we took our stuff and went back to our camp.

In a little while the dance started and a boy came to tell us to come. You can see just how friendly they were and how they liked

32

us. Wasn't it wonderful that they could believe us? Then we were invited into one of the Indian houses and had dinner: roast meat, lamb and ribs, bread, and coffee. The ceremony was over when the sun went down, and as far as we could find out that was the prayers for rain on their crops. That was July.

From there we went up to Santo Domingo and Taos. The Spanish told us the Santo Domingo Pueblos were mean and they wouldn't be nice to us, so we didn't even go near their village the first day. We just camped out on this side of the river, built a nice little bonfire, and played our music. I've often wondered what they thought when they heard the first few strains of some of those songs we played. They came just like shadows, just way out there, and stood around. After we'd played two or three pieces Father went out and told them to come closer to the fire and Mother smiled that nice pleasant smile of hers. The children appeared and the candy came out and was distributed around.

I know they've been done so many times that they thought, "now here's a new gag," but it wasn't. It was just some people who wanted to know them so bad and wanted to like them so much. They couldn't help but like us because we had nothing to sell and we bought whatever they had. Mother occasionally bought pottery and Father fixed a little box and sent it home to Kansas. Our approach was so different from any people they had ever met, see. We wanted to know them and they realized it. We stayed there and I learned how to drill oyster shells and turquoise into little beads.

In the spring of 1885 we went into the Mogollon Mountains [south of Albuquerque].[1] My father had heard about some great ruins in the mountains, and so we went always by mouth to mouth and from ranch to ranch. That was the way we traveled. We did find some ruins, but not the ones we were looking for. Some Mexicans working for us said it was Willow Springs. I've never been able to find that spot on the map, but probably some old timer would know whether there was a local name for it. Maybe it was Willow Creek.

These ruins were inaccessible and we had to lower our wagons over cliffs with ropes between there and Magdalena to get to it. I have a picture of us doing that. You can see it was awfully cold because Mother was wearing a sealskin coat. Look at my curls. I look like a big girl of twelve or fourteen, but I was just a little girl [of nine] wearing my mother's wool skirts that came down over my legs. We each had a rope end. This is my brother here and that's my father there. I don't know where my little sister was.

We camped several days a few feet from a spring. It had a good deal of water in it and it made a little creek down below. Sometimes a few cattle or horses got in the water and stomped around and we'd have to clean it out and wait until the water got clear before we dipped our drinking water. You know how people did in those days. We camped there several days and Father got some men to help him excavate in those ruins.

We had two small tents. Father got them in Albuquerque, for what purpose I don't know, to make more trouble I guess. We used one for sleeping and one for cooking. I guess it was on account of the cold that Father got them. Father got up in the morning before everyone else and built a fire before the open tent while the rest of us stayed in our bedrolls until the tents warmed up. Snow gets to be five to six feet on top of the Mogollons.

One morning Father wouldn't allow me to go out where the men were digging in the ruins because I hadn't got my lessons the day before and he said, "Whenever you get your arithmetic done and can read certain pages in the reader, why then you can come out." I wasn't interested in reading that morning and instead I played on the sunny side of one of the tents. I found some buffalo pumpkins, those gourds that grow wild all over the country and have such an awful stink. By putting little sticks in them I made horses and cattle out of them. I had to create my own toys.

I was making a little corral for these horses when I looked up and saw this bunch of Indians riding toward me, and one rode right up close to where I was playing there.

"Where is the water?" he said to me.

I thought he was talking Navajo and I answered him. I was the one to always pick up the languages because of this thin tongue of mine, as the Navajo always said. I pointed to the spring. "The water's there and the buckets are in the tent."

He got down off his horse and he turned to some of the men and said, "Water the horses, the buckets are in the tent." Then he said to me, "Do you speak Apache or Navajo?"

"I speak both, I guess." Oh, so proud that I was so smart, you know, and not a worry in the world about them being Indians.

"Where you come from?" he said.

I told him Kansas was my home, away off. That didn't mean anything to him at all. "You're an Apache girl." You see I had this black hair and Mother parted it in the middle and it was braided down the back in two long braids.

"No, I'm a white girl."

He laughed and said, "You awful dark for a white girl. Where's your people?"

"They're up there digging in the ruins." He sent a man up to look and he skulked around the hill and came back in a few minutes and he said, yes, there's two white people, two white children, and some Mexicans digging up there."

"Why aren't you playing with the other children?"

"I didn't get my lessons and my father made me stay here to study."

"I'm going to take you with me," he says. "They stole you to do their work here."

"No, nobody makes me work anywhere. I don't work, I just play all the time, but I have to get my lessons."

I noticed they had those big mules, large as some of ours. I had never seen any Indians with big mules; most had small ones. But, you know, kid-like I didn't think anything about it.

I stood up and he says, "You're a nice big girl, but you're an Apache. You can go to my camp. I'll give you a pony."

"I have a pony."

"You can play with the other Apache children."

"No, my mother wouldn't like that. She'd cry. I'm my mother's little girl."

"We're going to take this girl with us," he yelled to his men.

"No, we're in a hurry," one of them said. "We have to go fast. We don't want to be bothered with a girl."

"We can come back and get her," he said. So they decided not to take me. "What do they give you to eat?" he asked.

"We have bread and meat, everything we need."

"Do you have fresh meat?"

"No, we have ham and bacon but the Mexicans are going to bring us a sheep tomorrow."

"Go and get some beef for my Apache girl," he said to one of the men.

The man threw the tarp off one of these mules that was packed quite high and big with stuff and took out a quarter of dirty looking beef. He put it on the cook table, then they repacked the mule. One said, "We'd better hurry."

They started right up the road trotting right along, like Indians do. They got a block away from our camp and they turned straight up the mountain. It was kind of slag, loose rock and they had an awful time getting those big mules and some of those horses up that mountain. They had several extra horses, too. But they finally got up and went out of sight. Lazy as I was, I stood up and came around in front and watched them go up that hill.

I went on with my playthings and of course I had my book handy in case Father came down to camp, but they didn't come until it was time to have dinner. Mother went into the tent first. "Where'd all the meat come from?"

"The Apaches brought it," I said.

"Apaches. There's no Apaches in this country," Father said.

"These were Apaches. They talked Apache to me and I talked Navajo to them."

"I don't want to hear any fairy tales," he said, so I shut up.

"The meat's awful dirty," Mother said. "I'll have to cut off an awful lot of it."

"The dog will love it," Father said.

So she carved up the meat and we had steak and potatoes for dinner. We were sitting down in this cook tent eating our dinner when a bunch of soldiers rode up. Quite a bunch, I'd say ten or fifteen, almost as many as there were Indians, maybe a few more because I didn't count either bunch.

One man got off his horse and came up to the tent. "What in the world are you doing, camping here with your wife and children with Geronimo on the rampage?" he demanded.

"Geronimo?" my father said. We'd never heard of him.

"Yes, they killed a bunch of freighters right down here at Willow Springs, burned everything they had and took their mules. We followed their tracks here."

"My daughter was here at the camp getting her lessons and she said some Apaches were here today," Father said. "They left a quarter of beef because they thought she was an Apache."

"Well, you better get out of here right now because he's sure on the warpath and he's liable to be back any minute."

"My daughter will know which way they went."

I was in the limelights then and I just stood up and said, "They went right up the road." Now why did I do that? I didn't tell them that they turned off and went right up on the mountain. Geronimo surrendered in the following year in 1886. They say five thousand soldiers chased Geronimo all over the Mogollons but we never saw any of them. He went from Fort Bowie in Arizona with five hundred more Apaches to Florida and they brought him to Fort Sill in Oklahoma.

We went to Fort Sill in the fall of '86. We set up camp near the fort and in the evening as usual we made our fire and played our music. Some of the soldiers came there and they told Father and Mother that they had captured Geronimo and they had him there in the stockades.

"Well, we want to go and see that man; he was supposed to have been at our camp," Mother said. They told me to stay put while they walked over to see him. I'm sorry to say I didn't always mind. After they got nicely established over there and I knew they'd stay some little time, I threatened my little sister to stay behind and not to tell. It was about 6:30 or 7:00, just dusk in September. I chased over and looked around the fort. They had Indians, quite a few of them, and there was one that I picked out that I thought was Geronimo but he was quite different. You know he looked different a prisoner than he did a victor.[2]

NOTES

[1]Marietta confuses the dates of these trips so much it is difficult to discriminate between which events happened on which trip. She said she met Geronimo in the spring of 1885, which happens to be the same year they first came to New Mexico, and impossible since she says she was able to speak to Geronimo in Navajo. A version of this story appeared in *Sun Trails* magazine, May 1952, in which she said the year before she met Geronimo, she and her family lived among the Navajos at Pueblo Pintado where she learned the language. Several versions of this story exist in her taped recollections.

[2]Geronimo, Spanish for Jerome, was born in Arizona in 1829, under the name of Goyathlay, or "one who yawns." He joined a fierce band of Mexican Apaches, known as Chiricahuas, in raiding northern Mexico and the U.S. territory. He became chief, and his highly publicized raids provoked a national clamor for his capture. He and his followers were forced by Federal authorities onto "Hells Forty Acres" at San Carlos, Arizona, in 1876. He escaped three times after 1881 and a fourth and final time in 1885 with thirty-five warriors, eight teenage boys, and 101 women and children to care for. For a year, five thousand U.S. troops and five hundred Indian auxiliaries chased Geronimo and his band all over New Mexico and Arizona until he surrendered in 1886. He was imprisoned at Pensacola, Florida, and resettled at Fort Sill, Oklahoma. He died in 1909.

|| ▲ ||

3

Proposal on the San Juan

IN 1895 FATHER FINALLY decided it was time we saw those Mesa Verde ruins. When the spring warmed up sufficiently, we headed out toward Mancos, Colorado, where the Wetherills lived. We followed the Uncompaghre River in Colorado, the loveliest, most boisterous river I had ever seen. The water didn't flow, it leaped. It bounded from one rock to another and in some places the water looked like whipped cream. It wasn't a river, it was alive.

When we arrived at Mancos, our outfit created interest, as usual. Father went into the store and asked the man there where the Wetherill ranch was. He told us to go two and a half miles down this other road and we'd come to it.

When we came in sight of the Alamo, Father stopped the team and said, "Now that looks like a ranch. There's the haystacks and the big barns and everything neat and clean. There's the big plaza right in the center with the house on one side, the gardens and fruit trees at the back and the great alamo trees and a ditch running right through the yard." The house didn't impress us too much, but it was so comfortable looking, just like you'd dream a farm should be.

We drove into this center plaza and my father got out and knocked on one of the doors of the house. An elderly man answered and Father said, "I'm Sidney LaVern Palmer and I've come here to go see those ruins you've discovered."

"Oh, yes," he said. "Actually my eldest son, Richard, and my son-in-law, Charlie Mason, found them, but they're not here at present. Charlie, he's down at McElmo where he lives with my daughter, and Richard is with his brother, Clayton, on a trip to Arizona to see the Hopi snake dance."

"I'm equipped to take care of myself, don't want to bother anybody, have all my resources right in the wagon," Father said. "I need a place for my mules and the children's saddlehorses. I'd like to give them some hay and grain if you have it. If not we can drive back to town for it after we turn out."

"We have plenty of hay, and plenty of corrals," Mr. [Benjamin Kite] Wetherill said. He directed us behind the house where we could camp among the cottonwoods on a high grassy bank above the river.

We decided to stay and wait for Richard Wetherill to come home so we could see Mesa Verde with its discoverer. There were quite a number of people around—tourists outfitted at the Alamo before going to Mesa Verde. The Wetherills provided the horses, saddles, and food to take people up to the ruins. Everyone in the Western Country had heard of Mesa Verde by then because Baron Gustaf Nordenskiöld had excavated it. I rode with Win through the fields to look for deer and I accompanied Father Wetherill to town a number of times for the mail and groceries for my family. I liked Mother [Marion Tompkins] Wetherill and right from the first she liked me. She was quite a talker and very friendly.

"You're the most unusual girl I've ever met," she said to me.

"How do you mean?" I asked.

"You seem to have been so many places and are so interested in all the things we're interested in."

"I was born a pioneer," I said. "I've traveled all over the United States. I ought to know something because I've been learning all the time."

I told her about how we homesteaded in Kansas when I was a small girl. Our first house was a one-room dugout, about twelve feet by twenty feet in size. People lived in dugouts around there because they were afraid of cyclones. Father made a bed that took up the entire room when it was unfolded. He called it a Mormon bed because he slept in it with Mother and her two sisters, and my sister and brother and myself. When we laid the bed down at night we had to hang the table and chairs from the ceiling on big hooks.

The room had no floor, just dirt, same as the Indians. Rained harder in the house than outside, and brought in the mud, too. The dirt roof always leaked after the rain stopped and we had to put boards down on the floor to walk around. The dugout had a double set of doors with a bar across one and the other being a storm door in case of cyclones, but that didn't stop the rain from pouring down the walls. I said, "That looks like Niagara Falls," and Mother was so mad she said she would spank me if I said it again. I renamed the cascading water Bridal Veil Falls and then I got the spanking.

Father Wetherill and I went to town and on the way back he said, "I kind of feel the boys are going to be in today. They've been gone six weeks and they're ten days overdue." When we drove up, we could see that a pack outfit had just pulled into the big plaza and he whipped the horses and drove in and sure enough that was the boys.

I'd heard so much about Richard and Clate from Mother Wetherill, but I was perfectly satisfied with Win. He was the young one and he'd taken me around a lot and I thought he was a pretty nice boy myself. He was only a few years older than me. Clate and Richard were dirty and travel-worn and had long beards on. I wasn't impressed with them.

Mother Wetherill was so delighted the boys were home she invited us over to dinner that evening. "We'll make a little homecoming party of it." She loved to do this better than anything in the world. The dining room was long and the table ran full length of it. I suppose it would easily seat twenty people and Mother Wetherill always kept several girls to work for her and they had so much to eat. It was quite a treat for us. The evening was just one never to forget.

When I saw the boys again they were all cleaned up and looked quite different. I was absolutely enthralled with the stories that Richard told us about his discovery at Mesa Verde. The Wetherills ran cattle with the help of the Utes and Richard learned to speak Ute so he could talk to them. The Ute kept telling him, "Up on that mountain there's big cities." The Wetherill brothers had found and excavated a few small ruins down in the flats, including Sandal House, maybe ten or twelve rooms. But they didn't pay any attention to the talk of big cities, it seemed so ridiculous.

Acowitz, a Ute, who worked in the barns and gardens one day offered to help Richard find some cattle that had strayed up on Mesa Verde. That range belonged to the Utes and they made it unpleasant for people who tried to go up there to get their cattle. Acowitz took Richard Wetherill and Charlie Mason along a well-marked trail where they followed cattle tracks clear up on top of the mesa and across for several miles.

Old Acowitz patted Richard on the shoulder and said, "Come see the big city." Richard followed him to the edge of the cliff and right across the canyon was Cliff Palace. Mr. Wetherill was speechless. He had never seen anything like it. He motioned for Charlie Mason to come see it. Charlie rode up on the other side of Acowitz and he, like Richard, was dumfounded. He just sat there on his horse and looked and wondered what in the world he was looking at. After awhile Old Acowitz patted Richard on the arm and said, "You no like?" "We like but we don't understand," Richard said.

The day after the dinner party we went down into Weber Canyon to do some excavating in Sandal House. I think that Mr. Wetherill was rather selfish about his ruins. He loved those ruins so that he hated to see them excavated and torn up. If he could have found out all about the people that lived in them without taking out all that dirt and stone it would have made him happy indeed.

Father was the first to fall in love with Richard Wetherill. They were of like mind. I didn't think much about him because he was so much older than I, and there were several other cowboys around there that were my age. Richard would never tell how old he was and I said, "Are you ashamed of your age?" But according to his mother he was thirty-seven. I was nineteen. Once I got to know him I couldn't tell that he was twice my age. He was such a young, vigorous, quick, energetic, ambitious man that you never thought about his age. He didn't have any age. He was the same age when he died that he was when I married him. Many times I felt much older than he because he was real boyish.

He had a mustache. His hair was black and slightly gray in the temples and his eyes were black and penetrating. He looked a hole right into you. He wasn't a big man, about five feet nine or ten, and never fat. He didn't have time to put any fat on. He was too busy working night and day. Sleeping was something that he never did unless he had to.

There was a Mormon man with two wives down in Weber Canyon with about eighteen children between them. I had never known a man with two wives. We got well-acquainted and swam and fished together in the creek. It was hard for me to be grown up when there was a chance to play with the children. I could be two years old or twenty; it didn't make any difference.

We felt we were far away from everything and everybody. All the sounds we ever heard were natural. The water trickled down the river there and we'd hear the birds all day and at night we'd hear all the squeals and squawks the wild animals made. The coyotes serenaded us every night. I knew how to answer a male coyote as if I were its mate.

We camped there quite a little time and Mr. Wetherill came often to our camp to see if we had everything we needed. He was interested in us. Once in awhile he'd come by and he'd have his packhorse with him with a bedroll on it. He'd stay for supper and then we'd sit by the campfire until bedtime and Mother or Father would say, "Well, why don't you just throw off your bedroll and sleep here, Richard?" By that time we were calling him Richard. Only me, I never called him Richard in my life. Even the years I was married to him I called him Mr. Wetherill. And still do.

He'd stay all night and have breakfast with us and we'd get up extra early so he could get an early start and I don't think he was going anywhere special. Just to come see us. One time I went with Father up to the ranch to have the mules shod and Jim Ethridge was there.

"Where'd you'all say you come from?" he said.

"From Kansas," I said.

"Humph," he said.

"Why?" I said. He was one of those tall, slim, pasty-colored fellas with boiled gooseberry eyes and blond hair but because he worked in the hay his hair was always dusty, and kinda gray-like. Didn't say much.

"You're the first gal I ever saw Dick Wetherill ride down that canyon every day to see."

"He doesn't come down to see me."

"What's he go for then?"

"He comes down to talk with Mother and Father." That made him laugh and he made me so mad I could have clawed his eyes out. They all got to teasing me about it and I just got so I didn't pay any attention to it.

Mr. Wetherill finally took us to Mesa Verde on horseback and saw the ruins and we were up there five days. By this time Father began talking about Chaco Canyon. Mr. Wetherill had never been there and they both wanted to see it so bad. He said, "I've got an expedition next spring but I haven't anything to do during the winter. How'd it be like for us to combine forces and take that trip down to Chaco? I know I could guide you down there."

"Well," Father said, "I've tried to get there and couldn't so I guess I need a guide." We had made it as far as Pueblo Pintado once. They talked it over and Mother and I thought it was wonderful. After the decision was made we couldn't get ready quick enough.

Mr. Wetherill drove a light spring wagon pulled by two nice little jet-black mules and he put his saddle, a bale or two of hay, some grain and his plunder in the back. We went to Durango and finished our outfit. From there we started south toward Aztec and visited those great ruins, then went over to Farmington. We forded the river at Bloomfield and went to Dick Simpson's.

Dick Simpson was an Englishman that had been there quite a number of years, well-educated, and with an Indian wife and some little children around there. Found out later the Navajo called him Stallion because of the impression he made on the ladies. He had a nice store and a good business and was making money. He directed us as near as he could to Chaco Canyon. He never had been there but he knew it was an awful long way and that there weren't any roads or any way of getting food or feed for our horses and mules, but he guessed we'd get there. Mr. Wetherill assured him we would and Father didn't say anything.

I rode my horse alongside Mr. Wetherill's spring wagon occasionally and talked with him. It reminded me of when we moved from Illinois to Kansas. We took the train to Dodge City and from there took a stage, a concord coach with four horses, to Scott City. Being a little girl, I asked the driver if I could ride up in the front seat with him. I couldn't see anything out of the coach because everybody wanted to keep the curtains closed so the ladies wouldn't get tanned. He said, "Sure you can if you'll hang on." He was interesting looking, but I was a little bit afraid of him because he had a gun. He cracked a whip over the horses as he drove. I watched him because I thought it was bad to hit horses with such a vicious-looking whip. Then I noticed that he rarely ever touched them, he just cracked it over their ears or their backs and it worked just the same as touching them.

There were miles and miles of prairie dog towns, and they sat up on the top of their little mounds and barked at us as we went by. I saw the prairie dogs bunched around a fat rattler. The driver hollered back as he pulled to a stop, "The little girl wants to see a rattlesnake-prairie dog fight." The prairie dogs ran up and bit the snake on the back and on the tail and ran away before it could strike them. The snake finally went in a hole and we went on.

After about three days of pulling through sand behind Mr. Wetherill, we got to Swires's store. Here were these two old German brothers who had been there a good many years and their main business was selling great quantities of Germantown wool to the Indians to make rugs. When we were there they were down to a dirty green and an ugly brown yarn. The old men just shook their heads when we asked them for directions to Chaco Canyon. They had never heard of those great ruins and they couldn't have been twenty-five miles away from them at the very most. These Swires boys said the Indians talked about a trail going right along the Chaco Wash up on the hill. The trail looked like it was made by wagon wheels and then it periodically narrowed to a one-horse path. What happened was the Navajo man and woman rode side by side until they thought someone might see them and then she rode behind him. The water runs in the trails and wears them down. It looks like a good road, but generally there's high centers and bushes growing in them. In fact, it was very slow going. Most of the time it was a one-horse trail and only one of our mules walked in the trail at a time and the other struggled along as best he could.

Later, when we lived in Chaco Canyon, I found a road those ancient people built. I was up on the mesa near Pueblo Alto with a woman friend scouting for bushes they made their different dyes from. It was early spring and I looked across the hills toward the San Juan and I said, "Do you suppose we could find the sumac bush on the Escavada Wash?" Just as I said that I saw a twenty-foot wide swath of different-colored grass going over the hills. I had never noticed that before.

"What is that *ch'il*, that grass?" I asked my friend. She looked up and said she'd never seen it before. We rode across the Escavada to see it more clearly and it looked like it went on for miles. We followed it all the way back to the Alto ruin. Then my friend showed me the trail on the rocks that went from Alto straight toward Pueblo Bonito. On the second mesa for several miles there was a ridge twenty feet wide with a little wall in some places. We traced it to the stairsteps that the Indians had built through the crack in the rock down to Pueblo Bonito. Another fork went to Chetro Ketl and there on the other side of Chetro Ketl were a lot of stone steps. It must have been used for ceremonial purposes and the Indians that lived in the ruins went from Chaco Canyon to the San Juan to farm, I don't know.[1]

On our first trip out to Chaco Canyon with Mr. Wetherill, we finally found a Navajo that could talk a little English, but he said there was no way to get into the canyon. Then he said we'd have to go a long ways, from *hayíílká* (dawn) to *'alní'ní'á* (midday) to get up to a rincon that would take us into Chaco Canyon. My father hired this Indian as a guide and after awhile we went down into what is now known as Mocking Bird Canyon [the rincon behind Hungo Pavi].[2]

I rode ahead on my pony and said, "Well, there's slanting rocks here that I guess a wagon could drive over but I don't know what is at the bottom."

"Don't ride down there," Mother said. "You might not be able to get back out." I returned to their wagon.

"I'll see whether we can get down or not," Mr. Wetherill said. He drove off over the cliff and rattled and thundered down over the rocks. Then he hollered back, "Come on down, it's all right." Father's wagon had good brakes and good mules and we got down in there. The canyon was level and it was easier driving after that. We followed a trail through the canyon past Hungo Pavi. Off to our left as we turned into Chaco we saw Fajada Butte and the miles and miles of perfectly level country beyond it. We continued on past Chetro Ketl, but our guide kept trotting right on so we followed him to Pueblo Bonito. It's just a short distance from Chetro

Ketl, or Tseçqa Kintyèl (Broad House among the Cliffs) as we always called it.[3]

We knew Pueblo Bonito was one of the greatest things that we
had ever seen outside of Mesa Verde. Both Pueblo Bonito and
Chetro Ketl were built right flat on the ground in the valley of
Chaco and right up close to the cliff. There was only about a space
of thirty feet from the back wall of Pueblo Bonito to the cliff. An
immense rock hung over Pueblo Bonito and you could see there
was a crack behind it. It had been walled up and timbers had been
put up underneath it to keep it from falling over onto the ruin. Mr.
Wetherill tried all his life to get the government to send him some
steel rods to fix it to the main cliff so it couldn't fall over. The steel
came in the last ten years after the rock had fallen. That was one of
the most sorrowful things that ever happened.

Mr. Wetherill disappeared for hours and hours after we first arrived. He just threw the harness off his mules and turned them
loose and left. Next we knew he was up on top of the cliff looking
down. He found the water hole up there that people starved for
water never find. He scoured Chetro Ketl and Pueblo Bonito and
drew an outline of everything and he was so delighted he was
speechless. We all walked through Pueblo Bonito, talking about
what an immense thing it was and imagining what the people who
built it were like.

The Indians always claimed the back wall of Pueblo Bonito was
seven stories high. When we were there it was only five, but we
could see that it had been much higher. The ruins would have been
in a much better state of preservation, had the Mexican sheepherders not pulled the timber from the ruins. They bedded their
sheep between the ruin and the cliff and used the wood for their
campfire. That's why Mr. Wetherill took out a homestead there, to
protect the ruins, not to farm; there was no water. Mr. Wetherill
tried to get the government to do something about building fences
around those ruins or something to protect them just as soon as we
moved there, but they never would do anything.

When we rattled down into Mocking Bird Canyon that first day
we saw a stump of a tree on the first bench. It was then about
twelve or fifteen feet high and two feet and a half through. The
Navajo showed me others in the years I lived there. That was the

biggest tree I saw but I firmly believe that at one time there was plenty of pine timber in Chaco Canyon and all those mesas. I told Neil Judd about that tree. He was quite indignant, but I understand he went there and found it.

We made our camp in front of a V-shaped cave formed by two large boulders that had fallen off of the main cliff at one time. Father fixed a seat in there with some rocks. I was usually the cook because Mother loved to explore. One day I was sitting in there peeling potatoes with the butcher knife when suddenly an Indian jumped out in front of this little cave and let out a warwhoop. I jumped up, spilling the potatoes, and I charged him with the knife. He grabbed my hand, then laughed and made me understand he was just playing. He couldn't talk much English but he was one of several who visited us, usually around mealtime.

"You scared me," I said.

"You would have killed me, too."

"Sure I would." His name was Tomacito and he was a nice look-ing boy about my age with hair down to his waist. He sobered up and felt ashamed that he'd scared me so. "I'll get even with you," I said. "It might take a long time but I'll get even with you for that."

One day years later I was exploring a way to climb Fajada Butte and I got off my horse to look at something, thinking the horse was trained to stand, but he wasn't. He started trotting away. I yelled at him to whoa and started after him as he ran off and left me.

I began walking and when I came within three miles of home here came Tomacito riding a nice little buckskin pony. Oh, I was most affable, and I said, "Let me get on behind and ride with you."

"No," he said, looking horrified. "Don't you know that a woman never rides on a horse back of a man, much less a married woman with a married man. What would the Diné think?" They were very moral.

"Just now I'm pretty tired," I said. "I don't believe I care. I'll give you two dollars to let me ride your horse home."

"I couldn't do that," he said. "If the Diné saw you riding my horse home, what would they think?"

"I don't give a whoop what they think. I'm tired and hot and it's time I got home and took care of my baby." But that wouldn't do. I walked along the trail and he rode outside the trail right along with me, talking. Suddenly, I got an inspiration. I stopped and looked down on the ground and I got a little stick and scratched around. I kept between him and what I was doing and kept scratching and looking.

"What is it? What have you found?" he said.

"Come see." I kept working with it and he got down finally and dropped the horse reins and came over to where I was.

"I can't see anything. What are you looking at?"

"Look right over on the edge of the trail right over there." I got him looking good and I jumped and grabbed his horse's rein and got on his horse and rode home.

When I got home I tied his horse up in front of the store. There were several Navajo there and one, Bendi John, who always talked too much said, "Where'd you get that? Is that your horse?"

"Yes," I said. "You know I like the Navajo saddle. It looks so pretty with all those brass buttons." I didn't say anything more. I went on in the house and tended to my business and after about an hour or more here come Tomacito slouching in. "What happened?" the Navajo said. "How'd she get your horse. What'd you let her have your horse for? What's your wife going to say?" They were more than curious.

He wouldn't answer at all. Couldn't say a word. There wasn't anything for him to say. He was so mad at me he couldn't hardly stand it. He was grouching around and wouldn't speak and finally I said, "You know many years ago there was a little old white girl peeling potatoes in that cave right up there and there was a Navajo boy jumped in front of the cave and scared her almost to death. Do you remember she told you she'd get even?"

He put his head back and laughed, just howled.

I imagine we stayed in Chaco that first trip a month or six weeks. One evening we built our fire up against the cliffs, because we thought it would be pretty to see the flames lapping up the sandstone. Mr. Wetherill took his wagon seat out of his wagon and offered it to Mother and Father. Father was all fixed up comfortably against a rock, but Mother sat down on the wagon seat with Mr. Wetherill. We children were lying on a Navajo blanket near the fire and fooling with the sand. Suddenly we heard a crack almost like a gunshot, and a large slab of rock maybe forty feet up fell right off the cliff. Mr. Wetherill and Mother tipped over backwards. I was blinded with rock and my little sister and brother and I couldn't do anything. Mr. Wetherill jumped up and ran over to us children and pulled each one of us up. "If that had hit you," he said to me, "it would have killed me."

It was November by that time, and cold. That's why the rock cracked off. Mr. Wetherill was angry he let us children build that fire. Something else we always did when it was real cold. We'd pick out a solid, hard rock and put it on the edge of the fire during the evening and then wrap it up in a sack and bring it to bed to keep our feet warm. We tried to carry them along with us but Father wouldn't let us. He said we could always find rocks, which we did.

We did quite a bit of excavating while we were there. My mother got six or eight pieces of pottery out of one grave she found across the canyon. I started a handle collection and gathered over a thousand pottery handles that went to the Smithsonian, or it might have been the American Natural History Museum.

Finally we decided we'd better go on our way because those Mogollon Mountain ruins were still in Father's mind. Mr. Wetherill planned to go back to Mancos, but Father convinced him to come along. We revisited every one of the pueblos. Mr. Wetherill had never seen these pueblos and he wanted to compare them to the Hopi villages in Arizona. We didn't stay at them long, maybe just a few hours, and we got down to Socorro for Christmas.

Mr. Wetherill and Father rode off on our mules in the Mogollons [near Socorro, New Mexico] and Mother worried they were going to be lost and those Mexicans told her they never would get back alive, the Apaches would kill them. I was not allowed to go along, so I worried, too. They never found those ruins. Isn't it funny how elusive the things that you are hunting for are?

From the Mogollons we went on to Phoenix, and north to Montezuma's Castle, where we camped and excavated. Found a mummy of a child about four years old with light brown hair and a little shirt woven from cottonwood cotton, a miniature bow and arrow and pottery bowls that were probably once full of food. The soldiers had been stationed near there and they sure dug that ruin out. We didn't have ladders, just poles with some boards nailed to them and we climbed up there every day. I never did dig. I was an anthropologist, not an archaeologist.

We traveled on very slowly and visited all those ruins around Phoenix and Flagstaff. Then we crossed the San Juan River and traveled along the Elk Mountain fault in Arizona.[4] The fault runs eighty miles south of the San Juan, and on the opposite side of the river are what is known as Mule Ears. The fault is obsidian or volcanic rock squeezed up fifty feet in some places. We found interesting ruins in that country. The wind was terrible and full of sand, but there wasn't five minutes that went by that we didn't find evidence of ancient human habitation, pieces of pottery or skulls blown out by the wind. We found a number of whole pottery bowls and carried those along, of course.

One day we came to a cave along the Elk Mountain fault and Father thought that it would be a splendid place to camp for the night. We drove up to the front of the cave and saw that there had been a fire there not too long ago. We made our camp and we children began to find pieces of very rich silver ore. You could cut it with a knife. We picked up quite a few of those and put them in the wagon. We hadn't seen an Indian, although we had seen horses and Mr. Wetherill said, "There's Indians not too far from here; I can smell their campfire."

In the evening we played our instruments and some Indians came. We asked them about the silver, but they didn't know a thing about it. Mr. Wetherill asked them if there had been somebody camping here that might have left the ore. They couldn't tell him anything.

The next day we moved on a little further and one or two of the Indians followed along with us. We came to the camp of Hoskaninny, who was the chief of all the Western Navajo. There was lots of room in that country and we decided to rest our mules there a couple days because it was hard traveling in that deep sand.

Hoskaninny said one of his older wives was very ill and asked my mother and father to come up to see what was the matter with her, as the medicine men weren't doing any good. So Father and Mother went up to see her in her hogan, and Mother said she was having a serious bilious attack. Couldn't keep anything on her stomach. Mother made her some rhubarb tea and in a couple days she was noticeably better.

When we got ready to leave, Hoskaninny offered us six horses for curing his wife. Father said we had all the horses we needed. Then he tried to give us a couple of cows, and Father said he couldn't use the cows at all. "I must pay you," he said, "or else my wife will get sick again." Father told him he would take the meat of one sheep. Not the hide, nor the head, just the meat and two bags of corn. He also gave my father two bracelets with opals cut the white man's way. Father asked where the bracelets came from and at first he said he didn't know; then he said he found them at the foot of an old ruin. He said if I grew up to amount to anything to give them to me. I have them, now.

I must tell you what the designs on the bracelets mean. When my soul leaves my body and starts for the spirit world it will meet many enemies along the difficult trail and these turquoise will pay for my passage. When I meet these enemies I will use these teeth to gnash them and the horns to hook them out of the way. This ceremonial headdress means I'll always work and talk to the public. The turkey tracks show that I'll have plenty of meat and the indentations on the side mean long distance travel. These are the eyes of the Great Spirit that watches over and protects me. It keeps me from stepping on a rattlesnake. It's the subconscious mind, is what it is.

From Hoskaninny's camp we followed right on up the Elk Mountain fault. The wind and sand constantly stung our eyes. There were no roads to follow and we were always lost. "I know that if we follow this fault we'll come to the San Juan River," Mr. Wetherill said. He had planned to cross the river into Utah near Barton's Trading Post in order to meet a party at Monticello and take them some place to excavate for the summer.

When we finally got to the San Juan the water was high. It was late afternoon and we had run out of food excepting bitter chocolate and peaches. Nobody was hungry enough to eat them yet. We camped on the banks of the river, dug a well and got fairly clear water to drink. "We won't try a crossing until the morning," Mr. Wetherill said. "There may be Indians here by that time and we'll find out how the crossing is but it looks very bad tonight. I wouldn't think of trying it and you, Mr. Palmer, couldn't possibly do it with your heavy load."

But nobody came around, so the next morning, quite early, Mr. Wetherill decided he'd try to cross in the wagon. "Why don't you take the pony and ride across to see how it is," I suggested.

"That's a good idea, but I guess I'll just drive in," he said. "It's gone down a great deal."

"I think I'll ride in the wagon with you," I said, and climbed up next to him. As soon as we got in the river I could feel the wagon starting to lift. It was much deeper than he had expected it to be. "Those waves over there are pretty high," he shouted. "I can't go straight across. I've got to go up river. We have to be careful not to go downstream because we'll end up in a canyon, and then we'd be lost."

I was too scared to say anything. We couldn't turn around because the water was too deep. The mules swam a few feet more, got their footing, and then would have to swim again. "It may be possible that I'll have to cut these mules loose and when I do, I want you to step right out on the running gears and take hold of that mule's tail. You hang onto it because your life depends on it. He'll take you to shore. Will you do it?"

"Sure I will."

Then the wagon lifted again and he turned up the stream a little more and just kept going and we finally got over to the bank. The river was swifter against that bank and the mules couldn't jump up. He grabbed his rope from the back, ran out on the tongue of the wagon, jumped onto the bank, roped one of those mules and snubbed it against some driftwood there. That gave those mules a breathing spell for a minute until they could make it up on the bank.

We were used to being either too dry or too wet anyway, but we were soaked. Mr. Wetherill hollered to my folks on the other side of the river. I know they couldn't hear us because we couldn't hear them, "Don't try it," he tried to tell them. He walked down to the bank and waved emphatically to stay put and then he came back to the wagon. I was still sitting in it. "Were you frightened?" he asked.

"Why sure, I was scared to death."

"Where do you put your fear?"

"I guess I swallowed it. I couldn't say anything."

"No, you didn't say a word," he said. "Will you marry me?"

"I don't know. I'll have to think about it."

"I think we were meant to live our lives together. I'll do everything to make you happy."

"Well, then I will, I'll marry you."

We made motions to my folks that we would go on up the bank to get help. We drove up the Butler Wash to the trading post where Mr. Wetherill planned to go. Those two boys that ran the store had been murdered a short time before by either the Navajo or the Paiute and the store was burned down. It was a stone building, but the roof was burned with all the contents. That bothered Mr. Wetherill terribly. "I can't stand it," he said.

We went on to Butler Wash and the river had been so high that it had washed out the road. There was no way to get out of there, no way to go on. There was an Indian trail in the soft dirt, but we couldn't take the wagon through that.

We stayed there quite a long while and he finally said, "You know I'm going to have to leave you here because you can't ride that mule." One of them was mean as the dickens and had never been ridden. He put his saddle on the other mule and tied it up to the wheel. "I've never hated anything in my life more than I hate leaving you here but your parents have got to have help."

"I don't mind staying. I'll just stay here in the wagon."

"Oh, no you won't." He climbed the mountain to a little cave and dug around and in a few minutes he came back and rolled up two or three blankets. We had no food. We hadn't had any for a day or two. "Will you promise me you'll never leave this place until I come back for you?"

"I'll stay where you put me."

"Walk in my steps," he said as he led me up the hill. I did as I was told and the rocks rolled down. When we got to the cave he put the blankets down. "No matter what happens down there at that wagon, I don't want you to make one sound. If the Indians come along and steal the mule just let them have it. If they burn the wagon, just let them do it. Don't you move from here." He put me way back in the back of the cave and said, "You'll have to wait here a good many hours."

"I'll stay."

He kissed me goodbye and then he brushed out our tracks all the way down that hill so you'd never know I was up there. He arighted bushes we knocked over and brushed out every track I made getting out of the wagon and going up the hill, but left his own. He waved to me and rode away.

That was a long eight hours I waited there. I was frightened to death. I stayed right there and I was wide awake every second. Nothing happened, I didn't hear a sound, except mice. It was just about four o'clock in the morning when he came back with one of those great big double-box wagons and a team of great Percheron horses and three men. He hollered for me to come down and I picked up my blankets and went down and got in the big wagon. They gave me something to eat right away. They had to fix the road so they could come through there.

We went right on down to the crossing to my folks and Mother said she never was so happy in her life as she was when we crossed the river and drove into camp. It was morning and the water was down. We gave them some eggs and bacon and things for breakfast. Then they took Father's mules off entirely and took the heavy things out of the wagon and put them in the other wagon and crossed with those big horses and their big old padded feet. Then they went back and brought Father's wagon across the river.

We went on to Bluff, Utah, where we learned that the cave where we found the mineral was where the Indians had killed Myrick and Mitchell, the great explorers that went to the headwaters of the Mississippi and all over the West.[5] They had found the Indian silver mine and I've known men that have looked for it all their lives. We felt we'd just escaped death when we got through with that. We had a tub bath in Bluff, the first one since Chaco. It didn't kill us not to have one.

At Monticello, Mr. Wetherill met his party, and we agreed to meet in Sacramento, California, to be married. I spent the summer with my family prowling through the Pacific northwest and giving entertainments.[6] I rarely got a letter from Mr. Wetherill because he didn't know where we would be.[7]

NOTES

[1]Around 1050 A.D. the Anasazi started building straight roads about thirty feet wide. There are potentially fifteen hundred miles of road that extend to more than fifty Anasazi towns in New Mexico, Colorado, Arizona, and Utah, leading some archaeologists to believe the roads were a superhighway system connecting to Chaco Canyon, a ceremonial place. Only two, possibly three roads actually lead to Chaco Canyon, and archaeologists can only verify two hundred miles of road. Although some roads do lead from the different towns to necessary water or quarry sources, others seem to lead nowhere. There is no evidence of camping, and most roads are associated with shrine-like structures. One archaeologist says the roads were built to embellish the architecture. The Great North Road, which Marietta is describing, extends within a half degree to two degrees east of true north for fifty kilometers from Pueblo Alto to the dramatic banks of Kutz Canyon beneath Twin Angel Peaks. According to historical Pueblo beliefs, the road could have led to a symbolic *sipapu*, where the ancestors emerged from the underworld. On the other hand, Twin Angel Peaks is visible for many miles and could have been sighted on while circumventing the badlands. At the peaks, one would walk directly south to Chaco Canyon.

[2]McNitt says Richard and the Palmers sighted on El Huerfano peaks and rode directly south thirty miles, entering the Chaco Wash at the place where it opens on the Escavada Wash on the sixth day of travel, rather than entering Chaco via Mocking Bird Canyon. This way they saw Penasco Blanco, two other smaller ruins (probably Casa Chiquita and Kin Kletso). Marietta says they took that route the second time she went into Chaco with Richard.

[3]Nine massive pueblos, called great houses, surrounded by hundreds of small houses were built in the immediate Chaco Canyon area, beginning around 900 A.D. From west to east, they are Penasco Blanco, Pueblo Alto, Kin Kletso, Pueblo Del Arroyo, Pueblo Bonito, Chetro Ketl, Hungo Pavi, Una Vida, Wijiji. A tenth great house community has been discovered in an adjacent canyon. As many as a hundred and fifty Anasazi communities dot the Colorado Plateau, 100,000 square miles in area. These houses are characterized by "Bonito style" core-veneer masonry and massive construction and great kivas. Pueblo Bonito is the most celebrated, with five stories, as many as eight hundred rooms, and thirty-three kivas, including two great kivas. Between 1897 and 1899, Richard Wetherill and the Hyde Exploration Expedition cleared 189 rooms and several kivas in Pueblo Bonito.

[4]McNitt says that Richard led the Palmers to the valley of the Verde River where they explored Montezuma's Castle and other ruins, and then headed north for Oak Creek Canyon and Flagstaff. They stopped at many places along the way to give entertainments and explore. They crossed the Little Colorado and turned eastward to Tuba City to visit the Hopi villages. It was April 1896 when Richard took the Palmers up Marsh Pass, across the desert south of Chinle, and into the San Juan Valley.

[5]McNitt doesn't mention Mitchell and Myrick in the context of this trip. He said a traveler from Boston had been murdered in the area by a band of Navajos a few months before. The man had reached for his rifle when they demanded food. McNitt did confirm the story about the Bartons, who had been burned in their store.

[6]During the summer Richard went back to Chaco Canyon for a season under the supervision of George Pepper from the American Museum of Natural History. The trip was funded by the Hyde Exploring Expedition.

[7]In McNitt's notes Marietta tells about one of the few letters she had ever received from Richard:

> He was out in the Marsh Pass area, had been gone six weeks. I was just commencing to wonder where he was when a Navajo came in with a package for me. It had been passed from one Indian to another until I think three Navajos had a hand in bringing it on Anasazi's instruction to take it carefully to his wife at Pueblo Bonito. The letter was written with a piece of charcoal on a piece of pottery . . . he had no paper, of course. And to keep the charcoal from rubbing off, he had covered it all around with little sticks and then wrapped it in an old dishrag.

There is no mention in McNitt's notes of what the letter said, but somehow McNitt comes up with the note and includes it in his book on the Wetherills: "Dear Wife—Have been delayed ten days by windstorms. Will be with you soon—Your husband. Richard Wetherill."

4

Never Look Your Mother-in-Law in the Eye

IN BLUFF, UTAH, MR. WETHERILL made a formal application to my parents and told them he was very much in love with me and wanted to marry me. Father and Mother said they had noticed we were interested in one another and that as far as they were concerned the only thing was that he was much older than I. If we thought we could adjust, they approved.

Mr. Wetherill had prepared an appropriate and fine speech to make when he asked me to marry him. He hoped I didn't misunderstand him when he proposed so impulsively there at the river crossing after we'd come so near death's door, but he thought I was so brave, he couldn't help but ask me right there. I said I didn't know there was any specified time when a man should ask a woman to marry her, so I guess that was just as good a time as any.

The Navajo bartered for marriage. I read just the other day that the Navajo didn't sell their daughters, but I've seen it with my own two eyes. They sold their daughters just after they started menstruating, and they had a secret test for virginity. I can't tell you about the test because I swore I would never tell, but it has something to do with a measurement of the neck.

Children were a Navajo's wealth; the more children, the wealthier. I heard with my own two ears a mother say, "I'll take twelve horses for that girl. The first time I sold her, she brought fourteen because she's a good weaver and a good cook and a fine young, healthy, strong woman. She didn't get along with that man and I brought her home. In a year I sold her again and I only took thirteen horses that time, nothing else, not even a buckskin or a bead. Now this time I've got to have twelve horses. Just for friendship between mother-in-law and son-in-law I want a good buckskin and some jewelry to remember my daughter's married to this man."

A woman who had a daughter of marriageable age told the marriage bureau, the people who arranged the marriages. Often this bureau picked an older man for a young girl and a young man for an older woman. Smart when you see the reason of it because the older man has property: a good herd of sheep and horses and several hogans and nice fields of corn. He may have three or four other women. A young man has very little—maybe a saddlehorse, but no sheep or cattle. He isn't old enough to have accumulated things. If a young man married an older woman, she may have two or three daughters, and if he treated the old lady right she gave him livestock and he's pretty-well fixed. The arrangement may have been made that he has the right to buy her oldest daughter, and the girl doesn't have much to say about it. She could refuse to marry but that's quite a serious matter. The oldest daughter has to be married before the younger one can marry.

I think the people finagled it so that they marry the ones they're already attracted to. They had those dances . . . they called them squaw dances so the people can see each other, like any social club.

From the time a man and a girl's mother start making negotiations for the marriage they never look at one another again or they would go blind. They sit in a dark hogan each night with a black blanket over their heads. Later, when the couple marries, they build their hogan far away from the mother's so the husband's eyes would never meet hers. They can't look at each other but they sure could fight. The son-in-law might get mad over the mother-in-law making trouble between him and the wife and the wife was always threatening to go home to Mama.

Oh, the names they call each other when they're angry: Little Bear with Blue Eyes [blue eyes refers to the white man], Child of a Dog, House of the Devil, Coyote, Snake. Just hearing me say that could injure you. The names call up the spirits of those beings to harass you and keep you awake nights.

The Navajo wedding ceremony is simple and sweet. After the man brings the horses to the corral, the couple goes inside a hogan and sits on sheepskins. A basket of cornmeal mush sits in front of them. They each, in turn, reach across to the opposite side of the basket and take out a small handful of mush and feed the other. Then they each reach for a pottery dish of water and give the other a drink. The gestures mean they would each always provide for the other and share everything. Isn't that sweet? A medicine man talks to the couple and tells them what they must do to get along. The husband must see that the wood is brought in and when the

weather is bad he must herd the sheep. That's the end of the ceremony, except maybe they might exchange jewelry. The relatives
nibble up the rest of the cornmeal like children licking frosting off
a cake, for happiness.

We had two men working for us in the ruins at Chaco, Tomacito and Marcellino, names the Mexicans had given them. They
were both nice looking men and they both had nice looking wives.
The wives came quite often to visit me and have a meal and I'd sit
and talk with them. Mrs. Tomacito told me she was once married
to Marcellino and Marcellino's wife was married to Tomacito.
They'd each had several children. They didn't get along so they
traded husbands. "I didn't like Marcellino after I'd lived with him a
year or two," Tomacito's current wife said. "I always hated to see
him coming home. I get along with Tomacito so nice." She put her
hand on her chest and said, "He's so big here." There were no legal
obstacles in trading. When a woman wants a divorce, she just puts
the man's saddle and bridle and all his personal belongings outside
the hogan door. If he comes in she can chop him with an axe and
wouldn't get punished for it.

The women owned everything: the hogan, the sheep, the
daughters; and the men must do as the women say. I've seen the
women come and sell maybe a hundred sheep and the man would
be hanging around. You'd know who he was. She might purchase,
oh, great bolts of calico and a hundred pounds of sugar all done up
in little ten-cent packages. She'd be purchasing all day. You have to
lay the silver dollars along the counter and as she made her purchase she'd pay for each one. Maybe the man would finally come in
the store and be standing with other Indians and she'd throw a sack
of tobacco on the floor and he'd pick it up and that was her gift
to him.

Now the woman weaves but when the man comes home and no
matter where he's been she'll tell him to take the baby out and take
care of it. The men are very good nurse girls. He has his own work,
too, getting after sheep and horses. I noticed the average Navajo
woman was afraid of cattle and horses, never went around corrals.
They only rode gentle old scrubs. The women may give the horses
to the men, but they hung on to the sheep. That's their wealth,
wool for the blankets.

Mr. Wetherill met us in Sacramento, California, on December 12, 1896. I had written him that we'd be there around a certain date. He got there a day ahead of us and since we were not affiliated with any church and my father feeling the way he did about those things, Mr. Wetherill scouted around and found a nice justice of the peace. He asked Mother and Father if that would be satisfactory and they agreed.

Mother and I went down to the emporium and bought me a very nice suit. It was dark red, almost a maroon wool. It came with a little jacket made with a peplin below the waist trimmed with black braid and black embroidered frog loops for the big black buttons down the front. I bought a little black hat, gloves, shoes, hose, and underwear. Mr. Wetherill said I looked lovely. He gave me the loveliest silver bracelet he bought for me when we were among the Navajos.

Mother Wetherill gave us a full-blooded registered cow and Father Wetherill gave us twenty mares with the quarter-circle star brand on them. We got silver and napkins and tablecloths from my people trying to civilize us, you know.

I was scared to death, I just couldn't tell you why. I loved Mr. Wetherill and respected him, admired him tremendously, and had absolute confidence in him. We were going to leave my folks at Sacramento and meet them in San Francisco after spending a few days there by ourselves. I was so scared I couldn't eat or sleep. I was really sick. What was I scared of? I surely wasn't scared of a man I'd traveled with for months and knew as well as I knew him and feeling toward him the way I did, but still I was frightened to leave my people.

Mr. Wetherill said to me one morning while we were in San Francisco, "I think I'm going to take you out and educate you a little bit. You've been around a lot, but you don't know a thing about how the world works."

About nine that evening, three policemen called for us at the Palace Hotel. They were going to be our guides. We got in a cab and went down to the red light district of San Francisco and I learned a great deal in a few hours.

The streets were lined with cribs showcasing women. The district was so crowded with men, miners I guess, you could hardly get along. Then we went through the underground part of Chinatown and saw dope fiends and a naked woman that must have been beautiful once but was now repulsive. We went to the opium den and saw men and women lying on the floor. I saw a Chinese boss with corkscrew fingernails. He was dressed in magnificent Chinese clothes covered in gold embroidery and his hands were ladened with diamonds. That distressed me for days.

In Denver when I was much younger, we decided to get in the wagon and drive around just to see if we missed anything before we left. We got onto one street we hadn't seen before around twilight and there were women sitting out on little steps in front of their doors. "Mother," I said. "That woman is smoking a cigar." Most of the women were wearing Mother Hubbards, those old-fashioned dresses with a lace yoke and the bottom part was gathered up on bright red, green or pink satin. A policeman stopped us and told Father Market Street was no place to take women and children. I didn't know what it was all about.

Years later in Chaco Canyon, when Mr. Wetherill's sister, Anna Mason, visited, Bendi John, my Navajo informant, invited us to a dance on top of the mesa near one of the Bonito ruins. That was the mesa where we found shark's teeth lying around on the ground. I raked up a bushel basket.

"What kind of ceremonial?" I asked.

He put his finger to his lips. Secret, see. "It's a funny one. Maybe you won't like it."

"I don't see why I wouldn't like it."

"I'll take you and Anasazi's sister."

We rode up horseback wearing black blankets and he told us to sit down back of the hogan. After a while he called us into the hogan. "Sit close to the door and if you don't like it, you can get out." We sat on the bench close to the door and kept our blankets over our faces. There were women sitting clear up on the bench that circled the hogan. They wore only a skirt and their hair hung down over their bare shoulders and chest, very unusual. I whispered to Anna, "We're going to see something, but I wonder what it is?"

Men came in dressed only in a breechcloth and a G-string. Their faces were painted black. I don't care who it is, you paint a face black with a red stripe over the nose from ear to ear and some wavy lines around the mouth, that person is so disguised you wouldn't know him.

"Who are they?" I asked Bendi John.

"You know them. They work for you. There's one man here who works in your house." He wouldn't tell me which one.

They began to dance around and around. "You'll have to leave, now." We got up and left. Outside, I asked Bendi John what was happening. "I'll tell you tomorrow."

"No, tell me now. I want to know."

"They come here to be with these different men in the hopes that if they have a baby from this, the baby would be talented." He used a Navajo word for it that doesn't exactly translate, but I know what he meant. If the father was a good singer, the baby would also have that talent. These were married women and they were not supposed to know who they were with in that hogan. It was quite an honor to be invited to the ceremony.

The Navajo were afraid the tribe was going down because it wasn't getting mixed enough. I'd heard many a story where a Navajo would give a cowboy a gift for sleeping with his wife to get new blood. They saw what the Hopi had done with the inbreeding. I'd seen many an albino with gooseberry eyes and yellow hair and pink skin.

We went all through San Francisco and then went to Mexico City for our wedding trip. We came home earlier than we intended. Mr. Wetherill had hoped to go down to see the ruins at Milta and Oaxaca, but he got a wire from his father stating that the party who wanted to go into the Grand Gulch were ready to start the exploring expedition. We had to go back to Mancos the first of January and outfit for the trip.

Grand Gulch was out of this world. It was unexplored country, inhabited by Navajos and Paiutes and not too friendly.

‖ ▲ ‖

5

The Princess Mummy and Other Burials

MR. WETHERILL WENT to Grand Gulch [in 1893-94] and discovered the Basketmakers, another tribe of people who lived in the Mesa Verde country and also in New Mexico, Arizona, and Colorado. He named these early people for their great weaving.[1] Scientists thought everyone they dug up belonged to one tribe. Mr. Wetherill readily found more than one tribe; their heads were a different shape and they made different kinds of material in their homes. They didn't make pottery and they lived altogether differently than the Cliff Dwellers.[2]

When somebody tells me a tribe is pureblooded, I shake my head and say there ain't no such thing. Man is very promiscuous, you know. These Indians traded back and forth, and stole or sold slaves from the Horn up to the Bering Strait. You can't tell me there's such a thing as a thoroughbred Indian, whatever tribe he is. I look at those children that are brother and sister, and they don't look any more alike than my brother and I do. I've bred horses and I know how long it takes to get a thoroughbred.[3]

When we got into Grand Gulch there our trouble began. The trail used by the Paiute was in no shape to bring in pack horses and we had to stop for several days while the men worked on it to make it passable. The pack horses wore panniers, or side boxes, that carried pans, coffee pots, canned goods, and a keg of sourdough.

We had four or six Harvard boys.[4] One boy's parents decided the trip would give him something to do for the winter and he brought along a tutor to make sure he stayed out of trouble. They told us they would want crackers in their soup. Mr. Wetherill couldn't get oyster crackers but settled for soda crackers—about twenty-five pounds worth.

We had [forty] animals with us. We took along extra horses because Mr. Wetherill was such a horse lover and refused to push a horse further than it could go. We also brought horses for eating. We heard there would be no game down there and we couldn't drive cattle in, and they would be skin poor by the time we got down in there, anyway. I don't think those boys ever knew they were eating horse.

Bob Putney came down to see us at Pueblo Bonito when we lived there later and I brought up the subject of horsemeat just for fun. "I can tell when I'm eating it," he says. "It tastes much sweeter than beef." I told a Navajo to bring me a three-year-old mare and butcher it in the corral and hang it in my meat room.

We had plenty of horses worth fifty cents or a dollar and a half at a time and we couldn't sell them anyway. I fixed a nice rump roast with onions and potatoes on a good fire all day until it was as tender as chicken. When we were seated, I said, "Mr. Wetherill is busy in the store, so Mr. Putney will have to take his place and carve the roast." He sat in Mr. Wetherill's chair and carved great slabs of lovely, juicy meat.

Mr. Putney was a heavy man and a hearty eater. He sat back and said, "Mrs. Wetherill, they don't serve anything better at the Alvarado [in Albuquerque]. Fred Harvey can't beat that." That was a compliment because that was a real swanky place to go. I thanked him and took him out to the meat house and showed him the carcass. I had the Navajo leave the hooves on it. I told him I got tired of people telling me they could tell horse or burrow meat. He asked for a quarter to take home, to fool his wife. I know men do that, that's natural. We didn't eat horse too often because people don't like to eat something that's cheap.

After we got the trail into Grand Gulch fixed, we started down. One of the wranglers said, "It would break a snake's neck to crawl through that canyon." That's how crooked the trail was. Mr. Wetherill and the horsemen went first, followed by the pack animals. I should have been close to Mr. Wetherill, but I wanted to stay back to watch everyone as they went down the trail. Was I a coward?

Suddenly I heard a big racket up front and the horse that was packed with two boxes of soda crackers and a sack of grain across the top went over the side. The horse had gone around a narrow bend and his box touched the solid rock. It scared him and he tried to turn around but he slipped off. Crackers and grain and horse went clear to the bottom with a thump, killed him instantly, right now.

I was scared and so was my horse. Those trails were so narrow I was glad I parted my hair in the middle. There was no room to get off my horse because of the solid rock on one side and that drop on the other. "Billy," I said to the horse. "You be careful if you was ever careful in your life. I'll let you have the reins perfectly loose and I'll set square and steady on you and hang onto the horn of this saddle and I won't even breathe when we go around that place."[5] We made it all right.

Mr. Wetherill didn't want that horse down there dying, so he sent Clate down to see if the horse was dead and to take the pack saddle off him. A two-year-old colt fell off the trail before Clate could get to the bottom. I never could see any sense in it. He ran into the horse in front of him and his hind feet lost footing and he went down. I couldn't eat any supper that night. I just crawled into my bedroll and stayed there.

We got to the bottom that day with everything else and made our camp. There was a group of us and we needed quite a bit of room. The next morning everybody got up early to see this great gulch and we were never disappointed. In every curve there was evidence of people having lived there.

We came to a cave that went way back, and right in front of it were the remnants of a small room. We measured every cave, every grave, and took photographs of everything we did. If I make mistakes it's because I don't remember and didn't pay attention but I should say it was six or eight feet across. I was the one measuring and taking notes. "This looks like a turkey pen," Mr. Wetherill said, and he decided to excavate it.

They dug a little ways down and found they were coming to a body. Usually after they dug the first shovelful, they saw a rim of pottery or maybe a knee, and they got the brushes out. They used whisk brooms and a finer brush and then all the digging was done with a small garden trowel in those days. Mr. Wetherill insisted on photographing and measuring before he ever started to dig. I measured from front to back then the height by holding up a stick and measuring the stick.

They found this marvelous mummy in there. They called the mummy Joe Buck after one of the fellows on the trip. I don't know who did it but the boys all blamed me when [Orion or Oscar] Buck got mad every time anybody would say that mummy looked like him. The mummy was covered first in a plain turkey feather blanket. The warp of those blankets was yucca string, and the feathers were taken off the quill and wound around the string. That was covered with another blanket with little bluebird feathers in it. The marvel of marvels was a blanket made of cotton, beautifully woven and intricate as a design in red, black, yellow and white.[6]

The men lifted the blankets off the mummy and carefully laid them between canvas. Carefully, they took him out of his grave. He'd been a large man and his knees were drawn up. Mr. Wetherill found that he had been cut from hip to hip and sewed up with string made from human hair. You could see where it had begun to knit together. Mr. Wetherill turned him over and found a stone atlatl point six inches long sticking out of his hip. They had cut into his hip to get that point out and couldn't find it. The scar had begun to heal before he died.

We moved camp further down the canyon and went to another burial cave, this one more wide-mouthed and five or six feet above a stream that ran when there was water. These burials had been dug straight down into the bottom of this cave. They were two-and-a-half feet across the top but round and lined with mud and baked. And then they put the bodies in those little pots. They broke all the tendons in the elbows and the shoulders and the knees, and the back was bent over and the neck was broken and pushed right over. They mashed them down into those little earthen pots that they'd made there and then put a flat stone on the top. Somebody had been there before us and taken the bodies out of most of them. We only found a very few with the bodies still inside them, but the skeletons were lying in the cave. You couldn't walk in that cave without stepping on human bones they were so thick in there.[7]

I found one skull of a man who wasn't very old when he died. The teeth were still good and the skull was thick. It must have been shot right under the chin because the arrow point stuck out the top of the skull. Never knew what hit him.

We moved camp again and I'd been with Mr. Wetherill all day measuring some caves and we were just about ready to go home. It was getting warmer then and the sun shone in and it was full of soft clean sand. Mr. Wetherill looked around the cave and said, "It doesn't look like many people have lived in here, if any, but someone might have camped here occasionally." He walked behind a rock leaning up against the cliff wall, and thought it would make an awful good burial. "You're not in a hurry to go home, are you?" he said.

He dug a little and then carefully scooped away the wind-blown sand and finally brushed away the sand with a whisk broom. "Yes, here's a basket," he exclaimed. The basket was rather coarsely woven and at least as tall as I am, five-foot one-and-a-half. "I believe I'll dig a little bit around the edge here. Would you mind getting on your pony and telling Clate to bring the camera?" Everyone had already gone to camp and had taken everything with them.

I got down as fast as Billy would go and told Clate. By that time the sun was down and it was almost dark. I grabbed my flashlight while Clate saddled his horse. Clate tried to take pictures but it was too dark. They dug all around the basket and lifted it off. I was just in agony to see what was underneath it.

Under the basket was another basket and beneath that was a turkey feather blanket with bluebird feather spots. Under that was another feather blanket with yellow spots from wild canaries, perhaps. A smaller basket, which had a design similar to an Apache basket I have, laid at one end.

"Oh, she's alive!" I said when Mr. Wetherill lifted the basket from her face. I couldn't believe she was dead. You can't imagine how quickly these mummies begin to wither when the air gets to them.

"She sure does look asleep, doesn't she?" Mr. Wetherill said.

We called her "Princess." Her body was painted yellow, and her face was painted red and her hair was long. She had sandals [another time Marietta said she wore moccasins] on her feet and a necklace of shell beads. She lay in another basket a bit larger than the one covering her. Moisture never reached that little grave. She had just dried.[8]

One night it commenced to snow. This was my first experience of sleeping with a mummy. If we didn't get them in out of the snow, the mummies would have been destroyed. Our tent [made of large canvas tarpaulin] didn't offer much room and Mr. Wetherill was worried. "What would you like to do?" he asked me. "Would you like to have them at your head, or at your feet?" I said I would have them at my feet. So that night we slept with four mummies at the foot of our beds.[9]

We wrapped the mummies in muslin in those long tarpaulin bags and packed them with grass and snapped them all shut. It rained for several days and they sure did smell. Every time it was sunny I got our beds out and aired them.

We found very few burials in Chaco Canyon. We knew the Navajo wouldn't live in Chaco Canyon because of all the souls of dead people but we couldn't find where all those dead people were buried.

When we went to Chaco Canyon to live after our trip to Grand Gulch we found in some of our digging one room at Pueblo Bonito that had a great many tall vases varying in height from sixteen to twenty-four inches, perfectly round and flat on top with three or four little loops around the top where you could run a string through. There was a flat rock on many of them. The roof and two or three stories had caved in, breaking most of the vases. I never found out what was in them. It seemed like dirt. It didn't seem like human ashes.[10]

In the center of one room that had been lived in we found the skeleton of a man. He must have been the chief because he was decorated with many bands of turquoise around his head and arms. He wore a *nageezi*, one of those medicine pouches on a four-inch band covered with turquoise that came around under his arm and up over his shoulder. We found scarabs, ducks, and other things carved from turquoise, and there must have been a peck of turquoise. The skeletons of thirteen women were lying against the wall clear around the room and every one of them had a hole in their skulls. They were his wives, perhaps, to go to the afterlife with him.[11]

We did occasionally find a baby that had been buried just inside a door and it was reasonable to think maybe the baby was buried during warfare or sometime when they were afraid to go out. They dug into the floor and put this little baby there and just plastered right over it. That's all the burials that we ever found while excavating there and they still haven't found many.[12] [13]

Old Mother Cats[14] showed me a cave full of mummies once. They called her Mother Cats because she lived in the rocks and needed the cats to keep the rattlesnakes down. She said she didn't live in her house for years because it was full of snakes. She could see them hanging from the beams when she looked through the windows of her American Cattle Company home. She didn't have much, although the people said she was wealthy, so I brought her some flour that day. She wanted to show me something, she said, "But it may be something you don't want to see." I told her I wanted to see everything.

We walked up the trail from which we saw a cave ten feet above the canyon. I asked her if there were any houses in that cave, because I was always looking for cave dwellings. She said there weren't, but maybe I wasn't going to like what I was going to see.

We climbed up there carefully, watching for snakes. It was dark inside and I crawled in far enough so that I could see five mummies sitting in there. They were all leaning up against the back of the cave with their knees drawn up in front of them like anybody just sitting on the ground and some of them were practically skeletons, but they hadn't melted down much. Those toward the front were more mummified than those in the back.

There were beautiful baskets sitting all around. She didn't know who put the baskets there. I said, "Why don't you get those baskets and sell them?" She said she was afraid to. "There's plenty of Navajos who would get those baskets out and sell them," I said, but she said they'd be too afraid, too. She wasn't even sure if anybody else knew about the cave.

"Those are Apache baskets," I said. "Or Comanche." She laughed and agreed with me. The greatest enemy the Navajos had was the Comanche.

We backed out of the cave and I never went back.

Chaco Canyon had a great sand dune that moved. When I first went there with my parents, that big pile of beautiful yellow, almost white sand was down about three miles below where Chaco runs into the Escavada. I'd say it was half a mile long and a hundred feet deep. It blew right against the cliff and it got deeper all the time. It got so bad, we had to build a new road into Chaco, just about a half mile from our house. We used blasting powder and tore that cliff down and made a nice road going up over the cliff and then crossed the Escavada, cutting about six to eight miles off the trip into

Chaco. In ten years that pile of sand moved right up across from old Welo's house and the American Cattle Company houses and had completely covered some little stone cliff houses Old Mother Cats showed me.

Welo's family buried their babies and others that died in that sand dune. They'd bury the body right on top up against the cliff. In two years more, the sand had moved, and the Navajo would say, "What became of the bones of our people?"

"The Great Spirit took care of them when he was moving the sand," I told them.

In one of the hogans up on the mesa an old lady died and one morning some Navajos came down and asked Mr. Wetherill if he and some of the men would come up and bury her. The Navajo said they didn't want to bury her in the rocks because there were so many bad Navajos ruining the burials for silver and baskets. They thought that if we buried her in the ground like white people it would be better.

Mr. Wetherill took a couple of men and some shovels up to the hogan and I tagged along. They hadn't let her die in the hogan. Just before she died they laid her on sheepskins on the ground away from the hogan. If a person died in a hogan they would never use it again. When the soul leaves the body there's all these bad, evil spirits they've had in them that will go into the wood and make the living sick. The old lady felt she was dying because an Apache spirit was attacking her all the time. She couldn't sleep nights; all she really needed was some phenobarbital. If she just could have gotten a piece of Apache cloth, the medicine men could have shot it full of arrows and killed the evil spirit, but they couldn't find any, so they had to let her die.

Mr. Wetherill buried her in a deep grave, six or eight feet under. The Navajo didn't want a headstone because they didn't want anybody to know where she was buried. They filled the grave, patted it down, and covered it with sod so that they themselves wouldn't have known it was a grave. They were so afraid of the dead.

Normally, they would have put her in a little cave up on the cliff of the first or second benches. They would have laid her down on a couple sheepskins, covered her with a blanket, and surrounded her with her belongings, then put rocks over her to protect her from

71

being eaten by coyotes. The coyotes would associate with the dogs and the dogs would come into the house and bring with them the evil spirit of the dead person.

The woman died very early that morning, so no one ate that entire day. Not even the baby was allowed to eat. The husband and wife of the hogan were not allowed to speak to each other for three days and for three days they fasted as much as possible. After that the person was never mentioned again.

Another time I visited Old Mother Cats, she said, "I want to show you that I'm not poor." She drug out a box from behind a stack of firewood. The box was full of silver jewelry. There were at least four or five silver belts and all kinds of bracelets and rings. It was worth more than a thousand dollars. She laid it all out and said, "You can have anything out of here you want."

"No, I don't want."

"If you don't take a present from me I won't take any more presents from you."

I picked up a string of ancient beads that she said belonged to her great, great, great grandmother. The beads had worn in two as time went on and then they made buttons of them. They put *petascha* in the beads, a little ring that goes through the center to sew them on to a buckskin.

"This is what I want."

"Why do you want those?" she said.

"I like the thought that goes with old things and I like these."

She looked me straight in the eye for a minute. "You're just like I am." She realized that white people and Indians were alike in their love of treasures and the feeling we had and the love we had for our people that had gone before us. That is what I think she tried to convey to me. That was the way we were the same.

NOTES

[1]Richard gave the honor of naming the people to Talbot Hyde, who came up with "Basketmakers" since Richard always called them the basket people, but Richard was hoping for something that conveyed more of an idea of who they were. The name stuck.

[2]Grand Gulch, in southeastern Utah, is about fifty miles long and up to two thousand feet deep and harbors scores of ruins in shallow caves or under overhanging rock. Beneath the houses and basket-and-feather-blanket-graves of one set of people were the graves that were egg-shaped holes in the floors lined with clay plaster, belonging to a different people. Richard first found the Basketmakers in Cottonwood Wash in Utah in 1893. He was on his way to Grand Gulch to look for the people described by McLoyd and Graham in their 1890-91 trip to Grand Gulch (they were the first to note that there were different ancient cultures in the area). The people Richard found in Grand Gulch had long, narrow skulls as opposed to the skulls of the Cliff Dwellers (a name he gave to the Anasazi of Mesa Verde), which were flattened at the rear, making them appear shorter and broader.

[3]Archaeologists classify the Basketmakers as the predecessors to the pueblo builders in the course of cultural evolution of the Anasazi. Basketmakers lived beginning in 1000 B.C., and were nomadic but planted a few crops. By 500 A.D. the Basketmakers began building above-ground room blocks around their pit houses. By 900 A.D. they began building great houses and entered a period known as Pueblo II to III. The various peoples can be classified according to pottery styles such as McElmo versus Red Valley, or architectural styles such as Bonito versus Mesa Verde, or cultural affiliation such as Hohokam versus Anasazi. Mesa Verde Cliff Dwellers are considered to be Anasazi, although they did not use the meticulous core-veneer masonry seen at Pueblo Bonito, and their pottery was different from that at Chaco Canyon. After Chaco Canyon was abandoned in 1130 A.D., the Mesa Verde style of architecture and pottery moved into Chaco Canyon during the reoccupation of the 1200s, but the debate continues whether these people actually moved there from the cliffs of Mesa Verde or if the former residents moved back to the canyon with different tastes.

[4]According to Richard's field notes as reported by Frank McNitt, the trip was funded by George Bowles, a wealthy Harvard student, and his tutor C.M. Whitmore. Hal Heaton was a visiting member, but it isn't clear whether he was a student or not. Marietta took measurements and kept notes.

[5]In another version of this story on a later tape, Marietta said she got off her horse and walked around the fatal bend without looking back at Billy.

[6]According to McNitt's notes, Marietta gave him a different description of what Joe Buck wore:

> In another burial nearby, Mr. Wetherill found the mummy of a very tall man—he was different from the others we found there—with a long, thin head. Over him was a blanket of woven rabbit fur in a design as fine as that of this blanket here (pointing to Navajo blanket on wall). The background was a light yellow—we guessed it had been white and just turned yellow with age . . .

The mummy was found in a cave with eight other burials, including only the pair of hands and arms to the elbows and a pair of legs of one body, the torso missing. She doesn't mention this in her tapes.

McNitt's book reports that this and other mummies were found on Richard Wetherill's first expedition in 1893-94, before he and Marietta ever met, in which they excavated some ninety-six skeletons. T. Mitchell Prudden, wrote in *Harper's New Monthly Journal* in 1887, "Spear-points between the ribs, stone-arrow heads in the backbone, a great obsidian spear driven through the hips, crushed skulls and severed limbs—these secrets of the old graves show clearly enough that there were rough times in the canons [sic] now and then, and that these old fellows were proficient in the barbaric act of killing men—the art towards which some of our wind-and-paper patriots would fain have us climb back."

[7]This may have been the burial found in Cave 7, which Richard discovered in the 1897 expedition. Marietta would have witnessed this one.

[8]In a letter to Prudden, Richard wrote, "I believe it is the custom of the present Indians to build a fire and pretty thoroughly bake the linings of the cache. This, of course, would drive out all the moisture and make a safe granary." From Marietta's description of this burial cave in her oral history, one gets the sense that Richard had already discovered this cave and had returned with Marietta to collect more data and excavate further. Perhaps this is true with other finds for which Marietta gives eyewitness accounts.

[9]Paragraph from Frank McNitt's notes. He took license in the retelling of this sequence in his book on Richard, for the narration is embellished.

[10]The National Park Service checked the fire boxes in the great kivas for calcium deposits in 1974 and cremation was ruled out.

[11]The burial she spoke of was probably the celebrated Room 33, which was discovered by Richard and George Pepper in 1896, and described in McNitt's book as well as in *Chaco Canyon* by Robert H. Lister and Florence G. Lister. Adjacent to the room was a single, scattered skeleton. Pepper didn't say in his detailed report whether it was with or without a head. Twelve women had been found in a six-foot-square area, their bones widely scattered due to flooding or raiding. Not one, but two men were found *beneath* the floor of the room full of women, a detail even McNitt skipped. The skeletons were highly decorated with more than seven hundred pieces of jewelry containing nearly sixteen thousand turquoise beads between them. The HEE reported eighteen skeletons in Pueblo Bonito in all, in addition to thirty burials in the south side of the wash. They found that the lesser villages buried their dead beneath sandstone slabs in the trash middens. The difference in burial customs between the Basketmakers and the Anasazi was not lost on Richard. Richard was fairly certain the Anasazi cremated their dead.

[12]Prior to the HEE, a mummified body of a woman wearing turquoise bird fetishes was reportedly found by Col. D.K.B. Sellers of Albuquerque when he and another man broke into Pueblo Bonito. In the 1920s, Neil Judd's National Geographic Expeditions discovered the remains of seventy-three skeletons, usually entombed together beneath the floor of the great houses, sometimes adding bodies to old burials with varying degrees of accompanying wealth. Judd in particular was disturbed by a body count of a hundred compared to the thousand people he estimated to have lived there at peak times. In 250 years, five thousand deaths should have occurred, he reasoned, unless the Anasazi cemetery had yet to be found. He checked the vicinity for grave sites and the arroyos for evidence of carrying away the remains but found nothing.

According to Lister and Lister, by 1981, 325 burials had been found in the canyon, only about a third of them excavated from the great houses, and from that figure archaeologists extrapolated another 475 possible burials. The lack of burials supports the relatively new theory that the Anasazi were mobile, and heavy population in the canyon was seasonal.

On the other hand, the back of an old photograph Marietta gave Gordon Vivian noted that the wind exposed hundreds of human skulls at a burial mound at Pueblo Bonito.

[13]On November 16, 1990, the Native American Grave Protection and Repatriation Act, sponsored by the Smithsonian Institution, became law. The act prohibits excavating Native American burials. Archaeologist Joan Mathien with the National Park Service at Chaco Canyon said great care has to be taken when they even suspect that they might excavate a grave.

Some tribes prohibit the digging altogether, while others ask that the skeletons be replaced after study, and often with a tribal ceremonial.

[14]Also called *Shimáasani*, grandmother.

6

I Was Kidnapped by the Paiutes

I SAW A CAVE in a side canyon of Grand Gulch one day, about twenty feet from the top and two hundred feet from the bottom. I rode all around there but I couldn't find a way up so I took the old trail to the top of the mesa. This time when I came to the narrow place I got off my horse and led him past it. On top, I rode out to the point above the cave and my horse became very excited, so I got off and tied him to a tree. He tried to break loose and he just snorted and sweat.

I walked out to the edge of the mesa above the cave and laid down on the ground. In front of the cave were two of the cutest little mountain lions, just arunnin' and aplayin' catch with an old sage hen. In the meantime, my horse was apauchin' around and suddenly I heard something behind me and I turned around and there was Mama Lion.

She was just standing there looking at me. I was so scared I didn't know whether to jump over the edge or run. I thought she was getting ready to jump on me, but then I thought she had better sense than that because if she did she'd go over the edge. I laid still and never made a move. I never looked back.

Pretty soon I heard a stick crack and I eased around and saw her moving down toward me. I laid there like I was in a dead faint. She came down and looked at me and hissed, "*s-s-s-s-s*" like that. Then I wondered, where's Papa? I knew they traveled in pairs. She just kept looking at me because I was hanging over her kittens.

Finally I got the nerve to wiggle my toes and hands, then I backed up and got out of there. I went back to the horse and do you think I could get on him? After much struggle I mounted him and he ran like a scared wolf. I couldn't hold him. I thought "what in the name of God am I going do when I come to that narrow place," but I never knew we passed it he was going so fast.

I didn't dare go into camp. That horse was lathered from one end to the other. I took the saddle and blanket off and wiped him off with sagebrush. I wasn't going to tell a living soul about those lions because I knew those devils would go up there and kill them and I wasn't going to have it.

One morning quite early after my first encounter with Mama Lion at Grand Gulch, and after everybody went to work, I rode back to the cave to take a chunk of horsemeat to the kittens, thinking the mama would be out hunting. I tied my horse to the same tree and he didn't object, so I assumed Mama wasn't around. I fixed my meat on a string and lowered it. Just about the time the meat hit the ground, the mama came out of the cave. She ate the meat herself. I was so mad at her.

I didn't tarry because I thought she would take a notion to come and visit me and I didn't care to visit that day. I went home in a decent manner, walked past the narrow place as usual and got home after time for lunch. That made the cook mad, so I fixed my own. Everybody else was out digging.

The men went to work early in the morning and quit early in the evening because it was cold winter weather and the days were short. I spent my days exploring and the evenings with the men around the campfire. The mule herder told the most amazing stories about mountain lions which kept me awake nights because I knew he lied. I'd become quite familiar with mountain lions. I hardly ever saw my husband. I think I did more exploring than he did.

I went back three or four times and always took a lunch for the lions. The mama jumped up and grabbed the meat off the string as I lowered it down. One day while I was there the mama lion took a little lamb or mountain goat to the cave. She got so she wasn't mad at me at all. She looked up at me every once in a while, but she continued cleaning her kittens and if they acted kind of nasty she hauled off and slapped them.

The weather became warmer and the runoff got higher in the canyon; it was up to my horse's knees. I could see the water marks fifty or sixty feet up the cliffs and I told Mr. Wetherill I was picking me out a good tree to climb when it flooded. I knew he was worried so I didn't bother him anymore. It was about that time we found the princess and Mr. Wetherill worked into the night to get her out of the cave despite groans from the other men and an unfriendly reception by the cook. He knew the water was running. Right then

we commenced to make boxes. The difficulty of getting such frag-
ile and valuable things out worried Mr. Wetherill all the time.

Clate saw my horse tracks up on the mesa and became suspi-
cious of me so I had to tell him I'd seen a pair of sage hens. I'd saddled my horse up to go say goodbye to my lions and to see those
hens nest. Clate said, "You'd better hang around the camp or the
first thing we know you'll be off on one of those trips when we're
ready to go and can't find you."

I slipped out of the camp and saw the hens, anyway. It was peculiar the way the enormous sacs on the head inflated he strutted
around, and she'd stayed so indifferent. I left them and went on the
point of the mesa to see my lions.

I was getting back early, coming down the same trail, and just as
I got clear down to the bottom there were five Paiutes coming my
way. I didn't pay any attention to them and when we met in the
trail I stepped off so that they could ride by. But they stopped.
"Whatcha doing that for?" I asked in Navajo.

"You're coming with us," said one of them who could speak a
little Navajo.

"Oh, no I'm not. I'm going back to my camp." I reached for my
sixshooter, but one of them grabbed it. They were all around me by
then. "What are you doing this for?"

"*Yal.*" Yal is Navajo for *peso*, dollar.

"Come back to camp. My husband has money."

I tried to get off my horse, but one of them sat me back down
and they tied my feet under the horse so that I couldn't get off.
Then we rode away. There wasn't a thing I could do.

We went out of the canyon by a trail I'd never seen before.
I asked where they were taking me and they told me to their camp
on the Elk Mountain fault. It didn't do me any good to know. I
couldn't tell anybody. Nobody would hear my scream. I thought if I
could see some Navajos I would tell them who I was and they
would kill the Paiutes, but I never saw any.

We trotted right along quite a number of hours, maybe twenty-
five miles. We came to that country where there's all those mush-
room rocks. There were Indians standing all around a big one and I
prayed they were some of Hoskaninny's Navajos and I knew he
would make them let me go home. But they were all Paiutes, the

women and children belonging to the men who'd kidnapped me. They rode right up to the rock and a man untied my feet. They told me to get off my horse and climb up on the rock steps they'd put to the top of the big rock.

I told the Indians it would be cold up there tonight and asked for something to sleep on. They told me there was a nice warm man up there. I told them I had a nice warm man at camp. When I got up there here was one of those university boys. He'd been riding some place and they picked him up. That was Ben Bolton.[1]

Ben was frightened to death. I knew better than to be frightened because I knew I wouldn't have been able to think clearly. I knew they wouldn't kill us if they wanted money. I kept thinking Mr. Wetherill and Clate would figure out what happened and would try to track us. Then I remembered one of the Indians stayed behind and rubbed out our tracks.

Mr. Wetherill was late coming into camp as usual, and Clate said, "Did you know Asdzáni hasn't come in yet? She said she was going up to the mesa to see some sage hens nest." Mr. Wetherill started up the trail and found where these five men had stayed in the bushes until they saw me coming down the trail and then came out and met me. Clate found the track where I started to get off the horse and put one foot on the ground.

"If they're Navajo they won't hurt her because she will be able to prove her lineage to them in their language," Mr. Wetherill said. "If they're Paiute I don't know what might happen." They saw where the tracks had been obliterated and couldn't find any more because it got dark. They would have to wait until morning and you can't hardly read a twenty-four-hour track because of the mice and things that run up and down the trail. Mr. Wetherill was frantic.

In the morning four Paiutes came to Mr. Wetherill's camp. It was March and windy and colder than blue blazes. Being a married lady and Ben being a nice boy, we arranged that he slept on one side of an eroded part of the rock, and I slept on the other. We each had a sheepskin and our saddleblankets and that was all. Mother Wetherill had made me bloomers out of heavy jeans that went clear down to the ankles. They were big enough to allow me to wear two pairs of long underwear. But it wasn't warm enough. I woke up in the night frozen to death and tied up in a knot. I got up and went around to Ben and said, "Ben, I can't stand this. I'm freezing to death. Let's get together, what do you say?"

I slept up next to the rock and he cuddled up to my back. Instead of sleeping on the sheepskin lengthwise, we had them crosswise and draped the saddleblankets across our feet. It was hard sleeping on the slope. I had to keep claws out all the time to stay on those sheepskins.

"Are you asleep?" I asked, after awhile.

"No."

"Turn over. I'll hug your back awhile."

"Do you suppose they'll kill us in the morning?"

"They're not going to kill us." I couldn't make him understand that they had done this for money. "They might kill us after they got the money, but I don't know how," I said. "Mr. Wetherill probably went home to get the money to redeem us. My mother would give ten thousand dollars to get me out of this. Just be easy and do just exactly what they say."

By morning we were nearly frozen and we didn't get warm until the sun came up. "Tonight will be easier. We'll sleep on the side that's been soaking up the sun the longest." I knew the only thing to do was to make the best of it. There wasn't anything we could do with twenty people down there all around the rock watching us. We couldn't jump off because it was a long way down and we would break a leg. He was going to jump off anyway and run away into the night. "No, don't try it. They're keeping the fires up all night and they'll hear you."

I asked them to throw up some wood so we could make a fire and they said the Navajo would see it. They were pretty smart. They built their fires right up close to the rock so they wouldn't be seen. "The Navajo are my friends," I said, kidding them. "Old Hoskaninny will take your scalp if he knew I was here."

They gave us some terrible bread, burned elk—Paiute cow, we called it—and coffee for breakfast. That did us until night. They hadn't given us supper the night before.

Here we were sitting, not a thing to do. I can draw you a picture of that rock and those Indians all around it and the country as far as I could see in every direction because it was so imprinted on my mind. Ben was still worried about them killing us. The Indians were kidnapping children, and sometimes grown people, all the time in that country, and you never heard anything about it or you knew the people personally and there was nothing ever done. You paid what was asked and that was all there was to it. It was a common means of getting hold of money or horses or whatever the Indians wanted. The Indians ruled that country at that time; white people didn't.

After they gave us that delicious breakfast, we laid down and went to sleep in the warm sun. We were both just kids. I don't think he was more than twenty-two and I was just twenty. We asked for more bedding but they said their children needed what blankets they had. We were hungry enough to eat a raw dog. They did give us water and one Indian brought my horse around so I could see he was all right.

In the meantime, Mr. Wetherill and Clate rode day and night until they got to Mancos, and his family raised nine hundred dollars. Then Mr. Wetherill rode to Durango and got another thousand from his friend, Johnny Kirkpatrick. He was in the oil business and he told Mr. Wetherill not to tell anybody about it. Teddy Whitmore said he'd make up the rest and Mr. Wetherill threw in eleven horses. The Paiute told Mr. Wetherill they'd hold the boy and the girl at the top of the mesa the next morning and bring them down to the foot of the trail to make the trade.

The next morning, barely daylight, they handed up coffee and bread. There was no meat and it was just as well. "You come down now." We threw down our sheepskins and blankets and packed up our horses. They built up the rocks again so we could come down off that toadstool and Ben was just sure we were going to be killed then.

We just skipped right along and I tried to hold on to my horse. He hated the Paiutes just like I did and he was eager to get back. Those Paiutes watched that rocking-chair gait of his and asked me if I'd take fifty cows for him. I scolded them as we went along. "I hope you feel better. Isn't this boy going to have a wonderful tale to take home to the white people about how the Paiute starved and froze him up on a rock? How would you like to have your wife treated that way by the white people? That's why the white people get so mad they go out and kill the Indians." You knew they were a little bit sorry and I know they spent some sleepless nights wondering what was going to happen to them.

We stopped when we came to the canyon and finally one of the men came up and said bring me the *ba'ad* [girl], and of course they let the boy come along behind. I don't think I ever was as happy to see my husband as when I saw him. When I got down there I grabbed him and I just stood there and cried.

"Don't cry. It's all over now."

"I never was afraid, but it was terrible to freeze up there and not have anything to eat and wonder what you were doing and thinking all the time." Like all women I had to bawl it all out and then I was all right.

They made the trade and the Paiutes took the horses and drove them off and came back around and went up our trail. They took three sacks of silver dollars, fifteen hundred. They wouldn't take a check or paper money. I saw them fight over it as soon as they got up the trail.

As I say, those kidnappings weren't anything unusual. People didn't know how to get their children or wives back. They started to kill them with guns, but that wasn't the way to do it. The boy never told the tale. People didn't tell those things in those days. I've had old ladies tell me about how they used to steal their children by dressing up like deer or like mountain lions and creeping up to the house and snatching the baby. The parents would come out and the baby would be gone and they never saw it again and never did anything about it.

We had to get those mummies and all that plunder out of the canyon before we could leave. They put it all on travoises led by gentle horses and when they came to the narrow place, they unhitched the travoises and drug them around themselves.

We went on to Bluff City. Mr. Wetherill wanted to take a trip to Tsegi Canyon and the Marsh Pass country. "You know, it would be kind of nice if you'd go back to Mancos and be with Mother," he kept saying.

"No, I want to go with you and see that country."

When we came to Mrs. Allen's house where we took our room and board, I had a washtub bath in the kitchen next to the stove.

Oh, the luxury of it! I hadn't had a bath in three months. And to sit down at a table. This Scots old lady, Mrs. Allen, set a table with white linen and napkins and china and she could cook. I thought this was luxury personified. "I don't believe I want to go to Tsegi Canyon, after all," I said to Mr. Wetherill. "You go on and I'll stay here with Mrs. Allen."

NOTES

[1]McNitt said the two people who were kidnapped were George Bowles and C.M. Whitmore and not Marietta and Ben, who Marietta sometimes referred to as George. At the time, Marietta was supposed to have been with Richard's friends, the Allens, in Bluff City, Utah. McNitt said the Grand Gulch trip was cut short at the end of one month, not the three Marietta reports, because of the weather; and with the exception of Marietta, they divided into three groups to explore ruins. George Bowles accompanied two men to Mysterious Canyon. Three others went to Moqui Canyon just west of Grand Gulch and Richard and Teddy Whitmore headed toward Kayenta, Marsh Pass, Moqui Rock, and Tsegi Canyon in Arizona. The entire party, excluding Marietta, reunited at Marsh Pass, and it was there that Bowles and Whitmore turned up missing. A messenger, either Navajo or Paiute, showed up in camp and demanded ransom. Richard sent a rider to Bluff City for silver. Three days later Richard handed over a heavy sack of silver to the messenger and in a few hours Bowles and Whitmore rode into camp. Bowles and Whitmore were held captive on Moqui Rock northwest of Black Mesa in Arizona. Moqui Rock is really a cone, the base of which was three or four acres, which sloped gently to a hundred-square-foot point. It isn't clear where McNitt got his information on the kidnapping.

‖ ▲ ‖

7

Cleaning with the Great Spirit

WE HEADED FOR CHACO CANYON after the Grand Gulch trip in the spring of 1897 via Durango, Bloomfield (where we crossed the San Juan), Dick Simpson's, and Swires' Store. It took a lot of thought to outfit that trip just as if we were going to Africa. We bought a large wagon with three boxes about five feet high. We carried five hundred pounds of flour, one hundred pounds each of sugar and Arbuckle's Coffee, rice and tea, canned tomatoes, beans, peaches, asparagus. The asparagus came in square, pound cans nine inches high. We took dried fruit for the Indians, candy, crackers, vinegar. We packed tents and cots—couldn't sleep on the ground because of the snakes—and enough dishes to feed the Indians.

We camped right out in the hills. Once we left Swires' store, we didn't see a hogan or a living human being, but we hardly struck our campfire when guests arrived, the Indians, you know. We had several for supper that night. They asked where we were going and in our English and Spanish and a little Navajo, we told them we were going to Pueblo Bonito. They didn't know where that was, but finally Mr. Wetherill said, "The old houses, broken down?" And they said, "Oh, the Anasazi!" They began calling Mr. Wetherill Anasazi because he was always hunting the old people. He never had any other name among the Navajos but Anasazi.

Mr. Wetherill announced he needed men to work with him in the ruins for fifty cents a day plus room and board. The room would be their own sheepskin and their own saddleblankets on the ground anywhere they wanted them. They'd just kick the rocks out of the way, smooth the ground, put down their sheepskin and curl up beneath an *akidahinili*, or blanket, with their saddle at their head to keep the wind off. The board . . . I sure fed them good.

This time we headed into Chaco Canyon from the lower part where it runs into the Escavada Wash. These are just sand arroyos that run water during big rains. With a little digging we made a good road into the Escavada and we rode down that to Chaco. We didn't make it to Pueblo Bonito that day.

I had my cat along, this precious half-breed John Wetherill gave me. The mama cat had mated with a wild cat, and the kittens turned out to be big with stripes and tufts on the top of their ears. John gave me one he'd tamed. We always let him loose at camp and he'd never wander very far, but the next morning there was no cat. Mr. Wetherill told the Navajos who ate with us he'd give ten dollars to whoever found my cat.

It was three months before an old lady came in with the cat in a gunny sack, and was she scratched up! She'd seen his tracks in the sand and caught him in a trap she set. He bit her when she tried to release him from the trap. She just shook her head in absolute awe when she saw those ten silver dollars Mr. Wetherill put on the counter for her.

We went on our way and got into Chaco and settled behind the ruin near the cliff. We just threw things out of the wagon the first night and rudely made our camp. I have a photograph of the camp and you can see where we got our beds all made up on the cots right out in the open and the big wagon is there. It was a chuck-wagon with a big tailgate. We bought those Navajo blankets we used for shelter at Swires' store.

The year before, Mr. Wetherill had seen a cookstove at old Welo's place at the junction of the Escavada and the Chaco. He said the next morning he'd go down and see if he could rent it. It was a little four-hole cookstove with a nice little oven and they had never used it. The American Cattle Company brought it in when they were living in those houses near there and they gave it to old Welo when they left. In the picture you can see our tent and the stove right next to the ruin. Mr. Wetherill and I had one tent and George Pepper from the museum stored records and slept in the other tent.[1]

By the first evening we hired at least ten men, and they were ready to go to work by the next morning.[2] They helped build tables and benches for everyone to sit on while they ate their meals. We erected shade structures over the table with brush and the poles that were lying in the ruins. We unpacked all those boxes and put them in the ruins out of the sand and rain—should it rain.

There was so much cleaning up to do. We dug a ten-foot well in the arroyo and got ample water.[3] We walled it up and dipped water with two buckets and poured it into a barrel which we hauled to camp on a horse-drawn sled we brought from Mancos. Mr. Wetherill spent the first few days carefully photographing the ruin from end to end. He always pushed his diggings because he was so anxious to find out what was in those ruins. I guess it took ten days to get the camp straightened out to work that many men. Those Indians worked ten hours a day.

Word got out that we employed men and some of them came from as far away as fifty miles. They'd work six days a week and usually it was the first time they'd ever earned a wage. They'd have to go home and show their families and spend it at the store on sugar and flour and coffee.[4] But the Navajo were afraid to work in the ruins from the beginning. Whenever they found any sign of human habitation they threatened to quit.[5]

The Spanish Americans heard the Indians were getting paid and brought liquor in five-gallon kegs on their burros. One morning the men didn't show up for breakfast. Mr. Wetherill began looking for them and when he saw activity across the canyon, he knew they were over there drinking. He went over to investigate and found them sitting with three or four Spanish Americans, and they had liquor. Mr. Wetherill tried to get rid of them, but they wouldn't go away. They told him he didn't own the canyon. The Navajos stayed there until dark and then they hid in the trenches we dug in the kitchen middens for burials.

The Anasazi threw their trash in a great pile [south of Pueblo Bonito] that was fifteen feet deep and at least as long as the ruin. There were five or six or seven of them dead drunk asleep in these trenches. Mr. Wetherill poured dirt over their bodies and placed skulls all around them. He knew that would scare them to death and when they awakened in the morning and saw those skulls they were the most frightened Navajos you ever saw.[6]

They asked Mr. Wetherill what he could do to drive the evil spirits from them since they'd been surrounded by skulls. "You boys get cleaned up and come over and have some breakfast," he said. "This evening I'll do something to drive the evil spirits from you." That evening they came and Mr. Wetherill had them sit in a circle and in the center he burned flashlight powder and that cleansed them of the evil spirits. They weren't troubled by them anymore after that. "From now on whoever spends their money on liquor will no longer work for me," Mr. Wetherill said.

This bunch of men who'd been working for us rode into camp one evening. They said they wanted the stove back. Mr. Wetherill said, "I paid rent for the stove for this month and you can't take it." Well, they were going to take it anyway. He walked into the tent and put on his six-shooter with a belt full of cartridges and came out. He drug his foot in the dirt from the tent right across to the kitchen. "I'm sorry to do this but the first Navajo that crosses that line, I'll shoot and shoot to kill."

I'd never seen him do this before. Not a one of them went across the line. There he was that one man all alone against a dozen Indians.

We hired Juan to cook so I wouldn't have to. He cooked the meat in a copper-bottomed pot we used for boiling clothes. The pot sat on a couple rocks in a big fire pit and he'd leave the meat there to boil, replenishing the fire during the night so we'd have meat for breakfast. The Navajo rarely got to have boiled meat because it's a job and wood was scarce in the canyon.

Summer brought the hot weather and someone brought in a mutton and hung it up overnight. Juan chopped it up and put it in the kettle to cook. Mr. Wetherill came down from the diggings and looked in the pot. "What is that?" he said when he saw the big maggots crawling in the meat and floating on the water. Juan said, "I'll fix that." He poured a couple cups of rice into the water and continued cooking it and they ate it.

I cooked my own meat after that. The Navajo liked roasted ribs, but not oven roasted. We roasted them on a rack over a generous bed of coals, but they got tired of the same old food. We learned to get canned vegetables and preserves in glass jars over on the San Juan River. We hauled in boxes of it and varied the menu with tomatoes and onions. We bought green corn by the wagonload. You could see the Navajo getting fat.

The Navajo do not throw away any part of the animal. They even save the blood and make blood pudding that they stuff the stomach with, tie it up at both ends and boil it, seasoned with chile and onions. We introduced chile to them. They squeezed what was in the entrails out, but left the early digested food. They wrapped the entrails around fat and broiled it over coals. They didn't eat the contents of the stomach.

They put the head, the choicest part of the cow or a sheep, hide and all, on a bed of hot coals in a hole three feet deep and piled dirt over it. If they had an axe, they chopped off the horns because they're unwieldy. They tamped down the dirt over the hole and left it until breakfast. The hair was all burned off by then, and they skinned the hide and ate the meat. I like sheep's head myself if it's cooked properly and roasted in the oven so sand doesn't get into it. They'd eat the eyes, too, but I never could do that.

I didn't have to prepare any delicacies for my guests over the years because by the time they got to Pueblo Bonito and climbed the ruins and cliffs they were ready to eat anything. I loved to cook and plan meals and I had plenty of help. I had an Indian man who kept the wood boxes full and girls to prepare vegetables and wash the dishes. All I did was oversee the job, which kept me busy enough with my children and the extra children I had around to play with my children.

We always kept cows for fresh butter and the pancake kind of cream. We turned one room in the ruin near our kitchen into a cellar. We dug it out, put in new beams, a ceiling of cloth so dirt wouldn't come down, whitewashed the walls, and put in shelves. We didn't have refrigeration or ice. Mr. Wetherill wrote the government for plans for a desert cooler. He planted four posts, layered thicknesses of burlap between the posts and topped it with a board roof and tar paper. On that we put a barrel of water and hung down strips of burlap from the barrel and the room cooled as the water evaporated. I planted oats and grass seed all through the burlap sack and when that grew it kept the water ice cold. It took two barrels a day to run that thing and we could hang two mutton in there.

I told you about Mrs. Tomacito and Mrs. Marcellino swapping husbands, but I didn't tell you about the first time they came into camp. These two women were nice looking, heavyset, and I imagine around thirty-five. They smiled graciously and I invited them to get off their horses. I asked Juan if he would serve them dinner, and he said, "*Ha kon.*" That's "all right." He piled up big chunks of meat on aluminum plates Fred Hyde had sent out. I'd never seen aluminum plates before. He served a lot of rice and potatoes and generous amounts of bread. Juan just loved to have the ladies come, anyway. He was quite a beau. He fed them *dzidzetsos*, that's dried peaches, and more bread and coffee for dessert.

When Mrs. Marcellino and Mrs. Tomacito finished eating there was still quite a bit of juice left from the peaches and mutton tallow on those plates. Mrs. Tomacito said something to Mrs. Marcellino I didn't quite understand. They stood up and lifted up their velvet shirts and rubbed the juice and gravy all over their breasts and stomachs. They couldn't eat any more so they just rubbed it on to show me how much they appreciated it.

Working in those ruins was dirty because the dust was as dry as powder. When the Indians came out in the evening their hair was gray and they wiped their faces with handkerchiefs. They didn't bathe because there was so little water, just enough to wash their hands before they ate. They worked naked except for the breech-cloth and G-string. On Saturday night of the first week, they told Mr. Wetherill they'd haul the water if they could bathe in it and he suggested they take the tub to the arroyo where the water was. They wouldn't use the soap we gave them. They used roots from the amole, the soapweed. They came back with their hair long, some below the waist, and they put their clothes on.

After the men who worked in the ruins bathed, two or three old ladies came and sat nearby to do their hair. They parted the men's hair down the middle and pulled all the nits off. When they found a louse they cracked it between their teeth and turned it off like that and they pulled out another one until the men were deloused and ready to go home. I once asked them why they didn't go home and have their wives do that but they said it wasn't their duty. They paid the women a nickel to do that. They didn't have any hair on their bodies either, they pulled it all out. They bent a piece of tin in half, sharpened it on sandstone and pulled their beards and underarm hair out. They put horse fat on their hair and eggs won't even hatch in that.

We couldn't go into a hogan without getting lice and we had to delouse ourselves frequently. The lice really showed up in Elizabeth's blond hair. We called the lice "B-flats." One time Professor Pepper told Mr. Wetherill privately, "I don't know what's the matter with me but I think I've caught scarlet fever. I'm broke out all over and I can't sleep nights for the irritating itching."

"Well, I'll tell you what to do," Mr. Wetherill said. "Lay all your bedding and clothes on an anthill. Take a good bath with antiseptic soap and rub coal oil in your hair and under your arms." He followed the advice and didn't have any more trouble after that.

Frederic Putnam and his wife came to visit us a couple of years later. Mrs. Putnam was a petite, stylish little old lady and she did her hair beautifully and dressed for dinner in a semi-décolleté. It was low-necked and with my own eyes I watched the Indians pick lice off their bodies and put them down her back. They giggled and thought it was the biggest fun because she didn't have much confidence in them. She turned up her nose and passed around them like a cat does at what he's afraid of.

One of my special friends came calling one day. She was a very old Navajo lady, and a very smart old lady, and I admired and loved her very much.

Now in Chaco Canyon it gets pretty hot. I've known it to get as high as a hundred and nine when there's no wind. It was one of those days. I had taken a nice bath and I dressed in a white dress and shoes and I felt clean, cool, and comfortable. I walked on the porch and here my old lady friend was sitting right on the corner of the porch.

"Oh, you've come to see me," I said.

"Yes, I've come down," she said.

She walked all of ten miles to make this little visit. I told one of the girls in the kitchen to make some coffee and bring out some cake. I always treated the Navajos well when they came to my house because I was treated the same when I went to their houses. I was given a soft sheepskin to sit on and food to eat; it might have been just cornmeal mush or weak coffee, and I knew that was all they had or they wouldn't have brought it out.

The porch was raised a little and my friend was sitting there leaning against one of the posts. I offered her a chair but she said she thought she'd sit where she was.

"You don't need to think you're so much cleaner than I am just because you're all dressed in white," she said.

"Well," I said, "I hadn't thought anything of the kind."

"You look awfully clean," she said. "I don't look so clean as you."

"Course, you are," I said. "If you had dressed in a white dress you'd look just like I do dressed in a white dress."

"No, I don't mean it that way," she said. "This morning I knew I was coming down to see you so just as soon as the sun came up I went down to the arroyo and I took off all my clothes and bit all the seams." Of course, you know she bit the seams to kill the vermin. "I bit all the seams in my clothes and laid them down wrong side out all over the bushes so that the sun and the wind would cleanse them. I laid down in that nice clean sand the Great Spirit cleans all the time. I rubbed the sand over my body and it made me just as clean and then I went down to the water and I got some of the yucca. I had an old bucket there we always use to wash our hair in and I pounded up the yucca and I made good suds and I washed my hair and I washed the string and it's now white and clean as your dress. I went back to where my clothes were and I put the string out on the bushes to dry and I lay there in the sun and let the sun and the wind of the Great Spirit cleanse me and I thought about how nice it was going to be when I came down to see you this afternoon to drink your good coffee and eat your good bread and butter and sugar and jelly and things.

"And then I came and here you are just looking so white and pretty. I think that when you walked past me you had the thought that you were cleaner than I was. But you do your cleaning different. You go into that little dark room in there and light the light and then you get in the tub of water and you wash yourself all over with that water and that colorwash that you told me yourself was made out of the grease of dead animals. You wipe yourself with a white towel that's washed with the same thing because I've seen the girls do it and then you put on clothes that's cleansed the same way. Then you get a bottle and put something that smells like flowers on you and you comb your hair and get yourself all pretty and then you think you're cleaner than I am. But you could never be as clean as when the Great Spirit cleanses you."

Water was not easy to find in Chaco Canyon. You had to know where to look. I learned in Arizona to look near big rocks where water settled, but of course, that was a little brackish. Or sometimes we found a little spring by just looking for damp earth. The Chaco Wash only ran when it rained. I told you that we dug a well and walled it up, and every so often it filled up with muddy water. I stirred in a few big spoonsful of flour and that settled the mud. Cornmeal worked just as well. One year I ran out of flour, so a Navajo suggested I use *nopal*, this hand or mitten cactus. We held it over heat to burn all the stickers and then scraped the skin off. We pounded it up and put it in the water and it tasted green.

After we moved into our first house, we had a terrible rain. The rainwater usually ran over a deep gash in the cliff and collected in a deep hole. We learned to go up there to get water after it rained, before it spoiled and attracted mosquitos. But during this one big rain storm, the water poured over the cliff and drowned us out. All the plastering was washed off the walls. The water drowned every one of my chickens and turkeys we kept penned in one of the rooms at the ruin. You could see how the roofs had caved in and the rooms turned to ruin. When the Anasazi were living there, they fixed that with gutter spouts to run off the water.

One time we found a round wall off to one side of a big court about forty or fifty feet from a block of small rooms. Mr. Wetherill figured it was built to catch water. Old Welo showed me some ancient ditches that were built in the wash. He said the Anasazi built them to divert the water onto cornfields when the water flowed down the wash. At the end of the canyon was a dam they had built to trap water and make a lake. It was paved with big stones.[7]

One summer when we had several ladies and their children out to Chaco, I got complaints about the water. The well needed cleaning out. I took Pablo Wiggins, a Spanish American from Cuba [New Mexico] to a spring to fill up some five-gallon kegs. The spring was on the second bench where the Navajos went for water during the time of Kit Carson. Pablo was busy all day so we didn't get started until after supper. It didn't matter to me and he didn't know where it was so I had to go along. It took a long time to fill these kegs.

Mr. Wetherill came home from a trip while I was gone and the ladies told him I was out getting water. It was getting along about 9:30 when we started back, and I saw a man on a horse loping up. I was quite a ways behind Pablo when Mr. Wetherill asked him where I was. By that time I rode up and he had his six-shooter out.

"What's the matter? Don't you think I know my way home?"

"The women were worried about you."

"You go back and worry about their brains. I can take care of myself. I've a notion to pour this water on the ground and never let them have a drop of it."

I never went anywhere without a Colt .45 strapped on the horn on my saddle. Mr. Wetherill taught me how to use it. We had a big snubbing post in the yard, and Mr. Wetherill asked me why I always aimed for the top. I told him the only time I ever would use it was to kill a man and I wanted to hit him in the head.

"You might want to shoot a snake, but you wouldn't know how to shoot on the ground," he said.

"If I want to kill a snake, I'll stomp it to death." So you see, I was incorrigible even after I was married.

NOTES

[1]When Richard entered into an agreement with the Hyde Exploring Expedition for field work at Chaco Canyon in the summer of 1896, the Hydes brought in Frederic Ward Putnam, curator of the Peabody Museum and the American Museum of Natural History. Putnam slipped in twenty-three-year-old George Pepper to supervise Richard, to his chagrin. During the five-year life of the HEE, Pepper generally mismanaged the operations, and the ill feelings between them contributed to Richard's ultimate downfall. "He was a queer little man," Marietta told Gordon Vivian. "The less I hear about him the better." The Navajos dubbed him, *Hosteen Klish*, the snake man.

[2]Richard had hired Navajo men to work for him in 1896.

[3]In another tape Marietta said, "We got water from a pothole that was up on top of the cliff a hundred-fifty feet above us and carried it down in buckets."

[4]The expedition had problems with absenteeism, especially during ceremonial periods, and with pilfering of artifacts. Richard bought back the artifacts when they turned up in trading posts.

[5]Cultural taboo against working in ruins is still a problem today for those who work on the Navajo restabilization project of the ruins at Chaco Canyon.

[6]Another version of this story is that Richard lit the skulls with candles, and the Navajos were made to believe that the skulls belonged to people they themselves had killed while they were drunk.

[7]Marietta is probably referring to Los Aguages near Penasco Blanco, built by the Anasazi during the classic period.

8

Mother Nature Has Always Taken Care of Me

BY AUGUST OF THAT first year we lived at Pueblo Bonito I couldn't stand the smell of food and I'd get up in the morning sick to my stomach. After about a week of that, Mr. Wetherill said, "You'll have to go home to Mancos to Mother. Maybe she'll be able to doctor you." Neither one of us knew what was the matter with me. I'd been healthy as a pig, never even had a headache.

Clate and I started for Mancos on horseback.[1] We took our time stopping at stores and ranches and I couldn't eat a thing. I was sick to my stomach the whole way. At Aztec, we stayed at a hotel and I took a bath. I thought I was feeling better and had half a notion to go back to Pueblo Bonito, but I wasn't better.

"Don't you know what's the matter with you?" Mother Wetherill said when we arrived in Mancos. "You're pregnant."

In a couple of weeks I was better. It was the heat in Chaco Canyon and I'd eaten too much fat mutton. I kept myself busy, which Mother Wetherill advised. I fixed up the apartment back of the museum. She taught me to cook. I could cook on a campfire and make decent biscuits in a Dutch oven and I could roast meat and cook potatoes. I'd been raised in camps and didn't know much about housekeeping. My mother and her sisters and the hired girls did all that. I just went to school when we were at home. She taught me to make light bread and cake and how to serve it. She really made me a lady.

Mr. Wetherill and the outfit came the latter part of September and brought with them my three jackrabbits and my cat. Mr. Wetherill stayed all winter and I was anxious to show him everything I'd learned. He spent the winter packing the pieces they'd excavated from Pueblo Bonito. The wool we used was about three cents a pound.

Mr. Wetherill had four old bachelor friends, the Krumpineskis, who grew up with him. Their ranch was up on a mesa above the Alamo. The Krumpineski boys would come down and sit in the museum and talk in the evenings. One time they decided that now

oops wrong date — 1893

was the crucial moment to go bear hunting. It was the first of
March 1988.

So we went bear hunting in the La Plata Mountains. I didn't
know when I was to have this baby. I rode horseback every day and
just used my normal life like I always had and I wasn't inconve-
nienced any, except that I got fat. I started right out under the ears
and went in all directions.

We made our camp the first night. They wouldn't hobble my
little Ute pony, Billy, because he would run home during the night,
twenty-five miles away, just lope along with the hobbles on. Mr.
Wetherill tethered him to a steel picket with a swivel on top.
I could hear him running in the night. I woke Mr. Wetherill up
once saying, "What's the matter with Billy? I hear him running."

"He's just trying to get the horses. Can't you sleep?"

In the morning Mr. Wetherill went out and found that the
bears had been after Billy and they'd run around till he'd worn a
deep track in the ground.

They got a hurried breakfast and started out. I hadn't slept
much so I didn't go. I stayed in bed and decided to get my breakfast
when I wanted it. It was cold. The men came back with two old
black bears. "I guess Billy won't be bothered with bears tonight,"
Mr. Wetherill said.

We camped a week in the snow and they got all the deer and
bear they wanted. The pack horses were loaded to the guards. We
went back on the seventeenth of March, how well I remember it.

About 5:00 the next morning I woke Mr. Wetherill and said,
"I've got the worst pains in my abdomen. I don't know if it's something I ate. Go call your mother."

He brought Mother Wetherill back and I can remember hearing her coming wearing her bedroom slippers and a big heavy coat.
"What's the matter, darling?"

"I ate something that made me awful sick. I've got cramps in
my abdomen."

"Richard, hitch up the team and go get the nurse," she said. He
had to go down Weber Canyon to get Mrs. Jenkins, a Mormon and
very skillful. She'd brought more than a thousand babies into the
world she told me. Occasionally a baby would be born dead but
she'd never lost a mother. She was a tiny Englishwoman and had

taken her training in England before she joined the Mormon church and came to America. She was God's blessing to that country because there was no doctor.

She asked me a lot of questions to find out if it was time for me to have my baby and I had to tell her I didn't know, it was my first baby. Then I wanted to get out of the bed. I just felt my back would break in two and kill me if I couldn't get out of bed. I stood up on the floor and Mrs. Jenkins said, "I don't know why you want to get up. Most people are more comfortable in a bed than they are on the floor."

"I'm comfortable here. I'm going to stay here."

She got a chair and turned the back over and put it in front of me and in five minutes my boy, Richard, was born. Two pains, good ones, and he was born. He weighed twelve pounds.

When Clate went up to the Krumpineski boys' the next morning to tell them I'd had a baby immediately after the bear hunt, the older Krumpineski said, "My gawd, what if she'd had it up there? I wouldn't have known what to do." Nature's always taken care of me.

My next child, Elizabeth Ann, was born in early 1900. We'd made all the arrangements for the doctor and nurse at Tooksbury to come down when we sent for them. One night I woke up to the fact that I was in labor. Mr. Wetherill was gone, as he was quite often. Farmington people were afraid to come out on the reservation and it was difficult to get freighters. They were afraid of the Indians even though we were living so peacefully and happily there and Mr. Wetherill had to go back and forth as an escort.

I struggled by myself a few hours until I couldn't do it any longer. I saw there was something wrong. I called the Indian woman working for me and said, "Call that Indian boy in the barn to get a Navajo midwife and tell him to take an extra horse and hurry up quick, I'm awful sick."

There were times when I lived at Pueblo Bonito for six months at a time that I never spoke an English word and was there by myself with my children as they came into this world. It wasn't more than an hour, why here he was back with Mocking Bird and I said, "There's something wrong, I can't give birth to this baby. Go tie up your hair and take off all your clothes and wash way up on your

arms and clean and cut your nails." I told her to put six drops of
carbolic acid in the last water she rinsed her hands in. Then she
could make an examination.

"You can't have this baby," she said. "It's trying to come butt
first. We'll have to turn it around." So when the pains came she
turned it. She knew just as much about it as any doctor did. Those
lovely long, slim hands of hers. The little hand came and she put
that back and then in just a little while the baby was born. "I do this
for lots of women," she said. "I've even helped the sheep and goats,
I ought to know how."[2]

When a Navajo couple is sure a baby is coming, the father
works on a baby board made of buckskin and rubs it down smooth
as stone, and the mother gathers great quantities of cedar bark for
the bedding and clothing for the baby. The woman is shielded during her pregnancy. She can't go to any ceremonials and it's considered bad form for the husband to go to ceremonials, as well. If they
even thought about the spirit world it would be bad for the child.

When a baby is born to a Navajo couple there is great rejoicing
because it's the greatest sorrow not to have children. A large family
is a rich one, even if it means adopting or buying children. They
bought Paiute babies.

Grandmother or aunt or older sister come to take care of the
mother when she gives birth and they send for an old lady to midwife. It was very seldom I heard of a woman having difficulty deliv-
ering a baby. Either they're different than the average white person
or else they don't display their pain. I've known them to be on their
way to the store and get off their horses and give birth. They cut
the cord by pounding it between two rocks and tie it with some of
the hair off their heads. Then sometimes they come on to the store
and do their shopping and maybe they'd ask if they could stay all
night. They tried to plan their lives so that they would be at home,
but occasionally they made mistakes and were forced to come to
the store for some provision that they didn't have.

The assistant brings in a little fawnskin bag full of clean sand
and pours it out near the fire. (They made bags out of whole fawn-
skins and stored everything in them.) They pile up the sand and pat
it and fix it until it is the right shape and just as soon as the baby is

born they lay it on the sand naked with the head pointing downhill at a forty-five degree angle. They burn dried stems picked from a certain kind of a bush near the baby's head. I put my hand on a baby's head once to see how warm it was because it seemed to me it was going to burn it's hair, but the fire was just right. Indian babies have lots of black hair when they're born.

This baby I watched being born kicked and struggled and cried and coughed and cleared its mouth, throat, and lungs, and the women wiped it with cedar bark. The baby was left on this bed of sand for just about an hour and they kept a pretty good fire going in the hogan, too, because it was chilly weather. I asked several old medicine men why they put the baby with its head downhill. They said the baby has been curled up in a little ball. By laying it there on that sand, it kicks and kicks and the blood circulates. They must have the blood in the head first because that's where the brain is, that's where they think, they would say, and they have to have the heat up there to warm the blood so it would it circulate.

They rubbed the baby all over with ashes from the fire. It seems a queer thing to do because we know that wood ashes is what they make lye from but . . . I asked, "Won't that make the baby sore?" No, that's what gives the baby nice skin, they told me, and they rubbed it into the wrinkles. The baby is laid on its bed of cedar bark that has been rubbed up until it's as fine as feathers and as soft as down and layered on the buckskin baby board, the *'awee bits' aal.*

Then the care for the mother begins. She lies down on a sheep-skin that had been tanned with the sheep's own brains. They cover her up because you know how bad it would be if she got cold. The mother for the first ten days is allowed no food of any kind except-ing cornmeal mush. She can have all of that she wants as often as she wants it but that is absolutely the only food she's allowed to take. I never even noticed them drinking a lot of water. I ached to give them coffee or a nice broth but I learned the relatives ate it in-stead of the patient. One woman told me she'd like the mush better if it had sugar in it and I told her I'd bring her some sugar. "No, no I can't have it," she said.

If the mother isn't able to nurse the baby for the first few days, which many of them were not, some of the other women come in and nurse it. They told me they preferred a woman that just had a baby because the milk from the woman with an older child wasn't good for the baby. Fifteen years later they found they could give the baby goat's milk or sheep's milk or even a mare's milk. Gave it to them with a spoon.

The only thing I found that caused a woman to die at childbirth was getting cold. The afterbirth wouldn't come then and they had no remedy for that, and I didn't either. They used to come and ask, "Please come and see this woman that's going to die." I didn't know what to do.

While Mother Wetherill visited us a couple years after we'd been in Chaco Canyon, Joe Hosteen Yazzi came down and told me his pregnant wife was bringing in a load of wood on her back and she fell on the rocks and rolled quite a little ways. She had given birth to one baby and was getting ready to have another. Twins were bad luck with them. They thought it wasn't natural for a woman to have more than one child at a birth, and the mother and both children usually died. To prevent this they usually killed the weakest one of the two. The older members of the family tied a buckskin string around its neck and it didn't take but a minute.

I told Mother Wetherill two or three women around there had died from not being able to deliver the afterbirth. "That's foolish," she said. "Why do they let them die from that cause?"

"They don't know what to do. Their hogans are so open and the kids are going back and forth out through the door and she gets cold just after the baby comes and the afterbirth doesn't come."

"Let's go do something about it," she said.

We couldn't go up over the cliff to the hogan on top because she was an elderly lady and she couldn't climb it. We went around the canyon by buggy about ten miles out of the way. Mother Wetherill packed an empty five-gallon coal oil can and a couple buckets, carbolic acid, bichloride of mercury, and peroxide.

When we got to the hogan I could see the woman was very sick. I knew her well and she was in trouble. "Have you a tub here?" Mother Wetherill said. Yes, they had a little washtub. "Fill it full of water," she said. "Build a big fire around it in the hogan."

Land knows where they got the water. I guess they must have carried it from our well, I don't know, or they went up over the cliff about a mile. We got the hot water just as quick as we could and she poured it in the can. Then she cut a hole in the sheepskin about six inches across and placed it over the top of this can. Now the water in that was hot, boiling hot, and she put an old rag she found there around the can so it wouldn't burn anybody. We lifted that woman up and sat her on that can. We had to hold her, she was sick and weak, and we held her maybe twenty minutes and the after-birth came. The steam relaxed her. I don't know how many old women and medicine men shook Mother Wetherill's hand thanking her for teaching them. They hadn't realized that getting cold caused the muscles to contract. We saved the lady and one baby.

The first summer we were in Chaco Canyon one of our worker's wives had twins and he came to Mr. Wetherill in great distress not knowing what to do. "I'll buy them," Mr. Wetherill said. "My wife will buy one and I'll buy the other and we'll provide the food for them until they're able to get up and do something for themselves. This way you won't have twin babies and neither will we."

That was a satisfactory arrangement. We paid five dollars apiece for those two babies and then we sent down a fifty-pound sack of flour and sugar and coffee. The mother nursed one baby and one of her daughters nursed the other. They're still living.

NOTES

[1]Frank McNitt said the early August heat bothered Marietta in her initial stages of pregnancy, and she begged to be taken someplace cooler. He said Richard took her to Mancos, making the three hundred-mile round trip in a little more than a week. A letter Richard wrote to Talbot Hyde confirmed that he took the trip.

[2]The drought in Chaco Canyon in June 1902, forced the Wetherills to drive two thousand head of sheep and goat to Crede, Colorado. Marietta moved there as well because she had the mumps and was again pregnant. She said she had already lost a boy. Richard had gone before her and found her a house that belonged to a wealthy miner where she could stand on her porch and watch the trout jump in the Gunnison River. McNitt reports that she stayed with Charlie and Anna Mason, but Marietta doesn't mention them. She gave birth to Robert in Creede on August 6. They hoped to drive the stock down before the first snow, but it snowed the day they started back.

Marion was born August 27, 1907, and Ruth was born in Albuquerque, June 5, 1910, a couple weeks before Richard was murdered. She had two stillborns in 1903, both boys. The boy she said she lost between 1900 and 1902 may have been one of the two she lost in 1903 and she confused the dates. Later, in her tapes, she said she lost one boy before going to St. Louis in 1904 and the other six months after she came back from St. Louis in 1907.

RICHARD — 1898 ∞ Robert
ELIZABETH - 1900
ROBERT 1902
MARION 1907
RUTH 1910

|| ▲ ||

9

Of Homesteads and Hogans

DURING THE WINTER before Richard was born, we made up our minds we were going to make Pueblo Bonito our permanent home. Mr. Wetherill left it up to me. "I don't think I'll ever be happy anywhere else," I said. "Please take me back." The Hydes agreed to continue sponsoring the expedition because they were so flattered with the many beautiful things we found the year before. The Hyde Collection went to the American Museum of Natural History and they built a new wing to accommodate all that Mr. Wetherill found in Chaco and the Grand Gulch. We left Mancos in early May for Chaco Canyon when Richard was two months old.

It was quite an undertaking for us to start out with a new baby. I didn't know a thing about them and Mr. Wetherill knew less. Mother Wetherill said we should have an older person go down there with us, a lady who'd had children of her own. We scouted all over the country and couldn't find anyone. Finally we got a girl who was older than me by the name of Annie Wheeler whom I'd met when we first went to Mancos in 1895. Mr. Wheeler's the one who had two wives and eighteen children and Annie was the eldest. She knew what to do when babies had colic and she'd taken care of Mother Wetherill's house. We got along well together and we had a lot of fun on the trip down. Richard slept most of the way in a crib in the back.

When we finally got back to Chaco, we made our camp under the cliffs as usual and then we picked out the site for our house. Mr. Wetherill said he didn't want to put it anywhere where it would detract from the ruin or cause confusion when people were photographing it, so we put it down on the west corner away from the ruin a little ways. The sand didn't accumulate as badly there and we had a nice view out the [South] Gap in the canyon cliffs opposite Pueblo Bonito. You could see about half a mile back through there and watch the coyotes run the jackrabbits.

We had a nice home there but we didn't build it all the first year. We decided to build a trading post[1] at Pueblo Bonito so we built

the store and added a room next to the store which served as a bedroom and living room and kitchen.[2] Annie had a little tent outside.

The big room later became the dining room. The lovely beams
in the ceiling were from the rooms they excavated, and they knew
that if they stacked them up behind of the pueblo the Mexican
sheepherders would come along and burn them as they had in the
past.[3] The beams were fifteen to eighteen inches across and worn
smooth. The smaller logs were placed crossways and they'd been
used in those rooms so many centuries they were a beautiful rich
brown. Then above that we had cedar bark and dirt, just like in the
ruin. The Indians started the building when Mr. Wetherill was
away. They'd gotten it up about four-and-a-half feet when he came
back and said, "There's no necessity of building these walls that
deep and thick." From there on up they built the wall only eighteen
inches thick and then left this lovely bench along one side.[4]

Eventually we built on another store, an office for Mr. Wetherill, a bedroom, which became a sitting room for me, and a kitchen.[5]
The walls in the store were two feet thick and it had no windows,
but it did have a skylight. In the house, the windows were all in the
front. I just recently figured out two reasons why Mr. Wetherill did
this. In those days the windows were small and let the wind in.
I think he didn't want to let in the north wind or the dust. It was
for safety, too, because you must remember that at that time all the
criminals from Texas, Oklahoma, and God knows where were all
coming into New Mexico. Later on we cut a window into my sitting room, but Mr. Wetherill's office had only a skylight.[6]

It got hot in there, but we lived outdoors. I slept up on the roof
myself with the kids, moved up there when Elizabeth was just three
days old. I liked the outdoors and the wide open spaces with the
wind and the stars above.

I thought about why the Navajos didn't like to live in the
canyon. They said the evil spirits make you sick, that the air was
bad around the ruins. Well, I thought, it may be that constant
breeze up and down the canyon or maybe it's the pollen that causes
a cold or sinus problems.

The cliff behind Pueblo Bonito is about a hundred and fifty feet
high, bordered by a wide bench say fifty or sixty feet in some

places, and then the second bench [or mesa] comes on. The Navajo put their hogans on that first bench in sheltered places back in the little canyons out of the strong wind. One day as I rode on the second mesa I discovered a hogan down on the first mesa behind Chetro Ketl. It was made of rough cedar and piñon limbs torn down without an axe and pounded into the ground. Smaller pieces of wood were cut down to fit the little spaces as needed and chinked with other small pieces of trees and covered with mud. It was fifteen feet wide and quite a few years had passed since anybody lived in it.[7]

I found a place [where] I could get down to it and I saw there was an unusually long wall around the hogan. I judged when it was new it was maybe four feet high. It was laid up with stone, now broken down, and it curved out in front past the door which faced east and around the right hand side, turning south.

I rode on up the mesa a little ways to Yei Tsosi's[8] hogan. He once told me he'd lived there so many years and his ancestors had lived in hogans on the same land. The Navajo weren't nomadic—that's a misnomer. As the families expanded, they built their hogans out of sight of one another so that the mother-in-law and son-in-law could not come eye to eye. You'll find maybe eight or ten hogans in one little group and the families had lived with them more generations than they knew.

A woman came to the door and when I asked her about the wall, she said, "I can't tell you because I'm afraid. I'm going to all my life be afraid of what happened to my ancestors. Maybe Yei Tsosi will tell you."

I stayed until he came home, and she said to him, "Asdzáni Anasazi wants to know about our old hogan."

He looked sort of provoked as though I'd made a mistake in seeing it and that I shouldn't have asked about it. After awhile, he said, "You come back in two days and I will tell you the story of my people."

Well, not in two days. I was early and he began the story. "When the Comanches came into this country they robbed and killed us. We built those walls around the hogans so that if we had a fire in the hogan to keep us warm, the enemy couldn't see the fire as we came in and out of the hogan. Then the Spanish came and fought us and Kit Carson hunted us and made us prisoners. The wall protected us."

I asked one old woman if she hid from Carson and she said, "You won't tell on me?" I said I wouldn't if they came tomorrow and asked me. She wasn't so terribly old but she was gray-haired and wrinkled like they get from being in the weather. The women outlived the men and they were the few old, old people who re-membered Kit Carson. They kept track of their age by notching the seasons on a stick and some of the sticks started back when Kit Carson took them to Bosque Redondo. There were missing notches for brothers and sisters because many of the younger chil-dren died on the trip there.

The old squaws told me how the soldiers whipped their backs with ropes when they were ready to fall down from exhaustion and lack of food and driving through the snow and sand. If a squaw fell down, the soldier got off his horse and grabbed her by the nape of the neck and pulled her to her feet and said, "You go on or I'll kill ya." I always think of those things when soldiers tell me how brave they were. It doesn't sit well with me.

I think one reason the Navajos wanted to tell me so much about themselves was because of their experience at Bosque Redondo and the trip back and forth. It changed them. It broke their independ-ence. After that, the Apache were always trying to get them into trouble. If the Apache committed any depredation like killing or stealing horses, they'd leave something that belonged to the Navajo so the white people would accuse the Navajo of the crime.

To make the hogan circular they stuck a peg in the center of the hogan site and put a lariat rope around the peg and walked around to mark the circle in the dirt with another stick. I asked why the hogans were round and some would say there's more room and more places to put things. But the women told me the roundness accommodated being able to sleep without being bothered by the enemy. The people slept with their feet toward the fire that's built off-center in front of the door. The fire belongs to the Great Spirit and if an enemy came in while everybody was sleeping, he wouldn't touch the fire or the rocks around it for fear of dropping dead.

The smoke goes through a hole in the ceiling above. The fire-place hole was about three feet by four feet and they put a skin or an old blanket over the hole when it rained or snowed. The Navajo wished they didn't have the hole because the evil spirits came through the hole at night, especially when the fire went out while everyone slept. They were glad to get stoves with chimneys that would let through only the smaller evil spirits.

The roof was made haystack-style and starting from the out-side, they laid a row of logs and worked around with smaller logs to get the curve, and then packed it with bark and brush. The roof had to be substantial enough to hold a man working on top. De-pending on how much timber is left they built a hallway. A man or woman can stand off an enemy coming through that hallway. The Navajo said where they have trouble is from the top. An enemy can climb up and shoot arrows through the hole at whoever is inside.

There's no door, only a blanket hung over the entryway. Frank McNitt wrote to me, "I walked up to this Indian house and knocked on the door." I wrote back and said, "Mr. McNitt, no In-dian ever had a door and you don't knock." The way you go to an Indian hogan is you ride up within two hundred yards of it and you sit there awhile on your horse. If no one comes out and takes a shot at you, you move up a little closer. By that time all the dogs are at your heels trying to tear you to pieces and you stand there another ten minutes, talking kindly to the dogs. If you're welcome, some-one will come out and yell at the dogs. You can advance a bit closer and you holler and they yell out, "Good morning son-in-law, come on in." Then they throw firewood at the dogs, but you don't walk up to the hogan and knock on the door. I never knew one with a door.

The hogan always faced east. I've stayed many a night in a hogan and I never knew of a man who didn't get up from his bed and walk out the hogan at sunrise and thank the Great Spirit for taking care of his family during the night. And when the sun's set-ting, an Indian will ask it for protection until it returns the next morning.

When we tore down that old hogan there was a pit about two feet deep and a bench running around it where they stored all their plunder. The bench is made of dirt and plastered with adobe. I re-built the hogan I found, right on the same foundation, and copied it after Joe Hosteen Yazzi's hogan.

Fred Hyde made a trip around the world. He was very observ-ing, just out of Harvard. He'd tell me how the Navajo country re-minded him of several countries he'd visited, and he spoke of the similarity in homes. He'd live with the Navajo, sleep in their hogans on their blankets and sheepskins with mother and father and all the kids.

We built a hogan out of telephone poles for the Yeibichai we had for a sick old man. Mr. Hyde was so in love with the hogan he moved into it. He took some blankets in, some ordinary *hustlechusleys* [?], you know, bed blankets, and a pile of sheepskins to sleep on. We fixed it up real fancy. He was going to be a real Navajo.

He'd been there about a month when we had one of those awful rains. The water came down the canyon and straight into the hogan. It was waist deep. Both Mr. Wetherill and Mr. Hyde were gone and it took me several days to get enough Indians to help me drag the wet and dirty blankets out. I washed them in one of those 1776 cradle washers.

Fred Junior was a fine young man, but temperamental. He would work hard then lay off for a long time. After we came back from the World's Fair in St. Louis, Mr. Hyde and Mr. Wetherill bought a Buick in Albuquerque and they thought they could drive it to Pueblo Bonito. They got it as far as Corrales just outside Albuquerque and from there they pulled it with a team of mules with the help of Mr. Schmedding and Mr. Buck. Fred dropped a pair of pliers down into it and they monkeyed with it all the way as the mules were pulling it.

Richard [the son] tells me he drove thousands of miles in that car with Elizabeth and Robert. But it never moved from where it was drawn in there with the mules. That was the first automobile that came to Chaco and the last while I lived there. There wasn't a place where an automobile could go. The Navajo called the car "get-there-I-guess."

NOTES

[1]McNitt reports that Al and Clate Wetherill and Orion Buck, also referred to as Oscar, left Mancos the previous October to stay in Chaco Canyon for four months and establish a store and trade with the Navajo. They added a fifteen- to twenty-foot-square room directly onto the north side of the ruin where the kitchen had been, and it took several months to put up the walls of stone and adobe mortar. The items crammed into this small space included dry, canned, bagged, and boxed goods; harnesses; galvanized ironware and rope; lamps and fuel oil; chains; axes; and candy. The Navajos traded their wool or blankets or pawned their jewelry in the store.

As noted in his autobiography, *The Wetherills of Mesa Verde*, published posthumously, Al (Benjamin Alfred Wetherill) wrote, "I had my first store in two rooms of the ruin where this rock fell. B.A.W." Al wrote the comment at the top of a newspaper clipping (*Morning Kansas City Star*, January 23, 1941) about Threatening Rock having shattered a part of the north wall of Pueblo Bonito. On the back of a photograph of the store he wrote, "Mamie (Marietta) turned the store into a chicken coop" after she and Richard settled in Chaco Canyon.

Richard claimed the store as his own, however, and in a letter to Talbot Hyde, turned the store over to the HEE, retaining 10 percent for himself.

[2]McNitt said the three-room house was shoebox shaped, with the store in the largest room at the west end, George Pepper in the middle room, and the Wetherills in the east room, which was later converted into a dining room. The store became Mr. Wetherill's office, and a new and larger wing was eventually built for the store. Expansion continued as the family grew.

[3]The Anasazi had mortared the beams into the walls at Pueblo Bonito like rails in a fence to accommodate the five-story height. Marietta told Gordon Vivian that the stone for their house came from the wall between Pueblo Bonito and Chetro Ketl. She told him it was about four feet high and extended between the two pueblos. "Dick wouldn't let the Navajo use stone from the ruin so when they built some of the post and residence, the Navajo hauled in this wall," Vivian wrote in his report.

[4]Marietta told McNitt the dining room was long and narrow, about ten by twenty feet, with a bench running most of the way around it. The windows were set deep in the stone masonry. The room was lit by two lamps like those in Mr. Wetherill's office. The walls were decorated with squaw dresses and the sixteen original Navajo (clan) blankets.

[5]The Wetherills also built a hotel and a post office, and Pueblo Bonito became Putnam, New Mexico, after Frederic Ward Putnam. When Richard filed a homestead claim, he built several outbuildings to prove up the claim.

Richard filed his first claim on May 14, 1900, at Chaco Canyon "to keep people from trespassing on the ruins." He made a survey mistake and filed on Section 30, which included only one ruin, Kin Klizin. Then a few months later he refiled for Section 12, which included Pueblo Bonito, Pueblo Del Arroyo, and Chetro Ketl. The claim triggered protests by Hewett and others who accused Richard of vandalism. In December an investigation began, and Richard was ordered to stop all excavation until the results were in. Special agent J.S. Holsinger arrived at Chaco in April 1901, and he suspected that Richard changed his claim from good grazing land to the section with the valuable store and pueblos. The homestead issue was not resolved during Richard's lifetime.

Fred Hyde also filed a claim at the mouth of South Gap, which had only a large Navajo hogan on it. This claim was cancelled by the General Land Office.

[6]In his book, *Cowboy and Indian Trader*, Joseph Schmedding wrote, ". . . I never failed to be thrilled by the splendidly barbaric magnificence of the aspect upon opening the door and entering the bright wonderland . . . Wetherill was, undoubtedly, a showman at heart for somehow or other he managed to nearly always stage the first entries in the evening, when the canyon was wrapped in purplish shadows or when a brilliant desert moon created weird images among the ghostly remnants of the ruins. Then, when his guests were under the mystic influence of the outdoors, he brought them into the office, the brightly lit lamps placed advantageously and so arranged so as not to cast shadows."

In her oral history, Marietta said, "Mr. Wetherill was quite a hunter and he hung his trophies in there, the elk head, deer head, buffalo, mountain sheep, wildcats, and *jádi*, can't think of the English word . . . antelope. It was like a museum. There was beadwork from different tribes and my room had a library and a fireplace in it. We loved to read."

Marietta told McNitt the office was lighted by four lamps that each held a gallon of coal oil. They were dark bronze, suspended from the ceiling. On the left as you came in there was a big pot-bellied stove, with a big wood box next to it. One of the Navajo rugs in the office was a fine Ponca chief's blanket, the design in bayeta red, indigo blue, and white.

[7]Brugge stated that in 1886, special Indian agent William Parsons said Chacoan hogans "consist of a slight excavation in the earth, a rude unplas-

tered and unmortared stone wall about six feet high covered with a brush roof shingled with clay and containing but a single small room." In 1890, an agent for the Commission of Indian Affairs, C.E. Vandever, described in the Fifty-ninth Annual Report, the Chacoan winter hut as "a conical structure of tree trunks and limbs; covered with earth till it looks like an irregular dome-shaped mound . . . the average dimensions are about seven feet high at the apex and fourteen feet in diameter, and this uncouth dwelling may scarcely be called comfortable. At best it is merely weather-proof and habitable."

[8]This name was spelled Yeh Hitsosi in the text, but I am certain this was Yei Tsosi, a man she refers to often.

|| ▲ ||

10

Blanket Dynasty Gets Wet

WE HAD A GOOD STORE there at Pueblo Bonito and the freight was coming and going.[1] Sometimes the freighters would be such a long time on the road but when they'd come back in I wish you'd hear the stories they'd tell us about why they were four or five days late. Somebody stole their horse or the horses had run off. We'd investigate and find out that when they were in Albuquerque they had a big time and got drunk and maybe got arrested and put in jail. You know a cowboy always blames everything on his horse.

I noticed the Navajos' clothing changed after our stores got established. At first the women wore dresses made out of two blankets they wove themselves from wool, tied at the shoulder and belted at the waist. They had to leave the dress open at the sides so that they could get on a horse. They wore those buckskin leggings that came to the knee. The women were so shy and modest they'd try to cover the bare leg closest to you when they rode by.

Later when we brought in calico, they made their famous full skirts that were mid-calf length out of six yards of material. Calico was twelve and a half cents a yard, and they were glad when they tore the skirt on a bush so that could make a new one and wear it over the torn skirt. They observed that I wore an underskirt, see. They made the shirt out of a straight yard of calico, and later velvet, and folded it in half and cut a hole at the top for the head. They pulled it on to see how much they would have to cut off the sides. The fat women used the full thirty-two inches but most of them weren't fat. The pieces that were cut off the sides were used for the sleeves that were sewn on to the shirt.

At first the men wore buckskin chaps decorated with buttons up the legs like the Spanish. They were so skin tight I wondered how they got them off. Around the waist they wore a buckskin string from which they hung their breechcloth and wore it between their legs, and their bellies would be out open to the world. When the stores came in I noticed they bought the *manta*, the unbleached muslin and made it into a pair of pants cut open from the knee down. The white pants looked very nice, but they didn't stay white for long, although you can't fault that, and they covered up the breechcloth and G-string which was never very ornamental.

I never saw a naked man; the little babies ran naked around the fire, and everyone went barefoot at home. They wore their moccasins in public and were so vain and proud that if it were raining they would take their shoes off until they came within sight of the store. They didn't want to ruin their moccasins; they were quite a job to make.

Some of the wives of the men who worked in the ruins were nice weavers but wove an inferior blanket. Mr. Wetherill conceived of the idea of fixing a place where women could weave and be comfortable. He dammed off the arroyo cutting in front of the house and made a long shelter of logs covered with brush. He set up poles to hold the looms. Then he went around and found the very best weavers in the country and invited them to bring their dyes and weave for him. We had plenty of wool.[2]

We brought in red bayeta from Santa Fe. I remembered that when I was a girl in Santa Fe, I hid from the other children on a shelf in the basement. When I climbed down, I knocked a roll of moth-eaten, red flannel cloth off the shelf. It fell into a pile on the floor and a plow and one thing or another fell on top of it.

Years later, Mr. Wetherill said he wished he could find some bayeta for the rugs and I told him about the bolt I found at Candelaria's in Santa Fe. Candelaria was one of the early traders in Santa Fe who lived right on the plaza. He gave me Chimayo [blankets] for a wedding present. When we next went to Santa Fe to check on branding records, I told Mr. Candelaria about it. "I used to have rolls of it, but I thought I'd sold it all." We went down to the basement and sure enough behind an ox cart and under two plows was the roll of bayeta. It was even more moth eaten. Candelaria said it had come from Spain by way of Mexico. We issued it to the squaws, and some wove it into squaw dresses. We got the dresses just the same.

There were always five to ten women weaving their own design, sometimes more, while the husbands worked.[3] We never supplied the designs, but being great imitators they would occasionally put in a brand or letter and Mr. Wetherill would make them ravel it out.

Lorenzo Hubbell was doing the same thing at Ganado, but he had the Indians spin yarn on a spinning wheel, and we wouldn't allow that. We never used a cotton warp. Our weavers used few colors: blue, red, black, white, and gray. We worked up a demand for saddle blankets. Many of the Bonito blankets were thick, heavy blankets, about three-and-a-half by six feet. Some of our best weavers were the wives of such men as Joe [Hosteen] Yazzi, Tomás Padilla, and Hosteen Chee.

I also encouraged Mr. Wetherill to put in stock the right tools they needed for their silverwork: punches, hammers, tongs, and anvils. When we first came to Pueblo Bonito the Navajos limited their silverwork mostly to bridles and conchas for belts. They scavenged the blacksmith shops for whatever iron scraps they could pick up. The Navajo didn't want any Mexican silver dollars unless they were stamped with letter "M." We ordered the Mexican dollars from banks in Albuquerque and Gallup, getting about two thousand a month and paying fifty cents a piece for them. The Indians used these to make bracelets, rings, squash blossom necklaces—but they didn't have the fraction of turquoise that is available now.

There was a year of drought when the Navajos lost so many horses. So Mr. Wetherill said he would start a tanner and the Indians brought in the hides of horses that had died. He set up a tannery in the big warehouse and used canaigre grass in tanning. He put in big vats of two-inch limber staves that were bolted together. We produced some wonderful leather, shipping most of it to hide markets in St. Louis.

We got many good rugs, but the idea of the rug factory was not too practical because the women became lazy. After a year or two we discontinued it. Then Mr. Wetherill had the idea of giving them sheep on shares. We encouraged them to breed up their sheep and goats as well as horses and cattle. The Navajos didn't have many sheep when we first went there, so Mr. Wetherill brought in some fine bucks and the Indians prospered; their sheep herds increased. The Navajo had nothing much at all, but after the Hyde Company came, and began to branch out, the Indians began to get things they couldn't afford before . . . wagons for instance.[4]

We still bought rugs from the Indians after we closed the rug factory. They sure skinned me time and again.[5] They'd bring in a blanket and I'd weigh it up. I didn't know what a blanket of that size would weigh, and although it seemed awfully heavy to me, I'd pay for it.

In a day or two Mr. Wetherill came in and said, "What did you pay for that rug?"

"It's in the book," I'd tell him. "I paid so-and-so."

"I don't believe it will weigh up that much," he said. He threw the blanket on scales and it had lost maybe three or four pounds. It was wet, but you can't tell when a Navajo blanket is wet.

We planted four posts in front and hung some good-sized rope and we wouldn't buy a blanket before we hung it to dry a few days. After we dried out two or three blankets they never tried that trick on us again. The Indians would laugh at the one who got caught and say, "Ha-ha-ha, you didn't skin them, did ya, you big fool?"

Then they tried filling the blankets with salt and sand to make them weigh an extra three or four pounds. They'd bury the blanket in the damp sand overnight and then card it out and it would look fluffy and soft. We'd shake them out and sweep them off on a wagon sheet, and then hang them on those four posts and they didn't do it a second time. They also did the same way with goat and sheep pelts. They'd bring them in green. When they brought in "weight," sandy wool weighed with stones, Mr. Wetherill would just dump those bags of wool out and shake out several pounds of dirt and weigh that and pay them for the difference.

I wanted the squaws to make me some little square blankets I could stuff with hay and use as pillows for the camp that first summer we excavated there.[6] I tried to explain what I wanted, but they were hard to change. I finally asked an old woman if she'd teach me how to weave so I could show her what I wanted. She agreed, but she thought I would be teaching her something about weaving, and I tried to tell her I didn't know anything about it.

I sheared my sheep and I'm sorry to say I cut it in several places.[7] I cut the black spots out of a couple of their black-and-white sheep raised for that purpose, and I learned not to get too deep . . . it was pretty hard for me. Then I washed my wool and I made my loom out of cedar under her instructions. I spun my own warp and made this little blanket. It was eighteen inches square, just the size I wanted. I was a long time doing it, but I didn't have anything else to do and I got it done.

Years later after Mr. Wetherill's death I sold the last of my ordinary blankets to Candelaria in Santa Fe. When I was visiting my father at Riverside, California, we toured an old mission. The curator took us down through some subterranean passages where he stored Indian relics and I found my little rug in there. The curator had bought it from Candelaria. It was terrible looking, just like a kid made it, with a black diamond design in it. Imagine finding that rug thirty years after making it.

In 1911, I sold the bayeta blankets to Herman Schweizer, the buyer for the Santa Fe Railroad. At first he told me he never dealt with women because they would decide not to sell the things they showed him. "No, I can't sell that," he said the women would say. "I'm giving that to Grandma." I told him I already selected what I was going to sell and that I had a team of horses and a man capable of taking him to Pueblo Bonito from Gallup two days from now. "Anything I show you is for sale," I said. "I'll price it to you and if you want it at my price you can have it; if you don't we'll just pass it by; we won't squabble about it. But I'd like to have this taken care of as soon as possible."

He looked at me a minute and said, "I'll deal with you." When he came out and walked into Mr. Wetherill's office, he said, "My gawd, woman, where did you get these things?" And when he saw my dining room, he said, "That is the most exquisite arrangement I've ever seen in my life." I sold him a Ponca robe, with the split in the top for your head, for twenty-five hundred. He was there three or four days before he gave me a second check for thirty-seven thousand dollars. He said if he wasn't a married man he'd take me, too. I had the rugs bailed up and I shipped them to Albuquerque.

NOTES

[1]As Richard's homestead claim was being investigated, he used the time to develop mercantile operations. By the time investigator Holsinger wrote his report in April 1901, Richard had stores at Pueblo Bonito, Tiznatzin, Raton (Springs near Pueblo Pintado), Ojo Alamo (managed by Richard's brother John Wetherill), Escavada (probably Kimbeto), Sautells (unidentified), San Juan, Farmington, Thoreau, Little Water, Two Grey Hills, Manuelito, and Largo. In addition, freight, mail, and passenger services were operated on a regular schedule from Thoreau to Farmington. The company's wagons hauled merchandise to the stores and Navajo blankets, wool, and hides to the railroad.

[2]McNitt says Richard began to expand the Navajo rug and saddleblanket trade in the spring of 1899. The idea may have been stimulated by the hardships of the winter, with snows and extreme cold, and a 20 percent loss of stock overall, but especially among the cattle according to Brugge. Richard was able to get thirty cents a pound for the blankets, and he purchased the raw wool for eight to twelve cents and the sheep pelts for six to seven and a half cents a pound. The blankets went up to $1.10 to $1.25 a pound. He may have sold the blankets through a Hyde retail outlet at Times Square in New York in 1901. Another outlet may have been the John Wanamaker stores in New York and Philadelphia. Marietta said that stores in Dallas, Waco, and Austin, Texas, and in St. Louis and New York also took interest. "This manner of dealing with the Indians promises to revolutionize the Navajo rug and blanket trade, and make this ingenious product as valuable and as much in demand as the famous rugs of Smyrna," Holsinger wrote.

[3]The following paragraphs are from Frank McNitt's notes gleaned from an interview with Marietta.

[4]The order to stop the excavations became permanent and in March 1902, Richard's homestead claim was suspended. Brugge said that at the time Richard was expanding his livestock interests, and opponents wanting the same land may have used political connections to stop him through the Government Land Office (GLO). Also the Hyde trading empire may have aroused suspicion that the Bonito relics were being sold through the HEE stores.

By 1902, Talbot Hyde withdrew from the association after paying his brother's debts of more than forty thousand dollars. A former cattleman of Arizona, J.W. Benham, was assigned as manager to sever the relationship completely, McNitt claims. Benham continued to press the GLO to cancel

Richard's homestead through 1903 and then purchased the Hyde's interest in the mercantile business.

Richard continued to own the store at Bonito, and for a time, his brothers John and Al held out at the stores at Ojo Alamo, Two Grey Hills, and the freighting store at Thoreau. John eventually established a post at Kayenta, and Al became a postmaster at Gallup. Meanwhile, Richard improved the land, and another agent came in July 1905 and reversed Holsinger's report.

[5]Excerpts from McNitt's interview ends here.

[6]George Pepper claimed to have ordered the first table runners and pillowcases during his first season at Chaco and that the first sand-painting tapestry was made at that time.

[7]Marietta said that when the Navajos didn't have shearing tools, they ran their sheep through the bushes.

Marietta Palmer and her younger sister, Edna, circa 1895. *From Frank McNitt Collection, courtesy State Records Center and Archives, Santa Fe, New Mexico.*

The Palmer family, circa 1895, from left to right: Elizabeth Ann Palmer, Edna, Sidney LaVern Palmer, Sidney LaVern Jr., Marietta Palmer. *From Frank McNitt Collection, Negative 6559, courtesy State Records Center and Archives, Santa Fe, New Mexico.*

Marietta Wetherill, photographed by Joe Schmedding, during a ride in Chaco Canyon. *From Frank McNitt Collection, courtesy State Records Center and Archives, Santa Fe, New Mexico.*

Richard Wetherill with Navajos against Pueblo Bonito's north wall, 1896.
From Frank McNitt Collection, Negative 8659, courtesy State Records Center and Archives, Santa Fe, New Mexico.

A note on the back of this photograph reads, "Marietta Wetherill is too busy with kitchen chores to notice her picture is being taken. The small building she is about to enter is an appendage to Pueblo Bonito's rear north wall constructed the previous winter (1897) as the first Navajo trading post of the Hyde Exploring Expedition." However, a handwritten note says, "Not M.W., but is Roline Hatch, a Mormon girl hired to help cook for excavators." *From Frank McNitt Collection, Negative 8662, courtesy State Records Center and Archives, Santa Fe, New Mexico.*

Note on back of photograph reads, "The Chatelaine of the Chaco: Richard Wetherill's bride prepares an evening meal for hungry men after a day's work in the ruins, the summer of 1897." *Photograph reproduced through the courtesy of the American Museum of Natural History. From Frank McNitt Collection, Negative 8657, courtesy State Records Center and Archives, Santa Fe, New Mexico.*

Photograph taken by a Navajo, 10:30 A.M., 1896. Pictured left to right: unidentified Navajo, Orion Buck, George Pepper, and Richard Wetherill. *From Frank McNitt Collection, Negative 8660, courtesy State Records Center and Archives, Santa Fe, New Mexico.*

Navajo displaying long hair and quirt (from his right wrist), circa 1897. *From Frank McNitt Collection, Negative 8673, courtesy State Records Center and Archives, Santa Fe, New Mexico.*

Richard Wetherill showing off his trick shooting at Pueblo Bonito, 1896 or 1897. *From Frank McNitt Collection, Negative 8670, courtesy State Records Center and Archives, Santa Fe, New Mexico.*

Navajos at fiesta. Center man is Kli Klizin, or Black Horse, one of the tribe's influential men. *From Frank McNitt Collection, Negative 8676, courtesy State Records Center and Archives, Santa Fe, New Mexico.*

Marietta surrounded by seven unidentified men during 1897 Grand Gulch expedition. *From Frank McNitt Collection, Negative 8622, courtesy State Records Center and Archives, Santa Fe, New Mexico.*

Two hundred Navajos gather for the fiesta in Chaco Canyon September 4, 1899, surrounding the Wetherill home, seen here from north mesa close to the outer west wing of Pueblo Bonito. A brush-thatched structure in Pueblo Bonito near the house served as a workshop for anthropologist, Aleš Hrdlička, with the Hyde Exploring Expedition. *From Frank McNitt Collection, Negative 5813, courtesy State Records Center and Archives, Santa Fe, New Mexico.*

Navajos in Chaco Canyon, September 4, 1899. *From Frank McNitt Collection, Negative 8682, courtesy State Records Center and Archives, Santa Fe, New Mexico.*

Fiesta day, September 4, 1899. *From Frank McNitt Collection, Negative 8681, courtesy State Records Center and Archives, Santa Fe, New Mexico.*

South, or front, side of Wetherill house, September 4, 1899. Pictured left to right: T. Mitchell Prudden, George Pepper, Clayton Wetherill, Mrs. Clayton (Mary) Wetherill, Richard Wetherill Jr., Richard Wetherill, and Marietta Wetherill. *From Frank McNitt Collection, Negative 8690, courtesy State Records Center and Archives, Santa Fe, New Mexico.*

Resting in the shade of the Wetherill house in 1900. Pictured left to right: T. Mitchell Prudden, George Pepper, Clayton Wetherill, Annie Wheeler of Mancos, Richard Jr., Richard Wetherill, and Marietta Wetherill. *From Frank McNitt Collection, Negative 6564, courtesy State Records Center and Archives, Santa Fe, New Mexico.*

Looms were set up in the shaded structures in the arroyo near Pueblo Bonito for Navajo women to weave rugs for the Hyde Exploring Expedition. *From Frank McNitt Collection, Negative 8672, courtesy State Records Center and Archives, Santa Fe, New Mexico.*

Mummies from Grand Gulch. *From Frank McNitt Collection, Negative 5586, courtesy State Records Center and Archives, Santa Fe, New Mexico.*

Triangle Bar Triangle Ranch by Joseph Schmedding, circa 1905. *From Frank McNitt Collection, Negative 6567, courtesy State Records Center and Archives, Santa Fe, New Mexico.*

Marietta Wetherill, photographed at the World's Fair in St. Louis, 1904. *From Frank McNitt Collection, courtesy State Records Center and Archives, Santa Fe, New Mexico.*

Richard Wetherill, photographed at the World's Fair in St. Louis, 1904. *From Frank McNitt Collection, Negative 8696, courtesy State Records Center and Archives, Santa Fe, New Mexico.*

Hosteen Bí' al, who adopted
Marietta Wetherill as his daughter.
*From Frank McNitt Collection,
courtesy State Records Center and
Archives, Santa Fe, New Mexico.*

Marietta Wetherill, photographed by Frank McNitt at her home on Peach
Avenue in Albuquerque, New Mexico. *From Frank McNitt Collection, courtesy
State Records Center and Archives, Santa Fe, New Mexico.*

11

Hosteen Bí'al Could Read Minds

HOSTEEN BÍ'AL,[1] THE OLD MEDICINE MAN who adopted me, said he could read minds. I tested his mind reading by asking him to tell me what I was thinking and he said, "To fool me you're thinking of something way off I've never seen. It's some kind of wagon that goes in the air." I was thinking of the elevated trains in New York.

He talked about his abilities so much, Mr. Wetherill said, "The next time I lose something I'm going to call him."

We took in a lot of pawn in our store. When it came in, we marked it with tickets and hung it in plain sight on a row of nails back behind the counter up high. You couldn't reach the pawn if you stood in front of the counter unless you used the long stick with a hook. Seems like the Navajos would discuss the pawn more than anything else. "I see Asdzán Tsosi has put her silver beads in pawn," they'd say. "I wonder how much she got on them and how long she's going to leave them here? There's Hosteen Klah's old wampum. That's been in his family for generations. He always said he wouldn't pawn that. I wonder what's up?" It was just like a newspaper pasted up there. I'd say, "I don't know how much it's in for. I don't pay attention to that." I would never tell them.

Sometimes an owner would come in and look at the pawn and caress it. They thought so much of their beads. They'd look at the tag to find out how many more days they had to redeem them. We held the pawn indefinitely as far as that was concerned. We didn't sell anybody's pawn just because they were hard up; we didn't let it go [Navajo word] dead after six months like some traders.

We lost a string of turquoise and a string of silver, so Mr. Wetherill sent word for Hosteen Bí'al to come in, and when he did we showed him the nail where they once hung. We told him we never let anyone in the store alone. We kept the long stick with the hook on it in a certain place and there wasn't any reasonable way anybody could get those beads off that nail. He sat right down in the middle of the store, put his blanket over his head, and hummed a little song.

At last he got up and said, "I think I know who did it."

"I'd like to have them back," Mr. Wetherill said.

"Do you want me to bring the person who did it here?"

"Yes, I'd like to have him brought here."

"What are you going to do to him?"

"I'll ask him why he treated us that way and what we'd done to deserve such treatment."

"You won't have a white man come and arrest him and put him in jail?"

"No, I won't do anything of that kind."

Hosteen Bí'al went off and after three days he came back with the boy and both strings of beads. The medicine man sat down and chanted and laughed. The boy looked pretty frightened. He was young, sixteen or seventeen, but he wouldn't look at you. He always looked down. We always called him 'Ashdlá Kletso,[2] Five Cents, because he'd come in the store and stand there for hours and then he'd spend only a nickel.

Mr. Wetherill asked him, "Why did you do this?"

"I don't know," he said. "I'm awful sorry. I've been sick ever since I took them. After I got them and took them home I didn't dare show my folks. I just hid them around and I didn't have any pleasure with them. I was afraid to bring them back because you'd have the white man come and get me and put me in jail."

"I want to know how you did it?" Mr. Wetherill said.

"Somebody called Mr. Derrick outside," he said. Mr. Derrick was tending the store at the time. "Very quickly I ran around behind the counter and got the long stick and I laid it down right in front of the counter on the floor." Mr. Derrick was busy and when he went to the back room to get a blanket for a woman and she went outside to check her horse, he reached up and got them.

Maybe a month or two after that, Alfred Tozzer, one of the men from the American Museum, came out. I don't know what he did; I can't remember that I ever saw him do anything.[3] He came out a couple seasons. Mr. Wetherill sent him down the canyon with Mr. Swanson to look at a ruin just to give them something to do. They were gone three or four days and the wind began to blow terribly. The wind was especially bad because that big sandhill was moving. The wind blew so hard, it blew the glasses right off Mr. Tozzer's head. He didn't even realize they were gone because the sand was hitting him in the eyes so badly.

Mr. Wetherill called in Hosteen Bí'al to look for them. The old man made a little song over Mr. Tozzer and touched him on the forehead, on each shoulder, the stomach, the knees, the feet, and hands. He said, "I'll find them." The next day he brought them in. He found them a hundred feet from where the Chaco runs into the Escavada, knowing where the wind would be blowing the hardest. He rode up and down the trail a dozen times before he found the place to dig.

Hosteen Bí'al would be in the store standing at the counter looking pretty ragged. Most medicine men rather affected poor, dirty clothes, and kept their hair unkempt. They didn't make themselves dandies just because they got a hundred sheep for curing somebody. They were poor people to the public. A white person would come into the store and as soon as they saw him, they'd edge away. He would laughingly tell me later, "They thought they were cleaner than I was, but I just had a bath in the sand and I aired and bit all my clothes."

The medicine men were the smartest people in the tribe. They could hold their faces so still and expressionless you'd think they never had a thought in their head and all the time they were reading you.

I was anxious to get him to make a sand painting for me, just for me personally. "Are you sick?" he said. When I told him no, he said he'd wait until I was sick. It just so happened Elizabeth was a year old and she had a high fever and had gone off her feed because she was teething. I saw him in the store and asked him to do a sand painting for me.

He came and felt her and said, "*Neska*,"[4] meaning she was very warm. He told me to wrap her in a black blanket and tie the blanket to my back. "I'll come tell you when to come with me," he said. "We're going up in the canyon at Chetro Ketl where we can't hear dogs bark or chickens crow or men talk. The only noise we will hear is the wind the Great Spirit sends."

I put her in the blanket as I was told and we started into the canyon. "Don't walk little steps like you walk," he said. "Walk as far apart as you can." I walked as long a step as I could comfortably

135

make. "Do you believe I can cure the baby, because if you don't we better quit right now." I told him I believed he could cure her. Then he told me not to say anything more and of course that was hard for me.

We went clear up to the end of the canyon where the water comes over the cliff when it rains. It was shady and there were lots of green bushes. We sat down where he told us to and I got Elizabeth around into my lap. He got out his medicine bags and various things. He smoothed a little bed of sand into a flat square. He poured the colored sands from different bags. He colored in the four phases of the moon in yellow-dyed sand. On one side he drew a picture of a bow and arrow and then he put in another bow and arrow on the other side. He drew a snake that stretched clear around the smoothed bed of sand. All the time he was muttering and sometimes I'd hear a word I recognized like *ashanti biuway*[5] for little baby girl and *klush*[6] for earth.

He brought out a bottle of water and sprinkled powdered green leaves in it. When the leaves settled to the bottom, he told me to drink it and give the baby some. I drank most of it and gave the rest to the baby. He shook his rattle then and sang "*yi-yi-yi-yi.*" He sprinkled corn pollen on the top of my head and the baby's head and he held an ear of corn to her mouth and then to my mouth. That's all there was to it. She would be all right in the morning.

He raked up all that colored sand. He didn't take it to the four points like the others did. He dug a hole ten feet away and buried the sand and obliterated the tracks to the hole with a brush. "We will go home, now," he said. "Step in the same tracks you made coming up." That was why he had me make big, wide tracks. "When one's going towards home, they step further than they do when they're going away from home," he said. He walked behind me and obliterated all our tracks with little wave-like figures to make it look as though the wind had blown the sand.

When he got home he told me he knew I wanted to ask so many questions I turned red in the face. Now I could ask questions and I asked him what the medicine was. He said it was *cha tini* which would relieve the baby's fever and also mine. "You're just like a wildcat," he said. "You've always got your eyes wide open and you're ready to spring. It's you who are sick and not the baby." That's the reason he had me drink most of the medicine.

I asked him about the snake and he said, "It's the snake that makes you walk so fast. Everything you do you do at a dead run. You never sit still a minute. We buried that snake and now it won't bother you." He figured I didn't sleep so well during some phases of the moon and that's one reason I went so fast. I didn't have the time to do everything. "You try to live like a Navajo and you try to live like a white person, trying to take care of everybody. I have pled to the moon to make you rest."

Sure enough the baby didn't have a particle of fever the next morning. He took me back into the canyon several times and made more sand paintings for me to reduce my speed but it never worked. I told him I slept because he felt so bad if I didn't. He never used the snake again, but he always used the moon because he was afraid I was affected by the moon. "That's why you have a round head," he said. "It's full in front."

NOTES

[1]Also spelled Bí-al, Biyal, Beyal, and Bijal in Marietta's oral history. Marietta said Hosteen Bí'al was just a child when he went to Bosque Redondo, or Hweeldi, and must have been a very old man when she knew him because he had gray hair and gray hair comes late to the Navajos. National Geographic archaeologist Neil Judd says Brugge interviewed a Hastiin Beyal in 1927 who said his family had moved from the Bears Ears area of southern Utah to the Chaco region in 1841 or 1842. He was a boy of nine or ten then. In *The San Juan Basin, My Kingdom Was a County*, Eleanor MacDonald and John Arrington said a Hastiin Biyal, who had spent a part of his childhood in the Chaco region, was among a small band of Navajos who fled Fort Sumner during the early part of their exile and hid out successfully on the Escavada. According to Indian agent reports, a Hosteen Biyahl was one of three Navajos who witnessed Richard Wetherill killing a steer belonging to a fourth Navajo, Little George. Wetherill learned that he might be prosecuted and made amends by giving Little George a wagon.

[2]The *Saad Ahaah Sinil* Navajo-English dictionary says five cents is translated as *'ashdla' lichíí*.

[3]Alfred M. Tozzer was an ethnologist who built his reputation by studying the Maya culture.

[4]According to the Navajo dictionary, *neska*, or *neesk'ah*, means fat.

[5]The Navajo dictionary says little baby is *'awééchí'í* and girl is *'at'ééd*.

[6]*Nahasdzáán* means Earth; *leezh*, means dirt or ground. Perhaps Marietta meant *klish* or *tl'iish*, which means snake.

12

Bad Luck to Kill Snakes

THE NAVAJO CLAIMED that a woman with long, flowing yellow hair and a hundred-and-fifty-foot snake's body lived on Fajada Butte and if you climbed up there she would catch and eat you.

Fajada Butte is a strata of hard rock that stands right up out of the mouth of Chaco Canyon.[1] I could see it was flat on top and I knew Indians must have lived up there. Several times I rode around Fajada and finally found a place where it looked practical to get up. There was a ten-foot high crack in the rock and there was a space in there about four and a half feet wide and deep. I thought I could straddle the chimney with my hands and feet and kind of go up easy. Of course, if I'd fallen I'd have rolled quite a ways, but I hadn't planned on falling.

I found ruins[2] and I planted a small United States flag to prove I'd been up there and I spent a couple hours hunting for ceramic handles. I could see for miles. It was a wonderful view! I waited to see this woman and I thought, "Now she didn't eat me coming up, maybe she's eaten my horse while I was gone." I started down going frog-like.

Suddenly I heard a rattle. I looked all around and saw only plain rock. It sounded like it was right in my ear. As long as I stayed perfectly still it wouldn't rattle but as soon as I moved a hand, "z-z-z" he'd go again. I finally saw him coiled on a little ledge about six inches from my face. He was no bigger than my hand. I couldn't jump or let go because I would have rolled a hundred feet.

I stayed there so long he went to sleep and finally I was able to slide my feet down the rocks. Then I was in a big hurry to let go with my hand. He raised his head and rattled like the dickens, but I was out of reach. He knew better than to jump at me because he would have fallen.

A Navajo wouldn't kill a snake even if it's in their hogan. They moved out and let the snake have the place. A snake is a sacred enemy and it was the greatest of bad luck to kill one.

One day one of the Indians came to the house and said, "There's a big rattlesnake in our hogan. Bring the shovel and kill it." We built a hogan in the canyon for the Navajo to sleep in when they worked in the ruins or stopped at the store.

I grabbed the shovel and went down there. I was just as brave as a lion, I was going kill that rattlesnake. It was coiled up sound asleep on the bench and the men were packing their stuff and moving out. "Oh, don't move out," I said. "I'll kill him in just a minute."

I pushed the shovel hard down on him and quick as a flash that snake wound right up that shovel and ended up close to my face. I dropped the shovel, and Joe Hosteen Yazzi picked up an axe and chopped it in two.

He handed me the axe and said, "You did that."

"I sure did."

We laid the axe on the hard dirt in front of the hogan. I shoveled up one piece of the snake and two shovels full of dirt under him and I carried it out. I went back in and got the other piece and then I cleaned up every speck of blood and put it all in a pile by the axe.

"What shall I do now?" I asked them. They were frightened to death.

One old man went in and inspected the ground to make sure I got it all and then he came out. "We'll dig a hole for him," he said.

We dug a two-foot hole in soft dirt about fifty feet away from the hogan. They asked me to polish the blood off the axe with a rag and some sand. Then they buried the snake and the bloodied dirt and the rag with a mound of dirt at least two feet high and packed it like cement.

"The other snake will come tonight," they said. They moved all their plunder to another hogan. I didn't believe the other snake would come, so I got up extra early, and I didn't like to get up too early, and I went to the hogan. Sure enough there was a trail where it had come right down through the brush. You could see the trail in the sand and it went around and around this pile of dirt. We followed the tracks into the hogan a found the snake asleep.

I went back to the house and told Mr. Wetherill to come and kill the rattlesnake that was down in the hogan. I didn't try any more rattlesnake killing.

When I was a girl traveling with my family, we went to see the Hopi the snake dances. We ran across a Navajo who took us to the Hopi villages. I asked the Navajo guide many things and he would answer children's questions and be perfectly astounded when a grown person asked him anything. I asked him about the Hopi snake dance and he said he had never been to the snake dance and he shuddered at the thought of such a thing. I think they looked down on the snake dance and some of the Hopi customs.

We were miles and miles from old Oraibi but we could see it up on the hill and our Navajo guide pointed and said, "That's where you're going." Then he asked my father for the field glasses, and Father showed him how to adjust them. They were a mystery to the Indians. He got off his horse and steadied the glasses and looked a long time. "Me go back," he said. "Afraid of Hopi." He left us then and it wasn't very long until a man came to us and he proved to be an Oraibi man. He took us right to his village.

The snake ceremony was held at Walpi that year. I saw one Indian get bit right on the cheek. He was one of the attendants that stroked the snakes' mouths and faces with the feathers to attract their attention [while the dancers held the snakes in their mouths]. It wiggled out of the man's mouth enough so he turned and bit this fella right on the cheek. He immediately quit the dance and another man took his place. Father told me to follow him and see what he does. He went to the kiva and drank a bowl of medicine and went to the edge of the cliff and vomited. The next morning I hunted him up and there were only two little red spots just where the fangs went in, but there was no swelling.

Years later I found out the reasonableness of the ceremony that had been so astonishing to me as a girl. The snakes [turned loose after the ceremony] are supposed to carry messages with them as they go into the ground in these holes all over the country. They go into the earth and tell how good these people were to them, how they bathed and stroked them and danced with them and exposed themselves to their venom. It's something we don't understand because we haven't been taught that way, but that doesn't mean it doesn't work. It sprinkled on us some as we were going home and we hadn't been home long before it poured.

When we had lived in Chaco Canyon a few years, a twelve-year-old girl got bit. We were all getting ready to go to a wedding that was to be held in Mocking Bird Canyon when the mother of the bride arrived to tell us her other daughter, Des-pah, was dead. The family had sent her out early that morning to collect corn pollen for her sister's wedding. She stepped on the snake and it just coiled right around her leg and bit her several times on the calf. The snake was three feet long and had been eating. It was probably full and was sleeping when she stepped on it.

The Navajo remedy for snake bite is lamb's-quarter [pigweed]. We suggested they use it on her but they wouldn't do it. They said she was dead.

Dr. Prudden was there and he was very much interested in the different serums for people who'd been bitten by venomous snakes and so he asked, "How far away does she live?"

"It's just up here five miles," Mr. Wetherill said. "I'll have a man hitch up the buggy and we'll all go up and see what's going on."

We drove up to the hogan and asked, "Where's the girl?" They said she was out in the cornfield and she was dead. We rushed out there and sure enough there this little girl lay.

Mr. Hyde and Mr. Wetherill picked her up and carried her up in the shade of the hogan, but they wouldn't let us take her inside. Her mother kept screaming that she was dead. Dr. Prudden said, "She doesn't show any life and I can't feel a pulse." I tried to feel for her pulse and couldn't find any anywhere on her body. So he gave her an injection of strychnine and put some in her mouth and dropped it down her throat.

She never showed one sign of life for half an hour. "I don't dare give her anymore," Dr. Prudden said.

"Do you suppose some more would do her any good?" Mr. Wetherill said.

Just about then I noticed just a flickering in her nostril. "I believe I saw a little movement," I said.

They looked carefully and her eyelids fluttered and then Mr. Wetherill said, "She's alive!"

We were there a couple hours and in the meantime those Indians beat that snake to death. The ground was torn up and the corn was bent where they beat it. It looked like they'd been there with a team and a scraper. They had to give a ceremonial for having killed the snake because they're not supposed to do it but they did in their anger.

The wedding was put off and the bride was very upset because her little sister was dead. "I have no daughter," the mother kept saying. "She's gone."

"Shall we take her down to our house and see what we can do?" Mr. Wetherill said to me.

"Yes," I said. "Let's take her."

We brought her down and Dr. Prudden stayed with her about six or eight days. If I've ever seen human suffering I saw it in that girl. There were times I wished she had died and I prayed she would die before morning. She screamed with the pain. No matter how much morphine he gave her she screamed until she no longer had a voice, she'd just go through the motions. Her leg swelled up until even the skin broke and the meat cracked. She was just a living mass. She wasn't human.

"I don't believe we can save her," Dr. Prudden said. "Her vitality will give out from suffering this way. This is the most awful thing I ever witnessed."

But she lived, and at last, Dr. Prudden had to go away, so he showed me how to give her injections. When the pain drove her crazy, I gave her a shot in the arm. She never went to sleep. She still screamed but it seemed to ease her. I took care of that girl for several months and finally the poison settled down in the leg and it ran black stuff for weeks. The knee pulled right up under her breast.

After a while she could sit up and eat a little. She was there three months before she would try to walk. Mr. Wetherill sent for a crutch in Albuquerque and she would hobble on that crutch and one foot from her room into my bedroom.

I used to see a woman standing up on the cliffs, but she never came down. I know it was her mother. Not one of her people ever came near. To them she was dead. I went up there and told the mother and the sister that was to be married, "When she was sick she called for you to come and see her." And they would say they had no daughter or sister. She had died. They were that afraid of death.

Des-pah's leg was still drawn up and so I thought if she rode horseback with the children maybe it would straighten out from the exercise. The next spring I got it straightened out enough for her to ride. "We'll go up and see your folks."

She hung back and said, "We won't talk."

"We won't talk, we'll just ride by." We rode by and after that we rode by every day, or I'd send her with my son, Richard. Gradually her leg straightened out. She learned to walk but she still had quite a limp. I understand she's still living but she's quite a cripple.

I finally got her folks to let her come back but they never let her live in their hogan. She always slept and lived and ate in a separate hogan. By the time that little girl was fifteen years old her hair was as white as snow and she looked old. The girl finally left her people and went to live with Old Mother Cats. They made a medicine woman of her because she had died and then come back to earth, so she knew more than others.

NOTES

[1]Until recently an Anasazi shrine on top of Fajada Butte, which consists of two spiral petroglyphs behind three slabs of rock, marked the solstices and equinoxes. The unceasing traffic of scientists shifted the rocks so that they no longer accurately measure the solar events.

[2]There is a block of rooms on Fajada Butte which were built with a so-called Mesa Verde-style of architecture, leading some to believe the solstice marker was built during the reoccupation in the twelfth century.

13

Prayers Take Wing

MR. WETHERILL DIDN'T TAKE as much interest in the Navajo as I did. He couldn't. He had his living to make and he was responsible for the work there at the ruin, but he always encouraged me to learn what I could and help them in every way I could.

I soon learned the medicine men were the ones that I could get the most information out of, and if I knew the medicine men I could go to their ceremonials. A foreign medicine man would resent having an American watch a ceremonial and it would be bad for the patient. I always made it my special mission to get acquainted with the medicine men and invite them in to eat.

One medicine man told me that electricity, made in the sky by the Great Spirit, is the same kind of electricity that makes people alive. When a person dies, the spark of electricity leaves the body and goes into space again where it stays until another conception takes place. The spark comes back to earth and goes into a new body.[1]

Another old man explained reincarnation to me in a different way. "You went to school as a little girl?" he said. "And you went to different grades in school. When you started learning, you learned the ABC's, then you learned more and more. That is the way that spark of electricity grows. It grows sometimes in an Indian man whose father was a great singer and his grandfather was a great singer and his great-grandfather was a great singer and so on for a long time. Each one of these men were like a grade in school. When a child was born from all those singers, he was the greatest singer in the world."

Those sparks of electricity don't always go in the right baby . . . it's a promiscuous thing and sometimes it starts in a new singer by getting into the mother of that person. A talented person is an advanced soul. Sometimes great singers or card players or weavers reminded people of legendary figures in their history. Sometimes weavers didn't know how they learned to weave, but that maybe it was because their grandmother weaved.

Everything was by thought in the Navajo religion. They made prayer sticks out of wood and colored feathers. They said a prayer into the stick and then stuck it near the house or out in the ruin. The prayer stick was just a messenger, something to concentrate on.

At the Yeibichai we held I noticed that some wore owl feathers, others wore hawk feathers, some wore eagle or turkey feathers. All bird feathers had great sacred significance. Feathers connected them to the Great Spirit more than anything else. If in the hot summer days you could make a prayer on a turkey feather, you could send it up on a whirlwind and watch it rise to the Great Spirit. Or you could send a cornhusk and make a big prayer. You could get quite a lot onto a cornhusk. The best way to send a prayer into a whirlwind was to lay the feather on the ground and then run because it wasn't good to get in the whirlwind. They were full of bad prayers, too.

Any part of the roadrunner tails are good in ceremonials. An owl's feather is good. The owl is a snooper because he sleeps all day and stays awake all night to see what trouble he could cause, but he also kept track of things. It was better not to have anything to do with the owl's claws or bills.

It was a smart trick to keep away from owls because I picked up one once that wasn't quite dead. Little Richard had shot the owl and I went out and picked him up. It grabbed my arms with both claws and bit me. I killed him. I weighed pretty plenty and stepped on his head.

Most tribes I know anything about prize the eagle. They use every part of his body, feathers, skin, and blood in their ceremonials and medicine. Almost in every pueblo I have ever been in they have a good-sized cage where they keep eagles year round. They gather little ones in the spring when they're hatched and ready to fly. They put them in cages and it's the boys' jobs to feed them rabbits they killed with a bow and arrow. Of course, Indian children, like anybody else's children, need a great deal of urging and sometimes the children neglect the eagles. I noticed the water dishes were always empty and I've paid many an Indian child to run and get a bucket of water to put in the eagle cage.

The Navajo didn't keep eagles in cages because they tended to move around. They had to get their eagles when they needed them.

146

I went just once on an eagle hunt with Hosteen Bí'al. He went out beforehand and found a place about a half mile from an eagle's nest with young ones ready to fly. He and two or three younger men dug a hole, maybe six feet deep, four feet long, and four feet wide. They put every bit of the dirt they dug out into bags and dumped them in the arroyo. They covered the hole with four poles so that they wouldn't stick above the surface, and covered the poles with the grass roots and weeds they had carefully preserved.

Fifty feet away they dug another hole large enough to conceal a man with his knees drawn up. At night, one of the men crawled into that hole to guard the other hole to see that people or stray animals didn't fall into it, or a coyote didn't destroy all their work.

In the meantime someone caught two or three half-grown rabbits. One of the rabbits was tethered on the poles over the hole with four inches of string so that he could hop around. All this was done in the morning before light. Another man hid in the rocks with a rifle so that he could shoot anything that took the rabbit.

Hosteen Bí'al and I got up at three in the morning and walked a mile and climbed into the hole beneath the poles and the rabbit. I could see through a small six-inch hole, it was like looking through Venetian blinds. I was short and could stand to the side, and Hosteen Bí'al stood on a box so he could reach through the hole. He told me not to speak, but I could yell when we caught the eagle. I'd heard many stories about how few people could catch the eagles and how badly they got hurt. I was pregnant and after we got in the hole I realized two people could get hurt as easily as one and I started worrying about it. I squatted down in the dirt and waited.

Once in a while Hosteen Bí'al came close to me and whispered, "Don't be impatient, we'll get an eagle. I always do." He sang his little anthem just above a whisper. "Great Spirit help us catch the eagle." Several times he asked me if I was hungry, because we brought lunch. This was an uncertain undertaking. We could hear the dirt coming down a little bit because the rabbit was getting impatient, too. It wanted breakfast I suppose. This was in the hot part of the summer, August I would say, just barely daylight.

Suddenly we heard a *woooosh* and the whole cage tore off. Hosteen Bí'al reached up through the hole and grabbed that eagle's legs as he swooped down to get the rabbit. He had him by both legs and that eagle bit and fought like a tiger, you never saw anything like it. It was a grown eagle.

He put his feet on his head, and said to me, "Are you afraid to step on its head?"

"No, but let me get my feet on before you take yours off." I slipped my foot in between his two feet and stood on his head. I was a good, husky girl. Quicker than a wink, he tied that eagle's feet and wings. He took hold of the head and wrenched it so that he would quit fighting us, but he sure got some awful scratches. I suggested he use buckskin gloves, but he said they would do no good against the eagle knives. He wrapped the bird with buckskin string and put him into a buckskin bag head first. Then he got up on his box and called the men to come and help us out of the hole.

The man guarding the hole said he watched the eagle as it left the nest and flew directly to the hole. He began to pray because it would be wonderful to get an older eagle. The feathers were so much nicer. This was one of those bald eagles with a white head.

That eagle was still alive when we got back to Pueblo Bonito. Hosteen Bí'al pinched a two-inch patch of feathers from his neck right below the chin. Then he placed a bowl under the patch, and cut the neck there, so that the blood flowed into the bowl. They saved the blood, dried it and ground it up. Eagle's blood gives you strength when you're sick and can't recover.

He and his helpers plucked the feathers in little bunches off the body. They cut up the body like you would a chicken to fry and the meat was laid out to dry on the bones and ground up later to feed sick people. They used every part including the head and entrails and the contents therein. All of this was done behind Pueblo Bonito with a ceremonial song and outsiders were not allowed to watch, except me because I was in the hunt.

I was worn out when I got home. My husband said, "What happened?"

"Everything. Don't ask me now, I can't talk."

"That's the first time I've ever seen you like that," he said. I just had to go and take a bath and get my breakfast and recover from it before I could talk.

The Navajo are the greatest mental scientists I ever saw in my life. Some of the things they did mentally was unbelievable, just unbelievable. They fooled me. I was pretty smart, I thought, because I didn't believe in those things, but they fooled me just the same.

We had a *bijí* in my house, and it was a time I was fooled. Hosteen Bí-al had bought a nickel's worth of candy from the store. He gave each child at the *bijí* a piece; there were five there including my son Richard who was very small. He put the rest of it in his pocket. We couldn't have a fire in the middle of the room as is the tradition but we brought in a bucket of live coals and set them up on a couple of rocks so it wouldn't burn the floor and then the medicine man sprinkled horse mint he took from his little bag and it smelled nice and he hummed as he worked. After he sprinkled the mint several times the room took on a blue tinge.

"This is the Great Spirit coming into the room now," he said. "Can't you see his shadow there? He doesn't want to come in the hogan, but he'll come in the doorway."

The medicine men were always training the children what would happen to them if they didn't mind their parents. "Now I'm going to show you how powerful the Great Spirit is," he said. "I picked up a nice feather from Asdzáni's chickens and I'm going to make it walk up this stick and show you how powerful the Great Spirit is. We're going to, each one of us, give a prayer to that feather. We're going to make it walk up the stick and disappear. We'll know then that it goes to the Great Spirit."

This was a new one to me. I was sitting straight up in myself and looking with all my eyes to see it. We each one made a prayer and I made mine just the same as they did theirs. He brought this feather out from under his black blanket which he had up over the back of his head, so that when he leaned forward the folds of his blanket would obscure him from everybody for just a moment from time to time. He stuck the feather at the bottom of the stick. The stick was propped up against the back of the chair. Whether he'd made a hole there in the feather previously or not, I don't know. I watched him adjust the feather very lightly. Then he went over on the other side of the stick and stood, and, of course, he was singing all the time. Suddenly the feather started to walk up the stick. It walked up there very slowly, very carefully, moving by little jerks.

We were all speechless. I didn't understand it anymore than the children did. When the feather got up near the top it wobbled. He said it was getting kind of tired, it was such a long ways to get to the Great Spirit. He leaned over, the blanket fell and the feather disappeared. "The feather has taken all our prayers to the Great Spirit. All your prayers will be answered in the length of time it takes to answer them, maybe a day or a year, but they will be answered."

Then he did several other tricks. He poured a pile of sand from a bag in the middle of the room. He took off one of his moccasins and buried it in the sand. Then he made a line of corn pollen over the top of the sand. "You all saw me put the moccasin in the sand," he told us. "Now you leave the room and walk ten steps out in front of the house and say a prayer."

He followed us outside, but he was the last one to leave the house and we didn't pay much attention to him, there were so many of us singing and talking. We went back into the room and we all agreed that the moccasin was still in the sand pile. When he dug into the side of the mound the moccasin wasn't there. He dug into the other side and found the moccasin.

I gave this old medicine man five silver dollars for him to tell me his tricks. For the walking feather trick he cut a groove in the stick and pulled the feather up with two horsehairs attached at different places to keep it straight. No one could see the horsehairs in the dim room full of smoke. I tried it myself, but it took a lot of practice. The moccasin trick was just as simple. He skipped up to the front of our group as we left the house then he went around and came back in and changed the moccasin. "You were doped," he told me.

Every medicine man is a specialist. A medicine man that doctors the stomach can't doctor the head or set a bone. Many of them are mental physicians. They doctor you mentally because they say most illnesses are caused by mental condition. We make ourselves sick.

The Navajo believe in the transmission of thought and that people get sick by someone sending them a bad message. They had literally hundreds of remedies for all different kinds of ailments. Inhaling the sun's breath helps to remedy anxiety. I've seen them lay on the ground scooping their hands through the air to their open mouths. If a person was real sick they paint the entire body black using ground-up charcoal and horse fat, which was what they also did when they went on the warpath to keep the evil spirit away.

They chew charcoal and bread molds for a queazy stomach. They have a tendency to eat fruit while it is still green, like watermelon, and that gives them a bad stomach. Chewing roadrunner feathers helps to alleviate fainting. The claws of the wildcat are useful in treating body pain, but it is important to get right-hand claws for pain on the right side of the body, and left-handed claws for pain on the left side of the body. Banana juice is good for tuberculosis. The Navajo go all the way to Mexico for a stalk of bananas. A tea of pine needles and powdered yarrow cures headaches. They put that on a cloth or some cedar bark and cover their eyes with it or rub it on their head, hands, and the bottoms of their feet. They carry a lot of these remedies in a *nageezi*, the little bag . . . hung at their sides.

I've seen medicine men pick up these stink bugs, these old black ones that stand on their head. I asked one, "Are you killing them or what?" I knew that they wouldn't kill a red ant but if you should eat a leg from a red ant or one of his feelers it would kill you, deadly poison. They think those stink bugs are blind and they grind them up into a fine powder to put in the eyes. The Indians have very sore eyes. They get pinkeye. Dr. Hyde told me to use boric acid for their eyes, which I did. Another eye cure is powdered eagle and hawk eyes.

Puffballs you find around trees, cedar bark, and cobwebs stops bleeding. A coyote went mad and attacked an old lady who lived up on the mesa a short distance from us. She came to the house to show me that she was all raw and bleeding. "I'll put a poultice of ashes on it," she said. The swelling went down by the next morning.

Mr. Wetherill had been quite a hunter, and the Navajo would come in to ask for a little scraping of the mountain sheep horn or antelope. Hosteen Begay's wife had cramps in her stomach once and the medicine men said they needed the female organ of a buffalo and the hide. They begged Mr. Wetherill so hard to help them he finally wrote to some zoo and asked if they happened to have had a buffalo die and I think they sent the robe and organs for fifty dollars.

Pablo's wife came into the store with one breast swollen up with pain. She had been hit by her husband with an axe handle in a violent temper tantrum. We called in the medicine man who said he would have to operate. The medicine man came into the store later and bought from me a little bowl with blue flowers on it and also a pound of green coffee.

"Don't tell anybody I bought this from you," he said as he paid for it.

"No, I won't tell."

"Do you want to come to the ceremony this afternoon? I'm going to have to operate on Pablo's wife. I've got my knives out sunning now." They used obsidian knives and laid them in the sun two or three hours before they would operate so that they would be clean.

The medicine man made a cut in Mrs. Pablo's breast, and he lifted from her breast that white bowl with the little blue flowers full of green coffee and owl feathers. That was what was causing the troubles. He sewed her up and she recovered and never had any more trouble.

NOTE

[1]Just as there is no Supreme Being in the Navajo religion, there also is no recorded belief in reincarnation. When Navajos die, they believe they travel north for four days to an undetermined location underground. Pueblo beliefs are similar. The Hopis and eastern Pueblos travel north and return to their ancestors in the underworld through the *sipapu*. However, a Zuñi, after four successful incarnations through each of the underworlds, can return to this life as an animal.

|| ▲ ||

14

Pueblo Bonito Has a Yeibichai

WE LEARNED ABOUT a nice, old man falling ill, and Mr. Wetherill said, "Well, we should give him a Yeibichai."[1] We consulted with everyone that came into the store and decided that a Yeibichai would be the best thing for him. A Yeibichai is very expensive, about fifteen hundred dollars by the time you pay the medicine man and all his assistants and feed all the people who come.

The Yeibichai is always held in the fall, so it was the right time of year for one. Mr. Wetherill asked me which medicine man I thought should preside and I chose Long Man [Hosteen Hataalii Nez Begay, Son of Long Man Singer].[2] It took ten days of preparation to make the hogan, gather the medicine, recruit the singers and sand painters to help Hosteen Hataalii Nez.

I found a recipe for apple cider in the White House Cookbook and we had quantities of dried apples in the warehouse so I thought I could make four or five barrels and sell it for five cents a glass. I made the cider exactly according to the directions: ten pounds of dried apples in the bottom of the barrel covered with twenty pounds of sugar and water and two yeast cakes. We stirred it three times a day for three days and used it on the fifth. I made six barrels of it and Mr. Wetherill told me I was crazy but I never paid attention to what anybody said. With the help of two Navajo girls, we built a stand with a nice canopy over some poles and we put a lot of tissue paper waving around for the fiesta look. The girls made a penny profit off every glass they sold. I thought that was fair.

The men built a temporary Yeibichai hogan out of telephone poles they hauled in from the mountains. The Hyde Exploring Expedition was expanding business in Farmington and they wanted a telephone put in at the headquarters at Pueblo Bonito. They wired the poles together so they could reuse them. The hogan was more like a tepee, the logs came to a peak as opposed to being oval like other hogans. They made a smoke hole opening at the top of the tepee out of a big square of lumber wired together.

They brought in the singers and sand painters from many miles away. They all worked, sang, danced, and made sand paintings for many days, and all they asked for was a sheepskin out under the sky and some food.

They washed the patient all over and wiped him with cedar bark. They laid him on sheepskins with his head north and his feet south in front of a bed of sand five or six men prepared. This is the direction I sleep, too, being very sick. Then they painted his body black with powdered charcoal and horse grease and they washed and combed his hair back nice and smooth. They looked him all over for any visitors he might have on his body.

They had to find out why the old man was sick and when, exactly, the evil spirit entered his body. They worked up a history and went way back to see if his mother or father did anything wrong before the patient was conceived. I was there every minute for the questioning. They finally decided that while his mother was pregnant she had seen an Apache who made vicious moves toward her as if he were going to kill her. That frightened her very much and she always kept it a secret, but some old grandmother remembered the affair and came and gave her evidence.[3]

They sent a scout up to Colorado to look for a scrap of bone the Apache might have eaten. The man came back with a deer bone about four inches long and a piece of Apache shirt. He found the shirt hanging in the man's home, but he wasn't sure the shirt belonged to the man, so he had to hunt him up and question him about it. That's the story he told. The bone was from the front leg of a deer, the offender's favorite meat. It had touched his mouth, and so this was good. The medicine men put these articles on the sand painting and shot arrows into them and sprinkled them with medicine.

On the first day[4] they made a painting in colored sands, white, black, yellow, blue, and red.[5] The second day they began adding figures to the painting. The first was an elongated [yei] with a square head and short legs. The sand painter grabbed a handful of red sand from a pottery dish and let it trickle onto the bed through a crack in his fingers. He drew a red line all around it. And then the next man made a yellow line. Oh, they did beautiful work. There must have been six sand painting partners there. They had practiced as children when they were out herding sheep. If they're any good, they go to all the ceremonials and have plenty to eat for twelve or fifteen days. It takes a special talent.

Each day a new and larger sand painting with increased numbers of figures was created. At sundown four men came in and each man gathered up one fourth of the sand and took it off in the four directions so that the evil spirits can't get back together. I've heard people speak about how the medicine men were so careful about removing the sand painting before the sun went down. What else could they do but remove the sand painting? There it is in the middle of the only house they have to live in. They wouldn't want anybody to walk on it. Other people haven't any business even seeing it and the sick man has been lifted up off the sand painting and they've said the prayers for his recovery. Here it is getting time to cook supper. Of course, they built separate hogans for the ceremonies if they could afford it.

Singers and drummers also came in for the ceremony. The singing, chanting, and humming continues all day long. I call it humming because of the way they just carry the tone without saying anything. Solde came on the fifth day, I think, and sang by the door for eight hours without moving, unless somebody gave him something to drink.[6]

The main singers represent Hasch'eyalti and Hasch'ehoghan. After they have the fourth sand painting, they began singing "*hoo-hoo-hoo-hoo, hoo-hoo-hoo-hoo.*" Hasch'eyalti takes care of the verdure of the earth, the vegetation. Hasch'ehoghan takes care of the house. Ginis-kizhi is a sort of spiritual doctor. These three were to help the man get well.[7]

They passed twelve rings of reed over the man from head to foot. They pressed corncobs to his hands, mouth, and feet. It's a tremendous ceremony. Anything that lasts for [nine] days is a wonder it didn't kill him. That's if he was physically sick, but this man was sick from worrying, and the ceremony had the affect of curing him. Whenever I went to a ceremony, I'd ask the different medicine men what was wrong with the patient and they always pointed to the head. "I took the evil spirit out of his head," they'd say. Well, I should hope they did from what they did to them.

Everybody waited for the [ninth] day. That was the big day, the cure. On the [ninth] day they have the big sand painting. It almost covered the entire floor and the patient was sitting up by then. The

Yeibichai was a public ceremony by this time. No one was supposed to come in on the first six days because they would disturb the mind of the patient. After that they had him so worn down nothing bothered him.

Now at this time there were two thousand Navajos there, plus our white guests, traders, and freighters. Mr. Wetherill counted. We brought in beef and mutton and I suppose there were twenty women baking bread for four days. Everyone was supposed to come in and view the painting but most were more interested in the horse races and the chicken-pull.[8] They came the day before and they ate noon and night. They brought their sheep if they didn't have anywhere to leave them and hobbled their horses. The canyon was full of little camps. We provided firewood for their campfires, and the water.

Everybody was up bright and early on the [ninth] day, and by nine everything was going strong. Hosteen Hataalii Nez and the sand painters were just working like mad on that marvelous sand painting. There was a cross that started in the center, black, white, red, and yellow. On that cross is the swastika that goes the opposite direction of the German swastika. Then there's sixteen of those long figures around that.

Solde continued his announcing anthem. He sang about the mother of the sick man having encountered the Apache who had made cruel and bad motions toward her while she carried the patient. The patient was sixty years old by then, and of course his mother was long dead. When he came to the part when the Apache spoke badly to the mother, Solde sang high. He was a nice looking man and renowned for his singing. Then he sang low, the guttural tones down there to tell how bad it had been. It was a wonderful thing to hear that.

After breakfast, everyone went on to the racetrack for the relay race across the canyon from the house. The rider had to jump off the horse and pull the saddle off that horse and put it on the next horse which was already bridled, and then they ran the next half mile on the fresh horse. They changed horses five times and the first prize was five dollars and second prize two-and-a-half dollars.

Those Navajos are the greatest gamblers in the world. Here under a bush there was a game of two-card monte and over here maybe fifteen or twenty men and women played coon can. Some squaws sat under bushes with their blankets up playing that stick game. They use a big, flat rock that has to be perfectly level and you ought to see those big, old squaws get down on their stomachs to make sure it's level. Over the rock they stretch a blanket on four poles about four feet high. Outside the flat rock there's a circle of rocks, in groups of ten, one white and nine black. Then there are five flat sticks, which have up to ten stripes on them. Each stick is marked differently with red, black, and white stripes. They take those five sticks in their hand, raise them up and hit them as hard as they can on that flat rock, and they'll bounce clear up and hit the blanket. The sticks sprawl out on these counter rocks or on the center rock. The number of colors that show determines the points and they keep track of the points with the small rocks. That's a woman's game.

The enthusiasm really came when the horse races began. Young boys with lovely brown bodies entered the race wearing just their breechcloths. They tied chicken hawk or magpie feathers in the horses' manes to make them wise. They cheated, too. The night before, some of them look over the horses and note the best ones were brought in by a white rancher or maybe Jésus. These horses are guarded, but some fella invariably sneaks in and wraps three or four horsehairs around the horse's hoof real tight. The next morning the horse is lame. Or they turn the horse loose so he'll drink too much water or eat too much corn. Then of course they juggle for position and they like to run into the other fella's horse. If they get caught, they are barred from the race. But Paul Arrington brought over just a little bit of a horse and he won quite a bit of money. I bet a dollar against him and lost.

The chicken-pull was always popular. That was a Spanish game where you bury a rooster in the ground up to his neck. It was a little dirty and bloody for most of us and we didn't like it, so Mr. Wetherill buried a sack of silver dollars the size of a rooster, instead. The Navajo didn't eat chicken meat then and the money was real incentive.

Twenty or thirty men on horses got into position a hundred yards away. A man stood nearby with a bullwhip to prevent the riders from slowing down too much before they grabbed the sack out of the ground, or from the horses bucking as the man reached over on the right side of the horse. It annoyed the horse to have someone hanging over his right side when they are used to being mounted on their left. They came down one at a time, reached for the bag, and if they missed, they circled around to join the group again. Sometimes someone hung on to the sack and the horse went on. It occasioned so much laughing. When somebody finally pulled out the sack, everybody else took after him madly. They pulled each other off their horses and fought over it. The man who ended up with the sack wasn't the man who pulled it out. Mr. Wetherill thought it would be better to give the man that pulled it out two-and-a-half dollars, just to even it up. He was sure a Quaker, never liked to have any trouble.

The horse racing and the gambling and the anthems and the sand painting in the hogan went on all day and I really sold the cider. They were buying it by the gallons, trying to get drunk off it. I tasted it, but it wasn't hard enough to get drunk on.

At sundown, they laid the old man down on the sand painting and rubbed with an otter skin up and down his body.[9] These men went clear into Nevada, Idaho, Wyoming, California, or Mexico for their medicines and techniques. The fetishes, prayer sticks, the feathers, the sand, all of it was to help get the misery out of the man. Then he got himself up and sat on his sheepskin and the four men took the sand away, two loads each. Solde sang about how they killed the evil spirit that entered the body and the patient was well and strong through their songs to the Great Spirit.

Everyone ate then, boiled meat, bread, dried fruit, canned tomatoes, corn, potatoes, and rice we cooked in those copper-bottomed washboilers. We made coffee in the biggest tubs and it went down by the barrel. They all used sugar and condensed milk and crackers.

The old man told me he felt better, when finally I got to talk to him. I asked Hosteen Hataalii Nez if he could eat and he said he could eat cornmeal mush and fruit. I made him a bowl of mush; it didn't take long, and I gave him canned peaches and canned white grapes, which they called rabbit eyes. The man got up and I saw him dancing that night.

The dance was the supreme thing. Just as it got dark they built four fires, two on each side of where the men danced right outside the hogan. They smoothed off the area of all the stones that would bruise the feet. Eight singers lined up on one side and eight on the other. It was something they all practiced.

One bunch came in wearing masks made out of buckskin that hadn't been tanned. It was just a round cap that fitted right down over their heads and rested on their shoulders. There was a hole over the mouth and a tube for breathing. The tube was covered with fox fur so that it couldn't be seen. Around their necks they wore a big ruche of cedar boughs, and they tied cedar to their elbows and wrists. They shook dried deer hoof rattles wrapped around their ankles. Their legs were wrapped with buckskin leggings tied with the *janeezi*, a red strap they wove. They wore the breechcloth and G-string and a little calico or buckskin shirt belted with a silver concha belt. A fox skin hung down the back from the belt and almost touched the ground.

Every one of those eight singers reached down and shook their rattles vigorously and swooped up, singing "*hoo-hoo-hoo-hoo-hoo.*" Their voices reverberated from the cliff. I can shut my eyes and see their images and hear their songs. Bendi John, one of my informants, said they were calling the Great Spirit. There might have been four or five sets of dancers, and they sang and danced for about two hours. Around ten o'clock that night all the dancers gathered in front of the hogan for the final prayer. Hosteen Hataalii Nez led the song and the others hummed, "true, true."

The next morning the Navajo came and shook hands with me as they left. Hosteen Hataalii Nez came in. Mr. Wetherill had given him two or three mules, about a hundred dollars worth. He earned it. He was a big, tall, handsome Indian, and his father before him had been a medicine man, too, and so he knew a great deal.

He shook hands with me and I felt something in my hand as he pulled his hand away. I looked down and saw a silver box.

"Oh, this is a cute little box." It was Indian made, very crude. "Where did you get it?"

"I knew you were going to ask that. Many years ago when I was a young man, the police came with a school man and took my only son away from me. They never told me which school they were taking him to. He was gone many years and when he came back I didn't know him because he was a man.

"He walked up to me and put his arms around me. I was frightened. I thought he wanted to fight me, but I could see he was laughing. 'Are you my son?' I said.

"'Yes, Father, I am your son. Have you forgotten me?'

"I had forgotten what he looked like but every night he was in my heart and every day all day, even when the birds sang, I could feel him with me. I longed for him and wondered what happened to him and why he didn't come back.

"One day, when he was at Carlisle school he said, 'Father, I'm going to make you a little present.' He hammered out a piece of silver and made that little box.

"'Where did you learn to make a little box like that?' I said when he gave it to me.

"'White people have those to keep their stamps in.' And then he said 'I'm not going to live too many years longer because I have a disease that I can't cure. You'll keep this box always.'"

Hosteen Hataalii Nez said to me, "I'm giving this to you now and you'll always keep it." On one side is a [yei] and on the other is a sheep, so that I would always have meat. The turquoise tied on with sinew means I will always have wealth so that I would be able to make my trip to the spirit world. Inside were the ashes of a very bad enemy of all the Navajos. The ashes are gone in the years I've carried it around with me.

NOTES

[1]The Yeibichai, or Night Chant (*Klédze Hatál*), is one of six major groups of chants including Blessing Way, Bead Chant, Shooting Chant, Mountain Way, and Wind Way. The Navajos have a repertoire of more than fifty sings, chants, or ways, not counting variations, and between six hundred and a thousand sand painting designs. Most singers know only two or three curing rites. The Yeibichai is held when snakes are asleep and the danger of lightning has passed, and it is used for treating nervousness or insanity. The rite is called Yeibichai because of the many *yeis*, masked representations of supernatural beings, who appear on the final two days of the nine-day ceremony.

Alfred Tozzer witnessed a Yeibichai at Pueblo Bonito in November 1901, and in three separate works he described those sequences which were different from what Washington Matthews reported in his description of the Night Chant in 1902. He mentioned an incident in which a woman became hysterical because of Tozzer's presence at the ceremony. Tozzer was compelled to buy several yards of calico to cover her while the singer rubbed her body with feathered sticks. The woman and singer split the calico between them. The Yeibichai is a dangerous rite and any mistake can cause crippling, facial paralysis, or loss of hearing and sight.

Marietta remembers the Yeibichai lasting eight days, but does admit she couldn't remember the entire ceremony and referred to Washington Matthews as the ultimate authority. Marietta was so busy attending to guests, she probably didn't see the entire ceremony, and therefore, many of her recollections don't corroborate with the documented versions, which leads me to believe she added description from other ceremonies she saw.

[2]The *hataalii* directs the singing, sand painting, and dancing. Marietta said she selected Long Man as the head medicine man. I am assuming this is Hosteen Hataalii Nez Begay (Son of Long Man Singer) since Marietta refers to him as a medicine man everyone used. There was a Hosteen Nez Begay, or Son of a Long Man, who was involved in the circumstances surrounding Richard's death, but I don't believe he was a medicine man. Later in this chapter, Marietta says another man, Solde, sang in the Yeibichai, and in other tapes she translates his name as Long Singer. I get the impression he was involved temporarily in the Yeibichai, but was not in charge. See Chapter 15 for story of Hosteen Hataalii Nez Begay, and also Endnote 3 in Chapter 15, for a reference to a Hataalii Neez Bida', Tall Singer's Nephew.

[3]Tozzer witnessed a rite called *Ndelni*, in which the medicine man sprinkled lines of corn pollen on his right hand. During a trance, his trembling hand plunged into the ground, which was interpreted to mean that the patient had broken a tribal taboo by digging in a ruin and coming into contact with a human skull. "In this case, I am quite sure the shaman was sincere in what he did," Tozzer wrote. "I have no doubt that in many cases there is much humbug."

[4]Tozzer made a partial list of the different rituals during the Night Chant which included the consecration of the lodge, rites involving *kethawns* or wooden cigarette-shaped tubes, outdoor sweating ceremonies in shallow oblong holes, the preparation of medicine by a virgin, evergreen rites, Yeibichai talisman and masquerading, the initiation of children, the manufacturing of a gourd rattle, amole bath, the begging of gods, and rehearsal for the dance. On the sixth day, the first sand painting was made, a depiction of the four rain gods, or *Hastébaka*, or *Yébaka*. The second sand painting made on the seventh day was the picture of the *Naakhai* (Mexican) dance which depicted four tiers of figures totaling thirty-nine male and female dancers plus the *Hastséyalti* or Yeibichai (Talking God). The third painting made on the eighth day was the Gods with the Fringe Mouths, which included twelve figures. Another important sand painting was the Painting of the God of the Whirlwind, but he didn't mention what day it fell on in the ceremony. The number of rites depends upon the patient's ability to pay for them, Tozzer said. The painting Marietta describes on page 156 may be the God of the Whirlwind or the Whirling Logs.

[5]Generally, white represents east, yellow is west, black (a male color) is north, blue (a female color) is south, and red is sunshine.

[6]Marietta tells a story of how Long Man, or Hosteen Nez, was slashed in the stomach with a razor by his lover, Rose. McNitt repeats the same story but calls the man Solde. Rose was the sister of Pablo Wiggins, a Spanish American who worked for the Wetherills and whose mother did the Wetherill's laundry. When Marietta went to him, she found him in a breechcloth and G-string holding his entrails in with his hand. She sent someone for bichloride of mercury, hydrogen peroxide, cotton, her sewing box, and a book on physiology that she studied in the eighth grade. She cleaned his entrails, put them back in place exactly like the picture in the book, and sewed him back up.

[7]The two deities involved in the Yeibichai today are *Hasteseyalti*, or Talking God of the East, and *Hasttse-baad*, a female yei. Dialect and the person recording the dialect are responsible for the variation in spellings.

[8]Generally, there is much celebrating going on during the curing ways, but Marietta may be confusing the Night Chant festivities with the rodeo and chicken-pull fiesta the Wetherills threw at Pueblo Bonito, September 4, 1889, which was attended by two hundred Navajos.

[9]The otter skin relates to an episode in the Navajo legends in which the otter loaned its skin to the Twin War Gods when the Sun attempted to freeze them.

15

Death of a Singer

HOSTEEN HATAALII NEZ BEGAY AND HIS FAMILY always traded at our store and he was a prosperous and popular medicine man. Suddenly, the old fellow started feeling bad, but he continued practicing his medicine. He was always holding those *bijí*. He was the one who gave me conchas when I remembered the songs. My daughter, Marion, wears the beautiful conchas on a belt with other conchas I've collected. There's one or two conchas on it that were on Mr. Wetherill's chaps when he was a young man. When I look at that belt I think of poor old Hataalii Nez, how I had to see his terrible ending.

Hataalii Nez doctored a woman and she died. You see, you pay a medicine man for a cure. You don't pay him to die, you pay him to cure whatever's causing your trouble. When a medicine man loses a patient it goes against him.

Hataalii Nez failed to cure Welo's boy. Welo's boy had a broken arm, broken right at the elbow, and Hataalii Nez poulticed the arm and sang for him. Despite that, the boy didn't get better, and one night he got up and stumbled into the fire in the hogan. The boy's family had been digging in the ruins of Penasco Blanco where they had found enough turquoise to set them up for life. They thought that had brought them bad luck. Now, I knew the boy's arm was probably not set right and that it was inflamed and crooked. The pain probably awakened him and he got up and fell in the fire. But it was a failure for Hataalii Nez.

Hataalii Nez talked it over with Mr. Wetherill who told me he couldn't do anything for him. "He thinks some evil spirit is troubling him and he's not making any cures," Mr. Wetherill said. The trouble showed on the whole family. They stopped coming in and telling jokes and I wondered why they were so unhappy. Maybe the range was bad for the sheep or maybe they had run out of food. I talked it over with Mr. Wetherill and he said they hadn't asked for credit at the store so he assumed they had plenty to eat. A medicine man made quite a bit of money.

"He sits up at night and sings," his wife said. "Hours and hours he'll sit looking in the fire and asking the Great Spirit what is the matter with him. The next morning he's cross and yells at everybody."

I pointed to my head and told her the trouble was here. I asked her if he'd done anything to anybody and she said not that she knew. I said he's been successful, maybe somebody's mad about that. Jealousy is one of the greatest curses of humanity. It makes people lie about somebody and steal. It causes trouble between wives and husbands and it makes children worry that Mama is going to give them a smaller piece of bread than their brother. I told her that's what we call jealousy.

"You had sheep when you married him," I said and she nodded. "You've taken good care of your sheep and they've had lots of lambs."

"The reason why we have such nice sheep is because of Anasazi," she said. "He helped us get the good bucks so I could get better wool and now I'm a good rug weaver. Everyone in my family has worked hard for what we have. Nobody has the right to be jealous."

"There doesn't have to be a reason," I said.

I talked to all the women in his family. I don't remember if they were wives or sisters but they all lived in the hogan together.

All the time it was getting worse. He gave a Fire Dance[1] for a man and he died. I didn't go to it. Finally he had an *Oomtah*[2] to cure him of the evil spirit. Hosteen Didlewishin Begay, the Son-of-the-Man-Who-Is-a-Runner, gave the ceremonial.

They started the celebration in a hogan that belonged to some people not related to Hataalii Nez, who were willing to donate it and move out. They had ceremony and sand painting during the day and at night they sang until just before dawn and then quietly snuck out and drove their wagons in caravans to another hogan belonging to somebody else. They pulled Hataalii Nez on a travois behind a horse, dragging him over the brush to get the evil spirit out of him. They had to sneak out to get away from the evil spirit and all the time everybody kept chanting, "*Oomtah, oomtah, oomtah, ha, ha, ha, ha, oomtah, oomtah, oomtah,*" at high C to scare the evil spirit away. Everybody ducked through a piñon branch archway in front of the hogan, saying, "*Oomtah.*" The evil spirit wouldn't go through the arch because he would think it was a trap.

Some of the dancers painted their faces and others wore masks. Marcellino told me that the men who were dancing for women wore the face paint and the men dancing for men wore masks. The masks and face paint disguise the humans who might influence the effect of the dance with bad deeds or thoughts.

When the people moved to the next hogan, and there were at least a hundred, they really loped along. The women bounced high on the wagons. We finally came to a very nice hogan in a valley. They were like mad people. On each corner of the hogan were piles of dirt eight feet high. At each pile a man dipped a basket into the pile and threw the dirt into the air. Indians yelled and circled the hogan shooting their arrows and guns into the air.

They drug Hataalii Nez and four men, who had fainted or were injured during the frenzy, into the hogan. The medicine man rubbed the boys who had fainted on the backs with turtle shells and deer toes until they were raw and pretty soon they got up and walked out. He sang, not for the sick man, but to ward off any small evil spirit that might be in the hogan. The sick man was covered with cedar bark and piñons. Everybody laid on the ground and took a nap, and then after a while the women who could move began cooking. Hataalii walked out of the hogan completely cured because Didlewishin Begay told him he was.

Everyone was sure that the *Oomtah* worked and that everything was okay. He was cheerful after that. Hosteen Didlewishin Begay must have suggested something that cleared his agony. For another year everything went along just fine, and then everything went bad and another patient died. Hataalii and his family snuck away in the night to get away from the evil spirit, and while they were gone, their Paiute slaves stole their sheep. That winter, everything he did was wrong. Nobody hired him, everybody shunned him. Poor old Hataalii Nez became thinner with worry.

Hosteen Didlewishin Begay tried to find out if an Apache had ever said anything to Hataalii Nez's family, or even to his mother before he was born, because that might have been the cause of the misfortune. He asked if Hataalii Nez ever worked in the ruins or if he ever bought any of the turquoise from Welo that had worked in Penasco Blanco, and of course, he hadn't. I asked Old Welo if he ever sold turquoise to Hataalii Nez, and he said no. It wasn't the ancient people bothering him.

I try to imagine what it would be like living under that kind of strain forever knowing somebody didn't like me and I didn't know why. I can't imagine it. I can't imagine how I would feel if I had the fear of owls, fear of ducks flying over the house. Even the red ant and the coyote were your enemy. Even the tiniest piece of red ant leg or a coyote hair could cause an ulcer.

Hataalii Nez lived under this kind of strain for years. I went up to Colorado when Robert was born and when I got back that year, my brother and Mr. Colby who worked in the store, went to an *Oomtah*. The *Oomtah* was for a witch who lived way down on the Chaco thirty miles. They'd pronounced him a witch and dismembered him. I was curious because I never had seen one and I felt a little envious and I kept my ears open.

Mr. Wetherill found out that Hataalii Nez moved to a cave. It wasn't much, just a little rincon up in the rocks sheltered by a four-foot wall built as a hiding place when Kit Carson hunted the Navajo. Mr. Wetherill said I'd better ride up there and take him something. I packed a pound of coffee, a twenty-five-cent pack of sugar and a twenty-five-cent pack of flour, a can of tomatoes, a can of peaches, baking soda, a can of lard, and a box of crackers into my saddle pockets. I took the tracks from his old house and followed them up on the canyon about six miles.

I traced his tracks to a cave but I wasn't certain he was around there. I thought I'd just go see. Fool thing to do. I might have walked up to a robber who'd kill me. I looked behind the wall and there was that poor man.

He was sitting all bent over, back against the wall. He'd aged twenty years. He had been a fine, robust man. You know how these Indians are muscular and vigorous and they stand so straight. He'd had nice long hair he always kept so neat, now it was gray.

"*Ya ta hey, shidani,*" I said. "Good [sic], brother-in-law. What's the matter?"

"My father, my father," he said. He looked so sad. He didn't ask me to come in but I went around the end of the wall and walked in.

"Why are you living here all alone this way?"

"My wives, my children, my mother, everybody's left me."

"Why?"

"I'm in such trouble. That evil spirit won't leave. It's killing me."

"Where's the evil spirit?"

167

He looked at me astounded. "Where is it? I don't know."

"It's in here," I said, pointing to my forehead. "It's made a house right here."

"Maybe so," he said in Navajo.

"Come down to the store and stay with us," I said. "You can have that hogan there, the one right in front of the store. Anasazi doesn't care if you don't have any money. We're not afraid. Just come be our old man."

He thought about it quite a little while. "If evil came to you, I would cut my throat."

"Evil won't come. We have medicine to keep those things away. We have medicine for the cough and we open our shirts and let the sun cure us. You've seen those young boys with the bad cough come out here and get cured. Come live with us and you can become a good doctor again."

But he wouldn't do it. Think of the sacrifice.

"I brought a gift from Anasazi," I told him. "He asked the Diné where to find you. He sent me here to visit with you and bring him a message that you will stay in the hogan in front of our house."

I went out and untied the panniers off my horse and took out the food. Apparently he had nothing there to eat. I could see some husks of green corn, but it had been some time since there was green corn. I asked him, "Why did you break that hole there in the wall?" The hole would let in the evil spirit and certain death.

"Why do you ask questions that you already know?"

"I don't know that. I want you to tell me why so that I can help you."

"You know I know I'm going to die. I'd rather die right here but the Navajo have declared me a witch and you know how they kill witches."

"How do you know that?"

"I just feel it. When my wife and family left, I knew then they were afraid of the evil spirit in my body. I'd rather die here."

"You're not going to die here. You're going to come and die down by my house. Then we'll dig a nice grave for you and put you in a nice box and the Great Spirit will gather you up and take you into the spirit world just the same as though there wasn't any evil spirit in your body."

"No, I can't do that. I wouldn't let that spirit loose in your family. Maybe in a hundred years that spirit would come out and make your children's children sick like I am in the head."

I went to work after that. I stirred up some biscuits and baked them in the coals. I made coffee and I opened a can of peaches. He was ravenous. Ate every bite. I suspicioned he was starving to death.

I stayed and talked to him until the sun went low and made long shadows. "Please go," he said to me.

"Why?"

"It's getting dark. You're not afraid of the dark, are you?"

"Not in the least particle," I said.

"But the owls will talk to you as you go home."

"I'll talk back to them. We'll have fun."

"You're not afraid of anything, are you?"

"I've never had any cause to be afraid."

"Oh, I wish the Diné could be like that."

"They can if they'll get out of their minds this idea of somebody hurting them from a long distance."

He said he'd been too long trained in the Diné ideas. His parents and their parents always believed in that terrible curse of fear. Poor old man, you see me cry about him.

I went home and reported to my husband how he was. "Oh, that's too bad," he said. "I want to see he has plenty to eat if you have the time." I told him I had the time. It didn't take but just a little while to gallup up there and back. Next day I took him a hindquarter of mutton. He had a little kind of a suspicion of a smile in the corner of his mouth. I took a new shirt, a pair of overalls and socks. He had moccasins.

I went up two or three times a week that winter. "You'll get that evil spirit because he's a witch," the Navajo said.

"Witch, my foot," I said. "He isn't a witch at all. He's just sick in the head. He had the spunk to try to get rid of that. Look at the beautiful Yeibichai you went to. Weren't you afraid the evil spirit would jump out of his body and get into you while you were at the Yeibichai? No, you went to feast for a full week and kept your bellies full. You weren't afraid then to eat his food." It made me mad. I wouldn't treat a dog like they treated him.

I thank Mr. Wetherill's faithfulness to him because it was all his idea to take him food and tell him stories. He'd tell me stories, too. He'd tell me about when he was a little boy and how his father taught him to ride horseback, how he learned the Indian games. But he got to where he wouldn't shake hands with me. He'd just keep them at his sides. "Nataani Soto sent me a good friend too late."

"I just do what Anasazi tells me," I said. "He's too busy to come. He's all the time going to Farmington, Albuquerque, or Gallup to buy things to bring here to the Indians. It's a pleasure to help you."

"I didn't know white people were like that."

"The world is full of them. Your people are our neighbors. You trade at our store and we make a little money on what we sell you and then you come in and sell your sheep and you make a little money."

He thought the Great Spirit had deserted him, that he would never get well, that the Great Spirit had allowed the Navajos to condemn him as a witch. The only thing for him to do was to just wait his time, which he did. He waited and he suffered.

The day was set for him to ride down into the canyon. I wanted to attend the ceremony but Didlewishin Begay said, "No, it's not a nice thing to see. It will make you sick. You've never seen anything bad like that. There's only a very few Diné see this."

"But my brother saw one last year."

"That's different. A man can see those things, but maybe you're pregnant."

"No, I'm not."

"Doesn't matter. We don't want you to see it."

I went to Hosteen Bí'al, my old adopted father, and he told me the same thing. "You liked that old man. You took him things to eat when nobody, not even his own family, would go see him."

"I thought that was my business."

"Everybody knows. Maybe when the evil spirit as it is torn from his body . . ." That was the first time I'd heard that about the evil spirit being torn from the body. "Maybe the evil spirit will get into you. I don't want that to happen."

"Too many times you've told me that you wanted me to see everything that the Diné thought and did. Hosteen Hataalii Nez Begay and Didlewishin Begay both told me you wanted me to see everything so that I'll write it all down so that when your children are gone, their children will read it and know."

Mr. Wetherill finally interceded for me. He told them to let me go and they told him the same argument. "She's different," he said. "She's doing this for the people. She will tell the white people what kind of ceremony you had for a bad person that made people sick and took their sheep but was unable to keep them from dying. She'll stand it." I think five silver dollars changed hands and Hosteen Didlewishin Begay gave his permission.

I rode down on my horse to the place. It was on the right-hand side of Chaco Canyon as you go up to the Escavada almost where the canyon widens out on the south side and disappears a little before it does on the north side. I wore a black blanket as they told me to do. They painted my face black and showed me where to sit. Hosteen Hataalii Nez was sitting back and I went over and shook hands with him which made everybody mad.

The ceremony took place right below a sun symbol, painted recently. It was a yellow circle with feathers all around the face and it had eyes and a mouth, three or four feet wide. I remembered distinctly riding up the canyon for goat's milk and seeing this new painting on the wall of the canyon, but I didn't pay attention to it. Now I know why the painting was there.

I was so excited when I saw my poor old man laying there that I didn't notice anything else but him and two or three other Indians each one sitting by their own personal fire, chanting. Every once in awhile I noticed them reaching for a buckskin bag under their blankets and sprinkling the contents over the fire. I smelled the peculiar odor as soon as I entered the rincon.

I didn't see any horsemen. I'd left my horse outside the rincon tied to a rock. It was peculiarly silent. All the other ceremonies were noisy with everybody eating and talking and racing and playing games. This was just as silent as death. My extreme concern for the man made me sad and frightened. I didn't know what I'd gotten into. I think the medicine man had sympathy for him, too, because he'd realized how this spirit had taken charge.

A bed of sand had been prepared just like they were going to have a big sand painting and I thought that's what they were going to do. I was nervous and frightened about what I was going to see because they had warned me. But there wasn't going to be a sand painting. They'd exhausted all the power of the sand painting.

Hosteen Didlewishin Begay got up from his little fire and walked over to Hataalii Nez who was hunched over a rock. He spoke to him, and Hataalii Nez got up and walked over to the sand patch and laid down and just stretched out perfectly flat with his arms out a little ways from his body. He lay perfectly still like he was finally at rest.

Didlewishin Begay began chanting and rattling the rattles. "For the last chant, for the last time," he chanted. "For the last time I'm asking to send a sign. For the last chant, Nataani Soto, send a sign." The two or three other fellas repeated the request. They watched the sun as it set. They told me afterwards that if a lizard had run or a snake had crawled across that bed of sand or if a bird in flight had cast his shadow across the sand, they would have saved him. Hataalii Nez also prayed to the Great Spirit for a sign.

But nothing happened and I'll never forget how Hosteen Didlewishin Begay stood up and everybody held their breath. I did. "Spare this man, spare this man." And when nothing happened he just dropped his hands in desperation. There was nothing more to do. A very old woman, who I thought was a man all the time, uncovered herself and approached Hataalii Nez with something wrapped in a green leaf. I'll always think it was datura. She handed it to Didlewishin Begay and he put it in old Hosteen Hataalii Nez's mouth. He never moved, he just laid there. He swallowed it with difficulty. I don't know if he had to chew the leaf, I didn't see him chew, or if he had to swallow the whole thing in one gulp.

He was so thin, so wasted. He looked like one of the mummies we dug up at Grand Gulch. The skin was almost dried on his bones and he was that color brown. He just laid there and in a few minutes his whole body quivered twice.

Four riders then came out from behind the rocks. Their faces were painted black with white lines across their faces. You wouldn't know them if you'd been their own father. They got down off their horses and each one put a rope around an arm or a leg. They got back onto their horses with the rope in hand and just rode away. One piece of the old man, one arm pulled off. I don't know whether the other one did or not. I had to shut my eyes, I couldn't stand it.

The horses went off in opposite directions and all that was left was one leg still attached to the trunk. I couldn't look anymore. Hosteen Didlewishin Begay told me to go home. He brought me my horse and I got on my horse and went home but I couldn't sleep.

I waited several months before I asked Hosteen Didlewishin Begay to eat in my kitchen. "I must know the rest, it is my duty. You know how bad I feel."

"I know. You were a good friend and a brave girl. We were afraid you would try to do something, but you're a Diné all right. You sat perfectly still. You didn't know a man stood right back of you to restrain you had you got up to help the old man."

"No, I didn't know. Where did those men go?"

"North, south, east, and west. When a witch is killed it's a bad thing. His body must be dismembered so that it can never get together again. That is the bad part about it because when you are dismembered you can never be a human being again. You can never be anything. Even the spirit is torn apart so that it can't go to the spirit world and come back here in another body. It's gone forever. That's the bad part about it."

He told me to never mention the old man's name to a Diné. I never did. "But I will tell you . . . each horseman was selected by a different medicine man. Nobody wants to do that but somebody has to and they're working for their people when they do. No one knows who the other man is. That is a secret between Natani Soto and the medicine man who chose him and the horseman himself. None of them will ever tell, never. Each man drug his part of the body as far away from hogans or people as possible, staying close to the course. Their trails were obliterated with piled up sand and rocks so that the path would never be visible. After they started away, they never looked back. Just as the sun came up, they dropped the rope from the saddle and kept right on riding. Very seldom did they ride these horses again. They were chindee horses, devil horses."[3]

NOTES

[1]Marietta witnessed a Fire Dance, which is held on the ninth evening of the Mountain Chant or Mountaintop Way, a winter ceremonial held when there is still a chance that summer thunderstorms or spring windstorms might cause death by snake bite or lightning. The mountain is where the deities live. On the ninth evening a semi-circular corral of evergreen is built where medicine men perform magical feats. Men swallow arrows, yucca plants grow and blossom, and fire dancers smothered in white clay dance in and out of the huge central fire as a purification ritual. In two tapes, Marietta described in detail some lewd scenes involving clowns.

On February 5, 1903, the *Farmington Hustler* reported the following:

> Sheriff Elmer and John Wetherill both came in from the reservation yesterday morning and say the Navajos are making preparations to give the biggest fire dance in years, next Tuesday at Putnam Springs, about eighteen miles south of Farmington. Already large numbers of Indians have collected from various portions of the reservation . . . Huge piles of wood thirty feet in height have been gathered for the occasion. Only two Indians east of the Chucklock Mountains are capable of leading a fire dance and one of them, Hosteen Chung, known as "Bear Face," perhaps the most widely known Navajo in the country, who during an encounter with a grizzly had half his face clawed off, will have entire supervision of Tuesday night's dance. The fire dance is the most important of Navajo traditions, where spectators are not wanted as during the performance, gee strings, bracelets, in fact everything is discarded, and only the heat from the fire and bodily exertions enable to keep them warm . . .

Having seen the Fire Dance, Marietta became curious about the white clay, or asbestos, as she called it. She got an old woman to show her the fire retardant quality of the mud. She and a couple other women put long strips of the white mud under their arms and then they rolled hot coals in mud and held them in their armpits without burning them. She held hers the longest and the women said she was the bravest. She did get a blister and the women told her it was because her skin was not as thick as the Navajos'. Marietta stripped down to her petticoat to show Lou Blachly the scars.

[2]Marietta is probably referring to an *Entah*, or Enemy Way, which is held in the summer for people who are sick because of contact with a white or other non-Navajo. The three-day ritual begins at the patient's hogan, and moves to a new hogan each succeeding day. Between rituals, there is gambling, racing, and listening to talks by leaders. The Black Dancers, or

clowns, emerge through a smoke hole in the hogan on the third day and throw the patient into a pool of mud face down to exorcise the evil spirit. The ritual then becomes a muddy free-for-all with the spectators. The Squaw Dance occurs that evening and is a coming out for eligible females. Men ask the mothers for the privilege of joining the round dance with the young girls.

[3]This story first appeared in *Scribners Magazine*, May 1932, written by Grace French Evans. Marietta said Grace condensed several of her stories into one story and made many errors, but she didn't concede on the execution of the medicine man. "When the article was published I was greatly censored by various people that had lived a few years on or had passed through the Navajo Reservation. I haven't been to all the operas or all the circuses that come through this country and there's many things that's happened on the Navajo Reservation that all the Navajos haven't seen and there's some that are not allowed to see everything that goes on. It's very secret."

David Brugge lists a reference to a report by Indian Agent Stacher to CIA, February 5, 1910. The report mentions a Ho-tat-la-nez-be-ta (Hataalii Neez Bida' or Tall Singer's Nephew), who was the brother of a Navajo named Knockeye Yazzie (Nakai Yazzi, Little Mexican). Nakai Yazzi had been raised by Spanish-American Antonio Vallejos of Blanco, near Chaco Canyon, and possibly had been taken captive during the days of warfare. His own family lived near Gallup, and he had later settled with them and became an influential singer. His curing capabilities led to accusations of witchcraft, for around 1884, his life was threatened. He moved into Gobernador Canyon, where he lived as a hermit until the end of 1909 when Hataalii Neez Bida' visited him and convinced him to return home. He said he would as soon as he could sell part of his herd and collect some outstanding debts. By the time Hataalii Neez Bida' returned to the canyon, Nakai Yazzi had been killed. Two Spanish-Americans were arrested, and a third was released under bond as a witness at Rosa.

In support of Marietta's story, ethnologist Washington Matthews relied on a Hatáli Nez, Tall Chanter, who was "the priest of the night chant," for information on ceremonial rites, and who seemed "to have better knowledge of legends than any other member of the tribe." In 1897, Matthews said Hatáli Nez had become "unpopular as a shaman, owing to an increasing irritability of temper; but he exhibits no envy of his more popular rivals." Furthermore, before Hatáli Nez would confide in Matthews, he said, "The chanters among the Navahoes are all brothers. If you would learn our secrets you must be one of us. You must forever be a brother to me. Do you promise this?" From then on he referred to Matthews a "my younger brother," and Matthews called him "my elder brother." Hence, evidence of an adoption of sorts.

175

16

Origins

THE NAVAJOS TALKED about an ancient tribe of Indians who wore a blue cross on their buckskin moccasins. The Blue Cross people made their moccasins exactly like the Navajos made theirs. Now the Navajos wear a moccasin that is the same shape as the Pueblos', but they put the seam on the inside of the foot. They are so proud they all pinch their feet and cultivate the most marvelous set of corns, just to make their feet look smaller.

The Blue Cross people, according to the Navajo, came from the north and east often to play and gamble with the Indians who lived at Pueblo Bonito. The Blue Cross people were so successful at gambling, the Anasazi in their desperation traded off their wives and children to pay off their gambling debts. The Anasazi got weaker and poorer until finally they had to merge with other tribes because they could no longer support themselves.

I never took one Navajo's word for it. I verified it with other Indians. I had a pair of Sioux moccasins, white with a blue cross on them. I asked a Navajo in for a cup of coffee and I said, "Aren't they pretty?" We talked about them for a while and then we talked about the Sioux and what wonderful bead people they were to have done this work with sinew. I was so interested in the way those moccasins were made that I just couldn't think of anything else. Finally I got a lead pencil and drew the cross and said, "I wonder what that means?" The white people have one like it called a Roman cross. Then I colored it with a blue pencil, and we talked about the color.

The story finally came out. "There used to be a people that lived north and east that hunted buffalo and they were always fat and they were great raiders. They weren't satisfied with just hunting buffalo, they used to come down into this country and gamble with the Anasazi."

I heard that from a number of different people. But they had no history, they had no way of proving it. They used to say to me, "Do you believe what I tell you?" and look right into my brain. I'd say, "Sure I do or I wouldn't ask."

The Indians remember back easily three or four generations. I've tested them on this. Now I'm going to tell you something: never let an Indian know what you're after. Get him on the subject and let him tell the story. Don't ask him directly when his mother died, she'll be nine hundred years old by the time he gets through with his story. They're wonderful showmen, wonderful storytellers and their history is all word of mouth. You have to lead them up some other channel to get the truth, otherwise they'll tell you a fairy tale and enjoy telling it to you. If there's anything in this world they love to do is to fool the white man.

One thing I enjoyed with the Navajo were their legends. One day I was sitting in the shade along side of the ruin with three or four old Navajo men, who were doodling in the sand with sharp rocks and teaching me Navajo. They never came near me but what they would tell some word and then have me repeat it. If I made a mistake, they mimicked me and told me what it was I actually said. They'd shame me as much as they could.

I looked down at the ground and Klah Begay was drawing an elephant in front of a palm tree. "Where did you see that elephant, in a picturebook?" I asked. "Did you see one in Albuquerque or Gallup?"

"I've never seen it in a book," he said. "And I've never been to those places."

"How can you draw that if you haven't seen one?"

"My father used to draw it and his father showed him. That's where the Navajos came from."[1]

Well, of course my ears jumped off of my head and I said, "What do you mean where the Navajos came from?"

First he told me a story about worms.[2] The Navajos claim they lived for many centuries within the earth and they were worms about the size of my finger. They kept growing but it was so damp and wet inside the world, they cried loudly. There was a speck of light that enabled them to see underground. A turkey came along and told them that if they would not be so lazy they could dig through that hole where the light came through and they could live in a lovely place. "I'm going there now," he said, and left them.

The worms decided that was what they should do. They dug for a long time and finally pushed through the ground. At first the sun blinded them, but they learned to keep their eyes closed during the middle of the day and open them in the late afternoon. They grew to be big, strong Indian men, but although they were now living in that beautiful country with trees and grass, they weren't happy.

Seeing their despair, the Great Spirit arranged to have a woman from every known tribe walk before these men, and they selected the tall, slender women. From then on that had to be their wife, they couldn't have any other kind. They became very happy and relocated to different areas as the Great Spirit directed them.

Sixteen of these men started the original clans. When I was young and traveling with my family, we became acquainted with the Navajo near Raton Springs at Pueblo Pintado. They were having a ceremony and my father literally went wild because they wouldn't allow him to take pictures. We were in a strange man's country and we did what they said otherwise we never would have learned anything. But the medicine man allowed me to draw pictures of the sand paintings they were using in the ceremony. They thought that if a child did it, it would be destroyed in no time, and it wouldn't be done right, anyway.

I had to make the masks round to deceive the evil spirit who might come and copy them and use them in ceremonials to do great harm to me or the dancers. Father told me to name the colors. I'm no artist but I can copy a little bit and I had to go back many times to learn the right colors. I learned what every color, every animal, and every shape meant when I was a grown woman and married and living at Pueblo Bonito.[3]

Klah Begay told me the story of how the Diné moved from the land of elephants and tigers and palm trees. The rule of all Indian tribes is that you can't stay with your tribe if you find fault with the chief and disobey the medicine men. If you don't like the way the tribe is being run you have to leave. That is what happened to the Diné many, many years ago when they lived in the country on the other side of the big water. Little by little the people left to find a new tribe or a new place to live.

They wandered around the countryside and they couldn't find a place to live that wasn't already claimed by other tribes. After losing battles and experiencing more rejection, they came to a big water. They could see land on the opposite side, and connecting the two was a range of mountains. They decided to cross over on this mountain bridge, but the women were scared as they looked down at the water on both sides. The men drew me pictures to show how hilly the land was, these great black rocks that stood tall. They could see birds flying back and forth, so they knew they would not have to travel far, maybe a day or two. They came to a lovely green place with much grass, and game and berries. They thought they had found paradise. They knew that if some of the people from the old tribe came over and peeked to see where they were, they would be envious.[4]

They lived on all that game and the green things that grew there and just had the best time, but soon after they arrived the weather changed for the worse. The snow fell, *zas* they called it, frozen water. It snowed all night and the people chilled. They'd always lived in a warm country and didn't know what to do. Here there was no wood to burn, and they crawled into holes they dug beneath the snow for warmth. Finally they found rocks and moss, there's none like it in Navajo country they told me, and they tried building houses out of that. They then learned to construct houses out of the frozen snow. They suffered more when the game went away, and they even had to eat fish which none of them had ever eaten because the souls of the dead Montezumas[5] are in fish and that's just like eating a human body. But when you're hungry you can eat anything, and many of them died.

When spring came, those that survived decided they would go back from where they came but when they went to the edge of the water, the land was gone. Those high-peaked hills were all gone. That old black rock had sunk below the water's surface.

They then decided to travel further east and south and left their women, their elderly, their children, and their cripples with frozen feet all behind. "There's plenty of game now and you dry the meat for winter and get lots of skins for cover," they said. "We might not be back before the next snow." The strong men started south and they came, after many moons, to the place where the Diné now live, and they never went back for the people they left behind.

Aleš Hrdlička came to Pueblo Bonito to work with us.[6] He wanted to measure the Navajos to prove that everybody who lived in this hemisphere came from the south. I argued with him on it,

179

but he couldn't see how they could have come from the north. He was a Hungarian who spoke poor English and no Navajo. I told him the migration story the Navajos told me, but he discounted them as old man's tales.

I worked with him all summer there measuring the Navajos, when my responsibilities as wife, mother, and storekeeper allowed. He wanted to find a pure-blooded Navajo. I laughed at him and told him there was no such thing as a pure-blooded tribe on this continent and I told him he wasn't a pure-blooded Hungarian. I was a hothead, too. I told him how they fought and stole one another's women. I pointed out the Oriental slant to their eyes. Once he agreed the oriental features in one child was striking, he insisted I try to find out if any of these children were the progeny of Chinese in the area. I told him I refused to ask one of my friends that question, but he was adamant. I went to the family's bitterest enemy to discover if the mother of that child had ever been around Chinese people. Of course, she hadn't, and I told him so. He'd ask me then to get acquainted with the mother, and I went to the hogan and visited with the mother and asked her if she'd ever been around Chinese, and she hadn't.

In 1904, we set up an Indian exhibit for New Mexico and Arizona at the World's Fair in St. Louis. We brought sixteen Navajos with us who demonstrated blanket weaving and silversmithing. Often I invited one of them to walk around the fairgrounds to see other products of the world. We stopped in front of the Alaska Pavilion and watched Eskimos crack reindeer whips to pick up coins people threw on the floor. Without thinking, I turned to the Navajo next to me, and said, "*Ahlahani!*" (I'll declare!) One of the Eskimos closest to me stopped and said, "What did you say?" in English. I didn't realize what I had said. He told me I had something in a language he recognized, spoken by a people near his village. He introduced me to an old woman who traded with the tribe that spoke Navajo. I recited some words I knew like *shidani* for brother-in-law, a word Navajos use out of familiarity; Diné; *yal* for money. I counted: *t'áálá'í la'ii* (one), *naaki* (two), *táá* (three). Yes, she'd heard all those words.

When I saw Dr. Hrdlička again I told him the story and he invited me to go to Alaska to find the Indians who spoke Navajo.

I was going to have a baby but that was a long ways off. I told him I would go, and we made arrangements. I met him at Seward, a village on the coast of Alaska which I remembered the Eskimo mentioning. We spent a couple days riding around in a horse-drawn buggy to a number of villages. We finally found a woman who knew such words as *shidani* and *ahlahani* and numbers. She traded with the Navajo-speaking people and directed us to the inland village where they lived, about a day's travel from Seward. There were very few there, but they were undoubtedly Navajo because we could understand each other, not every word, but root words like fire, water, sun, and food.[7] Dr. Hrdlička immediately changed all his publications and claimed he discovered that the Navajos had come from Asia and I was never mentioned in any of that story. It was I who translated the Navajo and helped him cast their heads in plaster.

Just as we were leaving the village and saying our goodbyes an old woman emerged from the crowd and clasped a worn silver bracelet around my wrist. Dr. Hrdlička tried his best to get it away from me for his precious museum collection.

NOTES

[1]In another tape, Marietta said she often visited the hogans in the evenings and read them the animal stories of Seton Thompson and the story about Hannibal crossing the alps with elephants. She translated the stories into Navajo, and they were captivated.

[2]The Emergence Myth is a recurring theme among southwestern Native Americans. For the Navajos, First Man, begot from an ear, created the universe. First People made their way through four subdivisions of the underworld before emerging into this, the fifth world, through a hollow reed. A badger hole in the mountains of southeastern Colorado is believed to be the actual place of emergence. Another rumored place of emergence is around El Huerfano Mountain north of Chaco Canyon. First People worked to transform the land, which was covered with water, into an inhabitable place bordered by four sacred mountains. First Man and First Woman created the sun, moon, and stars from precious stones. Into this world emerged the monsters who killed many of the Earth People. According to one version, a deity, Changing Woman, married Sun and Water

and gave birth to twin boys, Monster Slayer and Born-of-Water. The battles between the Twin War Gods and the monsters are commemorated by natural land formations visible today. Changing Woman finally created human beings from flakes of her own skin. She formed six groups of people who represented the first clans.

[3]These crude drawings are in the Center for Southwest Research at the University of New Mexico General Library.

[4]The first inhabitants of North America migrated from Asia across the Bering Land Bridge ten to thirty-five thousand years ago.

[5]I don't know the meaning of "dead Montezumas."

[6]The story about Dr. Hrdlička first appeared in *New Mexico Magazine*, July 1954, the month of Marietta's death. Marietta read into the tape recorder the first draft of that article, written by Mabel C. Wright on her behalf, and therefore portions of it were used in this chapter to fill in the detail. According to this version of the story, Dr. Hrdlička (pronounced Hurd-lits-ka) first came to Chaco Canyon in the summer of 1899 and for the next five summers, used Chaco Canyon as headquarters for his work in physical anthropology among the Southwest Indians under the sponsorship of the American Museum of Natural History. McNitt says Hrdlička, the "crusty Bohemian," frequented Pueblo Bonito between 1899 and 1903, but Brugge says he first visited Pueblo Bonito a year earlier (giving no end date), according to a note Hrdlička made about finding some skeletons in abandoned hogans due to a smallpox epidemic the year before. He worked in a thatch-roofed room on the second floor of Pueblo Bonito. He called upon Marietta to assist him in measuring skeletons and influencing the Navajos to allow him to make plaster of Paris molds of their heads.

[7]The Navajos are classified as an Athapascan people, so named after an area in Canada, where they lived before migrating to the Four Corners area centuries ago. The Navajo language, *diné bizaad*, is part of the Na-Dene family of languages. This classification links the Navajos and the Apaches with other groups in Canada and Alaska. Navajos tell some stories that are similar to those told by people of the north. The Na-Dene family group does not include the Pueblo languages or most of the other languages in the western hemisphere. In fact, recent research by linguists suggests that there are only three language families in this hemisphere: the Na-Dene family which is closely tied to the Eskimo-Aluet family, and the Amerind family. The theory, however, is controversial.

‖ ▲ ‖

17

Sixteen Navajos Go to the World's Fair

MR. WETHERILL AND HIS BROTHER, Winslow, took sixteen Navajos
to the World's Fair in St. Louis in the spring of 1904. Hosteen
Klah, his wife and three children went. Hosteen Klah had stolen
the woman, Annie, from the Zuñi. She wove a rug that has a particular design that the Navajos said make the weaver crazy. Pablo and
his wife went. Pablo was the son of Kli Klizhin, Black Horse, a kind
of a chief who escaped Kit Carson and never went to the Bosque
Redondo. Solde, the Long Singer, went as did Joe Hosteen Yazzi
and his wife and one or two children.

We spent a year preparing for our concession booth and we in-
vested ten or fifteen thousand dollars getting ready. We'd been
around enough to know we needed to have a lot of small items for
people to buy. The Navajo women made literally hundreds of those
little pillow squares I originated and the little table runners. We
also sold the larger rugs, some of which came from the house. We
made little baby carriers, *'awéé bi-ts' áál,* bows and arrows, and
fawnskin and goatskin bags. We made dozens of moccasins in each
size. Everything was sewed with sinew. The silversmiths made rings
and squashblossom necklaces, earrings, and bracelets. Men always
wore the earrings, not the women, except when they had their
coming-out party after they'd reached maturity and were ready to
marry. After they were married they hung the earrings on their
beads. We had them make the men's earrings, a band of heavy silver.

At one end of our exhibit we had a replica of a cliff dwelling,
like Cliff Palace at Mesa Verde. Then we had to have a lot of that
ancient pottery to sell, so the Navajos dug those little shallow burial mounds and probably got a carload of that ancient pottery.[1] We
exhibited stone axes and hammers, turquoise drills, and *metates,* the
stones used for grinding corn. Someone bought the exhibit but left
it until the end of the fair. We packed everything in rough lumber
boxes.

I was never enthusiastic about going. I liked my home, and I had these children, and I'd had a baby that died and I felt badly over that. Mr. Wetherill thought I should go so I finally worked myself up to it.

Win went in April to rent a building down in St. Louis quite close to the Planters Hotel to open a store there. Later, they moved the concession to the manufacturers building.[2]

It was an enormous corner concession, fifty feet by hundred fifty feet, representing New Mexico and Arizona. We had thirty sales people in there at one time.

Mr. Wetherill sent for a seamstress from Gallup, and she made clothes for the children and underwear for me. You couldn't buy underwear in those days that fit. I sent my measurements to the National Cloak and Suit Company for my own dresses, which were supposed to be exclusive. I hired a girl, Jessie to take care of my house. We packed up all my silver, jewelry, and fancy things. My brother and Mr. Colby stayed at the house and took care of the store and supervised the shares the Navajos were running sheep on.

Mr. Wetherill went ahead with the Navajos to get them acclimated to living and working among a crowd of people. There were thousands of people lined up to watch them, and it always stopped the traffic. They were very timid. Some of them had never seen a railroad, much less rode on a train. Most of them couldn't speak English, except Annie, who worked in the house with me. The men demonstrated Indian dancing in the booth, but the women didn't do that. The law wouldn't let the men dance in their costumes— just a breechcloth, G-string, and headdress—because there were so many people who were so modest they couldn't stand it. They wore their overalls and their handmade velvet shirts with silver buttons. People gave them money and they fared well indeed. They received many nice presents and clothes, some of which were taken home for the kids to play with.

I started out from Chaco Canyon in two wagons with several trunks and three children. We made our beds at Raton Springs on a wagon sheet out in the open because there was no place to take cover, and it downpoured on us at midnight. We just had to lay there and allow ourselves to get wet. Everything was soaked, even the hay for the horses, but it was August, and we made a little fire to dry us off. We put on clean clothes and actually got civilized before we came to Albuquerque. I had to get the Navajos, who drove the wagons, loaded up and sent on their way back to Pueblo Bonito. It wasn't good policy to let them stay in town too long what with the gay lights, the city, and everything they could get into.

We took the train to Burdette, Kansas, where I planned to visit with my parents a few weeks before I went on to St. Louis. I had a Pullman and we ate in the dining car, but I brought along a box lunch for the children who ate like geese; they could never get enough.

I wasn't there but ten days when I got a wire from Mr. Wetherill telling me to come to the fair at once to meet his two cousins. It took a little planning to get enough money from my account in Albuquerque to the bank in Larned. Father thought five dollars would be plenty to pay for the train ticket and meals, but I took ten because I like to pay my expenses decently. I didn't even think ten was enough, and we argued about that.

It rained on the way and the train was delayed three days due to flooding. I had to stay all night in Wichita or Hutchinson, and that took money. I think we were rerouted through Texas. I wired Mr. Wetherill several times to let him know when I'd arrive. I finally got to St. Louis at eleven o'clock at night, penniless. I asked a patrolling policeman, a nice, elderly man, for directions to a phone to call Mr. Wetherill. I called the store, because I didn't know where they were boarding. I couldn't get anybody. I told my story to the policeman, gave him my life's history right off the bat. He finally got hold of the night watchman of the store who said he knew the Wetherills—fine fellas, real westerners, but they moved out to the fairgrounds a week ago.

"Well, now let's see what you can do, little girl." Here I had three children and he called me a little girl. "There's a nice Harvey House right here. I know the clerk and I'll get you a room." I told him I didn't have any money. He didn't think that would be a problem. He took me to the hotel and introduced me as a woman from New Mexico coming to the fair for an exhibit with her Indians and her husband who is already here but she hadn't found him on account of the flooding, and the whole story.

They showed me how to run the fan in my room, I'd never seen one before. It was so hot, I could hardly breathe, but I finally got to sleep. I'd been in hotels before but never scared to death like I was

185

because I couldn't find my husband. I thought of a motto the Mormon people hang over the door: "What is a home without a husband?" and I thought, my land, this applies to me. I am married and got a family of children and no husband that I could lay my hands on.

The next morning I showed the clerk the buckskin bag of jewelry I had and asked if I could have an advance of five dollars on it, like Navajo pawn. He gave me fifty dollars and put the jewelry in the safe.

If I'd had the children with me to hug up to me and give me strength, I would have felt better. I never had been in a city alone before. I took the streetcar to the fairgrounds and paid my fifty cents to get in. The ticket taker had seen a man with a gang of Indians come through, but didn't know where their exhibit was.

Oh, what a mess! They were still building the fair and there were lumber, trucks, horses, and people by the hundreds trying to move around. I hunted all day, went through every building, and I could not find the exhibit. I was so completely tired, I started back to the hotel when I saw a bunch of boys who had these wheeled seats they pushed old ladies and crippled people around in. I asked them if they'd heard of the exhibit. Yes, they had, in the Manufacturing Building. That was one building I hadn't searched. "I'll just sit in this chair, and you can push me there," I said.

I rode up and saw my lovely rugs hanging up in the booth. There wasn't one that was more beautifully arranged and colorful then ours. I saw the Indians and looked around for Mr. Wetherill. He looked up and saw me. "My dear, where have you been?"

"Looking for you." I told him the story.

"Why didn't you wire me?"

"I spent all my money wiring you." Well, he put his arms around me and said, "My poor little darling." We went right over to the telegraph office, and there lay all my telegrams. He was so angry, he was going to sue.

"Calm down. I got here, didn't I?"

I moved out of the hotel and we rented a whole house. The beds were full of bedbugs, but that's another story. Win and Mr. Wetherill slept in the booth to take care of the inventory. Mr. and Mrs. Dockarty, who were working for commission for us in the booth, also lived in the house. The Navajos lived in tents in a park we rented and they learned to use the street car. Within a few weeks, I had the children sent there. We had a lot of people to take care of, but I'd say we were making a thousand dollars a day in the concession.

As soon as I arrived, Mr. Wetherill turned his cousins from Pennsylvania over to me, and went back to managing the booth. He had a tremendous job taking care of everything. I walked around with his cousin Isaac, and we saw booths from Africa and the Philippines in that great hall.

That's when I discovered Geronimo.

He was an exhibit all by himself. He had a sign in front of him that said, "Geronimo, Chief of the Apaches." He had to pay his own way selling little beaded rings for ten cents. They weren't Indian-made. They were from Attleborough, Massachusetts. Geronimo was almost blind, the picture of misery. He told me later a man came every day to pick up the money, but he wasn't selling anything. He still had his pride.

We crossed the room and I put out my hand and he put out his hand and we shook. "You don't remember me," I said in Navajo.

"I don't remember much," he said. "I've had too much trouble."

"I knew you when you were a young man." I told him the story about him coming to the camp in the Mogollon Mountains when I was a little girl making horses out of buffalo pumpkins. He came by with his men and the one man put the beef on the table and I gave them buckets and they watered their horses and he said he was going to take me to his camp because he knew I was an Apache.

He thought a long time. "The reason the soldiers didn't catch you that time was because they thought they were very close to you," I said. "I told them it hadn't been but a little while since you'd been there and they galloped right on up the road and missed you. Maybe they caught you later because I saw you at Fort Sill."

"Yes, I was at Fort Sill," he said. "Yes, they had me chained to a post there. Tell me more."

"I only know that I was a very little girl and that they said you were bad. They said you killed the Mexicans and burned their wagons and that meat you gave me was meat you stole from them."

He stroked my hand. "You do know me. You are my friend from a very long time ago."

187

Over the months we stayed at the fair, I took him lemonade and ice cream and a nice sandwich from Berard's, the cafe across the aisle from our exhibit. I found a chair and pulled it up next to him and we talked for hours.

I don't know who kept him there, but he was still a prisoner. He said he was brought up from Florida near a swamp full of snakes and alligators and he'd been sitting in that chair for months. It was wrong to put an Indian in the humidity when he wasn't used to it. I talked about the injustice of the Indians being put in prison for killing the white man, yet the white man was not punished for killing Apache. Of course, they both killed, but only the Indians paid for it. I can't think of it. If I think of it I go crazy.

He told me one story about when the soldiers captured him. They were going to sign a treaty to stop the fighting. The soldiers all got drunk and he and his band got away and went back into Mexico and it was a long time before they got them back. He just laughed over that. He thought the soldiers were good boys, most of them, but they weren't raised to track or to keep their mouths shut. They hadn't been raised to hardships, they got tired quickly, and they rode their horses too fast. He said many of the soldiers had beards and were broad shouldered. "I think they were bad men from other places and they joined the army for protection," he said.

The stories about Indians mutilating their victims were absolutely in the imagination of the writer. They killed white men, that was a victory they were proud of. But after a man has been killed, the evil spirit comes out of the body, and you never know when that is going to happen. The Indians don't hang around. I often talked to the Navajos about taking scalps. "I don't see any scalps in your hogan," I'd say, and they'd say they didn't take scalps. The Comanches and some of the northern Indians did, and they learned it from the French, and that was because the French got the bounty, same as in Mexico. President Diaz gave the Spanish five dollars every time they'd bring in a scalp of a Yaqui. Every time I met a Navajo, or a Hopi, a Pima, or Papago, or Maricopa, I'd ask about scalping and they'd say, "Why would we want to have evil spirits in the house." The last thing in the world they wanted was the top of the head off a dead body. Possibly, if a white man injured a squaw, the Indians might have put him on an ant hill, but it was rare. There's just something about those stories I've never been able to accept.

When I read in the paper that Geronimo was going to be returned to Arizona I told him that very day. "I'm going to say goodbye to you because you're going to be taken home."

"Am I going to die on my own land?"

"Yes, there's where they're going to take you."

"The Great Spirit's good to me."

"Is there anything I can get you, anything you want?"

"I'm almost blind and I have plenty to eat, but I want something for my heart, something to keep me from thinking."

"I can't help you there."

He stood up and put his hands on my face and felt my hair. He felt of my arms, then said, "Goodbye my friend, but I still think you're an Apache."

That was the last thing he said to me. I never saw him again and then I read afterwards that he committed suicide. An Apache Indian told me Geronimo was so disheartened that they didn't take him back to his old stomping grounds in Arizona or New Mexico, but took him back to Fort Sill. He just wanted to live in the mountains and breathe that air. "How can people live here when they have no air to breathe or water to drink?" he'd say. "This stuff we breathe isn't air, this isn't water."

This Apache told me that Geronimo wasn't well. He had a bad cold. He ordered them to get his horse and it was raining and as cold as blue blazes. He just rode right out into the storm and rode and rode and rode and came back and died in a little while with pneumonia.[3]

On St. Louis Day I took Hosteen Klah up the tower so he could see how many people were at the World's Fair. As far as you could see there was nothing but heads packed solid in there. "You see, there's a lot of Americans. The Navajos can never kill them all, can they?"

He laughed and said, "We don't think that anymore. That was when we were crazy and thought we could."

We returned to Pueblo Bonito in 1907, after staying in St. Louis two and a half years.[4] It was time to come home. Elizabeth was losing weight from homesickness, and Robert had a cold. One of our girls, Jessie, was being fed liquor by a white man, and we had to have a policeman track her down in town and bring her to the train station. She threw her baby on the ground. Mr. Wetherill picked up the baby and gave it to me, then escorted Jessie onto the train.

I didn't see Hosteen Klah for I'd say six months after we returned. One day he came in all wreathed in smiles, and grabbed hold of my shoulders and shook me. "You thought I went off and died?"

"No, I was keeping track of you. You were out telling all the people what you saw." I had taken them to restaurants, and church, and vaudeville shows. They had even met President Theodore Roosevelt when he came by the booth. He visited Pueblo Bonito later and John Wetherill took him bear hunting.

"Before we went to St. Louis everybody thought I would die there. I had to tell them what happened to me."

"Did you tell them about how many white people were there?"

"Of course, I didn't tell them that."

"I took you up on that tower especially so you'd see how many there were."

"If I had told them that, they wouldn't have believed any of the other things I told them. If I told them I saw people as thick as the leaves on a tree, they would have killed me for a witch."

NOTES

[1]This is the first reference to the selling of artifacts I've come across in Marietta's oral history. In fact, she often took a stand against the practice. There is no mention in any other document that the Wetherills sold pottery at the World's Fair, although there was some question as to whether the Wetherills sold the pawn jewelry belonging to the Navajos. The World's Fair was so public, I should think there would have been protest against the selling of artifacts, especially by his enemies, George Pepper, and John Benham, who liquidated the Hyde Exploring Exploration in 1903. McNitt unearthed a letter to Talbot Hyde in which Pepper stated, "The Wetherills are sure to make a good thing out of the Fair. I wish there was some way of turning the stream of coin into your pockets, where it belongs."

[2]McNitt says Benham schemed to close down the Wetherill booth. When Win Wetherill arrived, he found that all the concessions in the Manufacturing Building had been taken, and so rented temporary quarters downtown. Then he met a Denver man named Dockarty who had a lease to a stand in the Manufacturing Building but had little to exhibit. Dockarty offered to share his well-placed concession, and the Wetherills took him up on it. Dockarty found he couldn't get along with Win and discussed it with Benham. Benham decided to take Dockarty into his booth, which also displayed an Indian making moccasins, thereby closing the Wetherills out of the concession. Apparently, Richard took over the operation of the concession and the plot was foiled.

[3]Following a drinking spree, Geronimo fell off his horse and died of pneumonia at Fort Sill, Oklahoma, in 1909.

[4]McNitt says the Wetherills arrived in St. Louis in August 1904, and returned to Pueblo Bonito that fall.

18

Crime and Punishment

I FOUND A SKULL right alongside the trail through these big grease-woods in the mesa above Chaco Canyon. I got down off my horse and picked it up and looked it over. I didn't see any marks on it. I thought maybe it rolled out of some ruins up on top the mesa, but after I stood there a few minutes I found a piece of a packsaddle and the handle from a frying pan. I picked up the skull and took it to the nearest hogan.

There was no one at the hogan but this old lady. I showed her the skull, and she said, "Take that away, that's bad."

"I want to know who this was and why he was killed."

"You won't tell?"

"No, I won't tell."

"One time before you and Anasazi came to the canyon, a man wandered through and camped right down there where you found him, but I don't know why he was killed."

"Who killed him?"

"I don't know that, either," she said.

Well, I knew better than to ask any more questions. She did volunteer that they, whoever "they" were, brought all his clothes up to her hogan. She threw away the clothes that had blood on them, but kept the soldier's overcoat and she showed me the buttons she pulled off it. Then she walked out of the hogan and looked up and down the canyon then came back and brought out a saddleblanket. The wool wasn't Germantown, it was unravelled material. "This brown in here was his socks, and the red was from the top of the socks. The gray was from the coat and the yellow was from the lining of his coat. The black was from the smaller coat he wore beneath it, and all this green was a wool blanket. We kept his two black mules and a nice bay horse. When you moved to the canyon we sold them to Anasazi."

I offered her ten dollars for the blanket. That must have been my high price, but she wouldn't take it. She later got hungry and came down and sold me the blanket. I gave it to my daughter in Tucson.

I never heard of murder or rape among the Navajos, and I'm sure I would have heard about anything that happened because our customers came to our store from more than fifty miles away. I will tell you this: I once found the body of a Navajo man.

I was riding down off the mesa into Chaco Canyon following a trail that squeezed between a large rock and the cliff. When we came to that tight place, my horse became frightened and refused to go on through no matter how hard I tried to force him. I got down from the horse and tied him to a rock. I walked in there and found a dead man laying face down with an arrow in his back. I couldn't see a track around anywhere, not even a horse track. There was a red garter about ten feet away from him, used to tie the buckskin leggings around the knee. I picked that up, tied it on the horn of the saddle, and rode down to the house.

When I rode up in front of the house, Bendi John came out and said, "Where have you been?"

"I been up on the mesa."

"What did you see?" He looked frightened.

"I didn't see anything."

"Where did you get the *janeezi*?" he said, pointing to the red garter.

"I found it."

"Well, put it away."

I did what he said, but the next day I went back up on the mesa and the dead man was gone. About a month later, Bendi John approached me again about the subject. "You didn't tell, did you?"

"No, I could tell by the way you looked that I mustn't say anything of what I'd seen."

"Nobody knows who kills a bad man or a bad woman," he said. "When you find one, don't say anything. It's none of your business."

That was what they called "working for the Great Spirit." Somebody has to be removed because they're bad, and there's somebody designated to do the job. They held court over it. I figured out who the dead man was by figuring out who stopped coming to the store, and it was a very mean Navajo. I made inquiries, but nobody said anything about it. "Why do you want to talk about him?" the women would ask. I'd tell them I just wondered why he stopped coming to the store. "Maybe he's gone away," they'd say. "I wouldn't talk about it."

Lots of secret things went on, and I told nobody. I respected their confidence.

They held court same as we do. They elected a judge by standing up and raising a hand. I indulged in politics and I backed Hosteen Didlewishin Begay, and he was elected. Now if a judge makes a poor decision he is censured badly, two mistakes and he loses his position.

One woman who came into the store about once a month, I knew to be a wealthy woman, but I couldn't understand why she looked so unhappy. She would never tell me why. Finally, I got her to come back to my kitchen for a little lunch. When I pressed her again on the subject, she told me, "I had a husband I disliked very much. I put his saddle and things outside, but he wouldn't give up. I didn't want to kill him so I ran away with another man. We ran far away where we thought nobody could find us. The husband reported it to the court and I was forced to live here away from my family, even though I am married to a new man and have children."

I told her I would tell her story to Didlewishin Begay. I told him, and once he heard the facts, he said, "She's had enough punishment." He told the first husband to leave the poor woman alone.

I bought goat's milk from a family who lived near Fajada Butte and had six or eight children. One boy I noticed always laid in the shade of the hogan and his mother always scolded him for not herding sheep with the other children. She worried over him and complained to me frequently about it.

This particular morning I rode up to the hogan and I could hear her scolding the boy. She didn't invite me in, she just kept berating him and saying, "This is the last time I'm going to tell you to go out and help the girls with the sheep." I knew by her voice something was very wrong. She was hysterical, half crying. It was so unusual to hear a squaw talk that way.

I hollered, asking if I could come in and she said, yes. I walked in, and the boy just laid there chewing on a bone next to the fire and paying her no attention whatsoever. She grabbed him by the shirt and jerked him into sitting position. "I've told you this is the last time. Are you going out to help with the sheep?" He never answered. She picked up a stick of wood about the length of your forearm and hit that boy on the head just as hard as she could.

Killed him instantly. He fell right over and blood ran from his mouth. She turned to me. "See what I've done? I had to do it. Death is better than disgrace."

I just turned and walked out. I pretty near fainted. I picked up a bottle of goat's milk from the children and rode home, and I never spoke a word to anybody about it. That was the custom of the country.

I started getting milk from Welo and didn't see the woman. About six months later I saw out in front of the house someone wearing a black blanket. I asked Des-glena-spah who it was, and she said it was the woman from Fajada who sold me the milk. I got curious so I poured a cup of coffee and walked outside. I greeted her but received silence in return. I lifted the blanket and sure enough it was that woman. *"Aszdáán,"* she said. I handed her the cup of coffee and walked back to the house.

She sat out there until I thought she was going to petrify. Finally she stood up and I walked out again, put my arm in hers and led her into the kitchen. I gave her some bread, meat, and coffee, and she took the blanket off her face. Tears rolled out of her eyes onto her dress. I couldn't hardly stand it. I put my arms around her and said, "Don't cry anymore."

"What do you think of me?" she said.

"I couldn't have done what you did, but you must be very strong to be able to do it," I said. "But I don't understand how you could have done that."

"I had to do it so he wouldn't grow up and kill other people. We live a very lonely life. Everybody knew I had this child that wasn't right. I kept thinking that he would get right when he got old. I gave ceremonials and the medicine men came and we did everything we could think of doing so that I wouldn't have to do what I did. I will never be happy again." Then she asked me, "Did you tell anyone? Have you told Anasazi?"

"No."

She looked at me a long time. "I didn't know a white woman would do that for a Diné."

"Let's not talk about this anymore," I said. "I will help you to forget it."

The most terrible disgrace was in getting caught because that meant that you weren't clever enough. Once I commenced to miss things and I suspected Bernice who had worked for me in the house for several years. I asked her if she'd taken anything and when she denied it, I asked to see inside her suitcase. She said she couldn't do it, so I pulled it out and looked inside and found pieces of jewelry and eight or ten silver dollars that she picked up in the store. She wouldn't say anything about it so I poured it into a pile and asked her to put the items back where she found them. She denied taking them again, so I told her she couldn't work for me anymore. That's when she went into hysterics. "What will the Diné say?" she said.

The custom was that if you stole something from someone, they would steal something back. One time I asked Bendi John to bring in one of our horses to eat, that was in 1903, the year of the drought. He brought a horse in, butchered it, and hung the hide on the fence for everyone to inspect. I never paid much attention to it. He knew our brand, the quarter circle star brand on the left shoulder.[1] Years later, the government wrote me that the Apaches had that brand and that I would have to counterbrand or sell my horses. I wrote back saying I had prior rights to it as I was registered in both New Mexico and Colorado. They continued to insist that I counterbrand, and I continued to refuse. It was finally dropped and I don't think I ever lost a horse.

Anyway, four or five days later, Tomacito came in and said, "Why did you eat my horse?"

I went out and pulled the hide off the fence and saw that it did not bear our brand. "I'll make Bendi John pay you for it."

He said he wanted ten dollars for it, so I found Bendi John and told him he was going to have to pay Tomacito for the horse. "Why did you kill his horse?" I asked.

"He ate one of mine," he said, but he repaid Tomacito and he had to work it out around the house chopping wood and doing this and that.

I kept a brand book for all the brands in the area and when Marcellino ended up with Tso's horses, say, I'd tell him how much he owed Tso for the horses, and he'd pay it, and that was that.

I have a picture of Vicente Cayitano, a Navajo leader, sitting on a pinto. He loved that horse, and he bought it from Jésus, who lived near Thoreau (pronounced "through"), New Mexico. Those horses over there were superior to everyone else's horses and they won most of the horse races at Chaco. We wondered where they got these thoroughbreds. Now, old Jésus was a Mexican slave who had been captured by the Navajos on the Rio Grande when he was a little boy. He stayed with the Navajos because that was where he grew up, and he married a Navajo woman and raised fine children. They were well-to-do. I asked him where he got the horses and he said he found them near a train track. A train with a carload of mares and stallions wrecked right near Thoreau and the horse car tipped over. Jésus just gathered up the ones that hadn't been killed and took them out of sight. The railroad intended to round up the horses, but the Navajos weren't so slow.[2]

Vicente traded a team of mules for a nice pair of turquoise earrings. Welo found a lode of turquoise in a room near his house at Penasco Blanco and it made him wealthy. I gave him ten flashlight tablets to burn so that he could chase away the evil spirit while he dug. There were eighteen of those big ruins in that country. Was it wrong for the people that were there first to go in and get a little out of it? The white man came in afterwards and took plenty.

NOTES

[1] The Wetherills also had the triangle bar triangle brand.

[2] Aleš Hrdlička had this to say about the Navajos in his 1908 report on the current status of Navajo crime:

> Among the Navaho crimes are rare, consisting of theft, desertion, and murder. In 1898 . . . some Navaho robbed one of their chiefs, Vicente; such an occurrence, however, from all accounts, is very rare. The Navaho steal stock from the Hopi, and on the border commit occasionally petty thefts from the whites; but the majority of the tribe are honest, as are most of the other Indians who have not suffered degradation. A murder in the tribe occasionally takes place, followed by the suicide of the murderer . . . A prospector on the reservation would run a serious risk of being killed; otherwise whites are never terrorized, and there is no instance on record in which a scientific explorer has been in any way molested. A medicine man who fell into disfavor was shot in 1900. A few cases of rape were heard of . . .

See *History of the Chaco Navajos*, for a more complete account of the crimes reported in the Chaco Canyon area for the past few centuries.

19

A School for the Navajos

WE FINALLY RENTED the store to the Gabaldons from Albuquerque.[1] "I'm tired of struggling with it," Mr. Wetherill said. "The way prices are, I'm going to devote myself to stock." We had lots of horses, sheep, and cattle after the panic of 1907.[2] I cut my expenses down as much as I could and did most of the work myself so we wouldn't have to hire extra help, although I did have a cook for all those cowboys and Des-glena-spah to help me with the children. Fred Hyde wanted to do more building, but Mr. Wetherill wouldn't let him; it was too expensive and would ruin our view of the Gap. Fred's family kept urging him back East to marry, but he was enamored with the Southwest.

Superintendent [Rueban] Perry came out to Pueblo Bonito that year with his good-looking stenographer and four or five Navajo policemen to get the Navajo children for school.[3] They stayed several days. "I never knew you needed police to make the Indians send their children to school," I said. Perry told me the police wouldn't be there if it weren't necessary. Plus, he said, he got five dollars for every child he got into school. They didn't tell Uncle Sam they used force. I've seen those police pull the children away from their mothers; they just screamed and cried.

A number of Navajo women came down and asked for help. I told them I couldn't do anything for them. "We'll just bury them," they said. I thought that meant they were going to kill them.

I followed them behind our barn and watched them dig a trench and lay the children in it. They covered the children's faces with wool and stuck oat or wheat straws from the barn in their mouths and covered them with sand. I'd do it if they were my children. The children had their instructions before the police came. They snuck down through the rocks in the cliff and stayed behind the barn.

When they caught the children, they sent them to the Indian school in Albuquerque, or Carlisle, Gallup, and Fort Lewis, and Christianized them. They kept them four or five years until they learned a little English. This is the thing that always riled my ire;

they went home after all those years in school without learning anything they needed to know to survive on the reservation, like blanket weaving or sheepherding.

It was so easy for the schools to lose those children. They'd get off the train at Gallup or wherever, and there weren't always school teachers there to meet them. These little kids didn't know their father's name, except maybe that it was Hosteen Yazzi or Hosteen Tso and that they lived near Kin Bineola. When they got in school, they'd get a new name, like Mary or Johnny.

Tomacito's only son was sent to Albuquerque for two or three years and then sent to Fort Lewis. I traced him there and learned he died of diphtheria. Nobody ever notified Tomacito. Nobody knew what terrible things, what injustice, what awful things have been done to those Indians. It just breaks my heart because I was so helpless to do anything. I wrote letters, I hunted children, and I'd have to tell their folks they were dead. I thought I would be smart and sent one little girl to school when she was five. When she came back at sixteen I took her to see her mother and there she stood dressed up in a cute little dress she had brought from school. She didn't know her mother and her mother didn't know her. Tears rolled down the mother's cheeks. "This isn't my daughter. She's yours, not mine." I've never gotten over that.

The other children would bring home two or three suits of underwear, a couple pairs of shoes, maybe some dresses from school. How long do you think those clothes lasted herding sheep? Did they adjust after living in a house with electric lights, steam heat, dishes, and beds with sheets?

There's how tuberculosis spread among the Navajo children.[4] They had lived all their lives out in the open, sleeping on the ground all summer long and in the hogan all winter with that big hole in the top. Plenty of sunshine and fresh air and wholesome food. They were taken to the school and shut up in the dormitories, fifty of them together. Mrs. John Wetherill and I kept track of thirty-seven children that were taken to Riverside, California, and I think three or four died from pneumonia that first year. After three years, nine came back and seven of those had tuberculosis.

The only grown person I ever knew who had tuberculosis when I first moved to Chaco Canyon was Bendi John. He was working for the Indian School in Albuquerque and he was put into the hospital there. As soon as he was well enough the doctors released him and a man took him as far as Thoreau. From there he rode horseback to Chaco Canyon. Several medicine men worked on him for free because they didn't know anything about the disease. He finally got well.

It was the most terrific, unjust way of education that ever was in the world. I guess we did the best we could.

The government tried to save the Hopi in the same way. The time we went to the snake dances, the governor, or "good," welcomed us. It hadn't been long since all the married men or men of marrying age had been taken by the government to Catalina Island where they stayed imprisoned for three years, but he was friendly anyway. Uncle Sam had built them some little one-room cottages at the bottom of the hill. Each cottage had a cook stove, with the warming oven in the top and the cooking oven down below, a set of dishes, a table and four chairs, a bed with springs and mattresses. Then the government demanded that they live down there off the unsanitary mesa. The Hopi refused to move out of their homes where they had lived hundreds of years to those hot little shanties at the bottom of the hill, so the men were taken to Catalina.

We made our camp near the cottages, and Mr. and Mrs. Lolo, bless their hearts, moved right down and stayed with us all those months. They were the dearest couple of old people that anybody ever entertained in the world. We didn't care to sleep in the house because we had our own sleeping arrangements, and they wouldn't either. One day I said to the old lady—I could make myself understood before very long—"Why don't you sleep here on this nice soft bed," and I bounced up and down on it as a young girl would. "Lolo, he no like," she said. "He think he on the ocean and doing this," and she swung her hand back and forth to explain to me how the wave made him sick when he crossed over to Catalina. Folded nicely away in the bottom oven were feathers of different kinds and some of those embroidered sashes and bits of this and that. Up in the top of the oven all the dishes were still carefully packed away. They had never used a thing. They left it right where Uncle Sam had presented it to them.

Mr. Stacher came to Pueblo Bonito with his wife and four children in 1909.[5] He was a short, heavy-set man, officious, like lots of young men who had no experience. He felt he knew everything about the Indians and he complained to me that the Navajos wouldn't come to him for advice. I told him it took time for them to get acquainted, maybe a year or two. "If you promise them anything, be sure you do what you promise. One mistake and it will go all over the reservation like wildfire. They'll never forgive you."

Des-glena-spah said to me one time, "I don't think Mr. Stacher is a good man."

"What do you mean, Glena?" I said.

"The Diné say he says bad things about Anasazi. He's jealous because they come to Anasazi instead of him."

Mr. Wetherill brought Miss Eleanor Quick back from one of his trips to Denver to sell what we didn't sell at the World's Fair. She was about thirty-five or forty and never been married. She was a wonderful schoolteacher, and the children learned just fine from her. I had three children in school and the Stachers had four children. She lived in one of the cottages where Uncle Clayton lived before he died and she alternated between eating with us and eating with the Stachers every two weeks. We fixed her room there next to the school with rugs on the floor and the walls. But I'll say this in a whisper, her company came through the window.

Little Richard came to me and announced, "I see men's tracks going through the window in Miss Quick's room."

"Some people just trying to scare her," I told him.

Mr. Stacher had a [stockman] by the name of T. H. Jones who looked like the early gambler, the tall sort of fancy-dressed man with the very loud vest and a watch chain that reached from one vest pocket to the other. He was very fond of the ladies. He liked me but he fell in love with Mrs. Stacher and she with him. He hadn't been there but a short time until it was quite evident to me.

Mrs. Stacher and I were good friends. I shouldn't tell you this because she is still living but once she told me she was pregnant and the father was Mr. Jones.[6] I scolded her for it, but she said she loved him so. I wouldn't have touched him with a ten-foot pole.

Miss Quick worshipped the ground Mr. Wetherill walked on. She liked all the cowboys but she had her favorites. She favored

John Arrington's brother, Paul, but she liked Will Finn best. Will Finn was Mr. Wetherill's pet. He just rode in one day on a good looking horse wearing good chaps, a good bridle, a wool shirt, blue jeans, a fancy pair of boots, a Stetson hat, two sixshooters and a rifle, all the common equipment.

I met him first.[7] "Howdy," he said. "Is the boss in?"

"No, he's not. He's gone up on the hill to look after some stock, but he'll be back soon."

"Could I put my horse up?"

"Just take it to the man in the barn and he'll take care of it for you."

"I prefer to take care of it myself."

"Suit yourself." I didn't tell him I was Mrs. Wetherill, but he looked me up and down pretty thoroughly and I thought he was rude.

"All right," he said. Never cracked a smile. He was a severe looking kid and I thought he was a runaway.

He told Mr. Wetherill he was from Waxahachie, Texas. His uncle was Dwight Moody, an evangelist, and his father had a big ranch, quite well-to-do, but he was murdered, or he died, I don't remember which. He kept running away and Dwight put him in the Roswell military school when he reached the ninth grade. He was there two years, and in the third year he ran away and hooked up with a man he'd known in the cow business, Joe MacFarland, in the Capitan Mountains, New Mexico. He said they were the two best cow thieves in the country, and got a nice herd together. MacFarland finally got arrested and he told the kid, "Leave the country and go straight." He went straight to Pueblo Bonito and told Mr. Wetherill of his good intentions. He worked for us a number of years and for me many years afterward.

He was faithful. Mr. Wetherill set him to riding broncos. The Indians were not bronc busters. Finn was good with a rope. No cowpuncher in the country could come close to four-footing a horse like him. He liked to work with horses, but he didn't like them personally.

Joe Schmedding left to hunt him a wife. We had Lee Ivy, Paul Arrington, Gus Thompson, Jack Dee, and Finn. They took care of the stock and looked after everything. An Indian kept us in wood and water. We built another well right straight down in front of the house and Mr. Wetherill put in a windmill there to pump water up to the house so that we could have water in the bathroom. We planned to pump water up to the hotel, but we never did. Far fewer people travelled out to Chaco country.

The range was getting poor and we sold off a lot of our stock because we needed the money. The range was overstocked. You can't feed it off and then expect more to grow if you feed it off before it goes to seed. That's what ruins a range.

I think Mr. Wetherill said we had eight thousand sheep, all out on shares. In the spring the sheep buyers came in. As soon as you lamb they come in and advance you ten cents a head on the fall market, so when the sheep went up for sale in the fall, many of them were already spoken for. As far as I know Mr. Wetherill paid off everything and everything was going along smoothly. We didn't have any worries out there that I know of concerning the slump in the market. When the sheep go on the market, there's lots of activity, lots of Indians come in with their herds and take their share and they pay up their bills and redeem their pawn in the store. Then you get settled for winter and then's when you really enjoy life, when you didn't have so much to do.

Mr. Wetherill tacked a paper bullseye to the seven-foot snubbing post about a hundred fifty feet in front of the store. He competed with Winslow Wetherill, Fred Hyde, and Finn and anybody that wanted to show off their marksmanship, and they wasted a lot of ammunition. Thousands of rounds, especially Fred. He'd bring it in those great big boxes. Fred could toss a can in the air and empty all six shots into it. Finn was as good as Fred.

We brought in ladies from Farmington and we all wore my white dresses to our dances. I loved dancing with Finn, and Mr. Hyde was a good dancer, too. Mr. Wetherill never danced. He'd come and stand with his hands up on the door on each side of the casing where we were dancing and say, "I've missed a lot, I see that." It was against his religion.

One Christmas Fred Hyde sent us a big box at least four feet high. It arrived in Gallup two or three days before Christmas and he wrote and told us when to meet it and to open it as soon as it arrived. One year he gave the cowboys each a lovely saddle and bridle, and a rifle and cartridges from Simms Hardware back east. But this time he sent three roasted turkeys, several hams, fruit cakes, plum puddings made just like big cantaloupes with the ridges in them, jars of jelly, canned cranberries, six mince pies, white cake, and candy. We ate on that stuff until I was sick to death of it.

We made it always a point to have the Navajos in to eat at our table, like Tomacito, Marcellino, Bendi John, Hosteen Tso, Hosteen Nez Begay, Joe Hosteen Yazzi, whoever was around. But they'd much rather eat in the kitchen at my little table where we could talk and laugh. They'd say, "Oh, I can't come, I'm not dressed," and I'd tell them not to worry, neither were the cowboys. "I don't know how to eat at a white table." I'd tell them to watch what others would do. You'd see them watching the fellas both sides of them and wiggling back and forth, and they'd take exactly the same amount of each food as did everyone else. I was always careful to put them among the cowboys and not next to a white woman at the table. But in the summer, if Joe Hosteen Yazzi or someone came in a G-string and breechcloth, and a white woman would catch her breath, why I couldn't be bothered.

It wasn't the best of times there on the ranch toward the end, but we were comfortable, and life was good enough. But Stacher insisted he was building a school at Chaco. Mr. Wetherill was against it. He didn't want the Navajos coming in there with their sheep and horses running all over the ruins stirring up dust. It wasn't the proper place and there wasn't enough water. He suggested Kin Ya'a, a ruin in open country out toward Gallup, which had plenty of water. No sir, Mr. Stacher wanted the school in Chaco and he said he would dam up the canyon for water and fence the canyon at both ends so that they could bring their flocks any time they wanted to visit their children.

Stacher talked about it at the table when Miss Quick ate with them, about how he was going to build a school and how Richard Wetherill wasn't going to prevent him from it. Miss Quick came back to our table and told us what Stacher said and made her own little additions. She was good at that. I disliked her. As a rule Mr. Wetherill paid no attention and changed the subject, but that didn't stop her from talking about how Stacher was going to build this school in Chaco Canyon.

NOTES

[1]In February or March of 1910, Wetherill sold his trading business to an "unnamed Spanish-American," according to MacDonald's book, and to the Wetherill tutor, Eleanor Quick. Miss Quick seemed to think the sale was prompted by the difficulties Richard had in collecting debts due to the Indian agents. Brugge speculated that the Mieras of Cuba purchased the store. Epimenio Miera indeed purchased the remaining Wetherill interests after Richard's death.

[2]In January 1906, Richard claimed his principal business was stockraising, and Brugge said that in 1907, the *Farmington Times-Hustler* reported that two parties went out to Pueblo Bonito to look over Richard's holdings. Richard may have begun thinking about selling his interests when the price of sheep fell sharply during the "Roosevelt Panic" of 1907, and Joe Schmedding confirmed this in his autobiography. Other factors may have gone into his thinking. He happily relinquished title to the ruins on January 14, 1907, making Chaco Canyon a National Park (due largely to the work of Hewett) because it meant they would be protected by the government. In doing so, he reduced his lands from 160 to 113 acres. Furthermore, on November 9, 1907, Theodore Roosevelt signed a simple withdrawal to extend the Navajo reservation until the Navajos could be given their proper land allotments. The extension included a major tract encompassing the Chaco region, which was later appealed and corrected, although Navajos still use the lands surrounding the monument. A separate jurisdiction was created at Pueblo Bonito in 1907 for a school and agency, but no bureaucrat was installed there until 1909.

Meanwhile, in response to the extension order, Richard wrote to the Commission of Indian Affairs offering to organize the Navajos' stockraising efforts, admitting, rather vaguely, that he kept his stock out on shares to the Navajos, perhaps as a way of coping with the government squeeze. He shot himself in the foot by admitting that he also had deeds to railroad land and that coal reserves existed on his homestead. He had mined some forty feet into the cliff face, but was not interested in coal. On April 1907, action to suspend his homestead entry had been dropped, but was promptly protested because of the coal deposits, and the entry was again delayed for another five years. Marietta had claim to railroad sections 11, 13, and 15, as early as 1901, although the patent to section 13, immediately south of their homestead, was not granted until May 1906. According to Brugge, land allotment agent George Keepers testified after Richard's death that Richard "knowingly made a false affidavit" regarding an allotment made to Jack Edway. Edway was a Navajo boy allegedly adopted by the Wetherills, and his allotment was made in an area Richard fenced for pasture.

Brugge says Richard's major problem was in the way he operated. Instead of protecting the Navajos in their claims to the range around Chaco Canyon, he competed with his customers for the grass, thereby reducing them to such poverty they couldn't pay their debts. When Chaco Canyon became part of the extended reservation and a National Park in 1907, his ranch was put in jeopardy, and his endeavors to retain control aggravated the Indian service officials.

[3]If Richard Wetherill were guilty of a crime it indeed was his inability to assuage the Indian agents. A chief duty of the CIA was education for the Navajos, and agents were to "induce or compel" Navajo children to attend school. The first schoolroom was established at Fort Defiance in the fall of 1867 by the Presbyterian Church, which sent out Charity Gaston as the first teacher. Over the decades, missionary and government schools were built, but few in the early days realized how difficult it was to gather children scattered across three and one-half million acres of reservation. School did not mean much to the Navajos who wanted to plant fields, build homes, weave, and trade their horses and sheep. The Navajos wanted what the schools could not give: to fit them for work. Although criticized for exploitation, traders like Richard Wetherill offered more than the government schools and the agents could provide at the time.

Rueban Perry became established as Indian Agent in the Summer of 1903. In November of that year, he expected Richard to help him recruit ten children for enrollment in school at Grand Junction. He also expected him to settle disputes between Navajo and Spanish-American herders, but the good relations did not last long. Perry was forced to inquire about a complaint made by a Navajo concerning a piece of pawn Richard and his brother, Winslow, had allegedly swindled from a Navajos. Richard told Perry it was none of the agency's business. This opened up other accusations made by the Navajos of having been cheated, and the romance with the agents ended. By the time Perry resigned in November 1907, he reported that Richard was a hospitable, cultured man, yet his reputation for honest dealings was not good. He said Richard was known to employ policemen to take Indian stock without due process to pay debts, and he sometimes imprisoned the Indians in underground rooms at Pueblo Bonito, all of which was only hearsay to Perry. Perry also accused Richard of convincing the Indians that no authority had more power over him than he.

Another important adversary to Richard was William T. Shelton, who became superintendent of the new San Juan School and Agency in August of 1903. Dubbed "Nat'aani Neez," he established Shiprock and directed the affairs of Indians in northern New Mexico with unprecedented firmness for more than a decade. His tenure was to be marked by controversy. Although Richard was eighteen miles out of his jurisdiction until 1907, Shelton was not inhibited from trying to oust him.

[4]A diphtheria epidemic spread through the San Juan in the fall 1903 or 1904, and death came to nearly every hogan in Chaco Canyon. Shelton denied medical help to Pueblo Bonito because it was outside his jurisdiction. Marietta quarantined her own children against exposure while Richard apparently set fire to the hogans with dead bodies in them, which, according to Brugge, may have started animosities between Richard and the Navajos.

Marietta doesn't mention the epidemic but instead related a time when two of her children and a Navajo boy came down with scarlet fever. She nearly lost her daughter while waiting for the medicine to arrive. She packed Richard's arms and legs in salt bags, but the disease settled in Elizabeth's ears. One day, while rocking the child's head in her lap, fluid ran out of Elizabeth's ears, and she became better after that. Marietta was up day and night for nearly two weeks giving her children shots of morphine when they screamed with pain.

[5]On April 12, 1909, Samuel F. Stacher moved to Pueblo Bonito, where he was superintendent of the proposed school and where he headquartered his administration of the eastern Navajos. He rented the Wetherill hotel for $18 (McNitt says $15) a month. In an early report, Stacher noted an absence of local schools, ten or twelve trading posts, fifty white residents, and about three thousand Navajo residents. His attention first turned to land allotments. Old Welo and Navajo George were granted allotments, and in the case of Welo, he received the land under the Homestead Act because he had made many improvements on the land around Penasco Blanco in Chaco Canyon. Trespassing was almost impossible to police, to Stacher's frustration, and Richard's behavior complicated matters. In the end, only Welo was able to keep his land. Stacher joined forces with Shelton against Richard.

[6]Of course, this can't be substantiated. By 1910, Jones was dismissed as the stockman and was married to a woman who worked at an agency substation at Blanco Canyon. In April 1910, Stacher requested her resignation, as well. Apparently she had become some kind of annoyance to him. Stacher believed the Joneses were sympathetic to the Wetherills after Richard's murder.

[7]Joe Moody, alias Bill Finn, began working at the Wetherill's Triangle Bar Triangle ranch at Pueblo Bonito in 1904 or 1905. Schmedding said he was the first to speak to Finn. He suspected Finn of being a bank robber or a murderer and noted he carried a Derringer. The two of them went on debt collecting tours among the Navajos. He was apparently rough with the Navajos and McNitt says his hostile style was transferred to his employer. McNitt says he was neither a murderer or a bank robber and

prefers Marietta's version of his story of origin. Other cowboys working for the Wetherills included Marietta's uncle, Fred Palmer, who worked for several years at Pueblo Bonito as a blacksmith and could outshoot Finn; Gus Thompson, who was crippled in one foot; slow-witted Lee Ivy; quick-tempered "Black" Phillips; and Richard's Uncle Clayton who had lost both legs in a storm in Canada and died while Marietta and Richard were at the World's Fair in St. Louis.

20

Navajos Go on the Warpath

I RETURNED TO PUEBLO BONITO in late June 1910, from St. Joseph Hospital in Albuquerque with my new baby, Ruth. The feeling of enmity between Mr. Stacher and Mr. Wetherill had undoubtedly been kindled.[1] To make matters worse, Mr. Wetherill rented out the north pasture to Sheriff Tom Talle of Gallup and the Navajos were upset about it.

I was home only a few days when Talle drove in the five hundred head of cattle he just bought in Texas. That was a long drive from Gallup, eighty miles. He came around by Seven Lakes, watered the cattle in the lakes that still had water, and drove them to Chaco.[2]

Stacher heard about Talle's drive to Chaco Canyon and told the Navajos, "You can see he's going to bring a lot of cattle in here and you won't have any grass or water left. He'll run you out of the country if you don't do something." The Indians told me that's what he said.

The pasture Mr. Wetherill rented to Talle was one he let the Navajos use. A Navajo came in and told us the Diné didn't like Mr. Wetherill renting that pasture. Mr. Wetherill told them there was plenty of grass and the cattle wouldn't be there very long. "He'll just leave them here forever," the Navajo said.

"You have to help your neighbors out," Mr. Wetherill argued. "When it rains [on his land] or he gets another pasture someplace he'll move them out because he don't want to leave them here. We haven't got much grass and they wouldn't get fat here and he's got to take them out before winter." But they didn't like it, you could see that.

The morning Talle's cattle was to arrive, June 22, Mr. Wetherill sent Finn and Lee Ivy to Hosteen Nez Begay's [Tall Man's Son] house to retrieve a horse.[3] The day before, some Navajos came in and told Mr. Wetherill that Nez Begay had stolen a colt of ours and he'd rode him pretty near to death. He was only a three-year-old and there wasn't any business riding him.

When Finn and Ivy rode up to Nez Begay's they found the horse tied in the back of the hogan. His head was down and he was covered with sweat. As was the etiquette when approaching a hogan, they hollered a time or two, and when no one came out of the hogan, Finn brought the horse to the front of the hogan.

Nez Begay[4] came out and Finn said, "What are you doing with this horse down here and who has been riding it?"

"I don't know, but the Navajos are mad." Nez Begay jerked the bridle of the horse [Finn was riding] right below the bit and the horse started to rear up. Finn pulled a six-shooter out of his chaps pocket and hit this Navajo on the head. He fell to the ground.[5]

"I oughtn'ta done that but he made me so damned mad when he took hold of the horse I just saw red," Finn said later. "I guess maybe I hit him harder than I ought to have but there was no blood so I guess he wasn't seriously hurt."

Then Chis-chilling-begay [Chiishch'ilin Biye', or Son of the Late Curly Hair] came out of the hogan followed by some women.[6] The boys started back home with the horse, but the horse [died]. The Navajo had hurt him badly. They left him at Marcellino's hogan.

The main bunch of cattle came in that afternoon and Talle and Mr. Wetherill sat in the office talking while the men counted the cattle in the corral. Talle had a beautiful six-shooter, and he took it off and laid it on the table in my sitting room. "It's so hot, I'm going to leave this here," he said to me. "You can use it if you need it." He was teasing me, you see. Then he went out to help his men drive the cattle up to the mesa.

Mr. Wetherill waited in the office for the last of the cattle, the tag ends [or drags], to come in. Finn and Ivy arrived and I was there to hear them tell the story of the horse to Mr. Wetherill.

"I don't understand why Nez Begay would do such a thing," Mr. Wetherill said.

"We'll go back after the horse in the morning," Finn said. "I see the cattle have come in."

"Oh yes, they're nice-looking cows," Mr. Wetherill said. "Talle's taking them around to water up on the hill."

By that time there was quite a few tag ends in the corral, and Mr. Wetherill said, "I'll take these last ones up." He sent Ivy up the

210

canyon to help Talle and then said to me, "There'll be some extras for supper. What time will we have it?"

"The usual time, six o'clock all right?"

"We may be a few minutes late." It was already getting late. Finn and Mr. Wetherill began driving off the cattle.

Chis-chilling-begay, in the meantime, went to George Blake's store [at Tsaya] which was down on the Chaco. Blake was a good friend of ours and bought goods from us all the time. Chis-chilling took his silver belt off and threw it down on the counter. "I want to pawn this for a box of cartridges. I'm going to stop Anasazi from bringing stock into this country."

"You better not do that," Blake said. "You'll get into a lot of trouble." But Blake gave him the cartridges anyway and took the belt in pawn. Indians talk a lot, they're always going to kill somebody. George didn't think anything of it. He didn't know anything about the situation at Pueblo Bonito.[7]

"The Navajos are awfully mad," Des-glena-spah told me after Mr. Wetherill and Finn drove the cattle down the canyon. "Let us go away. Let us take the children up to my house on the Escavada. We don't want to see what's going to happen."

"What is going to happen, Glena?"

"I can't tell you but let's go up to my house over on the Escavada. I don't want you to be here."

"I won't go away. I'm going to stay right here."

"They won't ever kill you," she later told me. "You're Diné, and your children are safe because they're part Diné."

I didn't heed her warning and I put the baby to bed and in doing so I happened to look out the back window through the Gap. I saw five or six Indians painted black with their hair down over their faces.[8] I called Des-glena-spah to the window. "What in the world are they fixed up like that for?"

"I told you they were mad," she said. "They're on the warpath, isn't that what you white people call it?"

"What are they doing that for?"

"I don't know, maybe they're going to kill somebody. They haven't told me but I know Stacher said that's what they should do so that there wouldn't be too many cattle brought to push our sheep off the range."

"That's funny," I said. Then I saw Mr. Wetherill and Finn stop right there by Pueblo del Arroyo and talk with this group of painted Indians. After a few minutes Mr. Wetherill and Finn rode on with the cattle. I found out later that one of the men was Old Welo and he was carrying an old gun that was falling to pieces. Mr. Wetherill said, "What are you carrying that old wreck for Welo, it's no good."

"I'm mad."

"What'cha' mad about?"

"We don't like these cows coming."

"Why, they won't do any harm."

"They'll eat up all our grass."

"Lemme see that gun," Mr. Wetherill said. "What do you shoot with it, anyway?" Mr. Wetherill didn't think Welo was serious. He couldn't believe his children that he thought so much of could act that way.

"You're an old man and you ought to have a better gun than that," Mr. Wetherill said. He took the gun and broke the stock off against the horn of his saddle.[9] "You come up to the store when I get back and I'll give you a new twenty-two. You're a good neighbor and you need a better gun than this to kill rabbits. I'll throw in a box of cartridges." He then threw the gun right down there on the ground. It was an old fashioned .44, and they weren't worth anything anyway after they wore out.

Mr. Wetherill and Finn rode on, and the Indians went down into the arroyo to the spot where Finn and Mr. Wetherill would have to cross the arroyo about a quarter of a mile below the fence [at Rincon del Camino]. They drove these cattle with leisure. They were tired and they had a hill to climb and it took them some little time to get them down there.

The Navajos hid in the dense brush in the arroyo. When Mr. Wetherill and Finn dropped into the arroyo, Chis-chilling-begay raised up from behind the bush. As Mr. Wetherill's horse reared up, the bullet went through Mr. Wetherill's right hand holding the reins. And then right through his heart.[10]

I had gone into the kitchen to see if supper was getting on the table. I'd put in a big roast and I knew we had plenty of food. Then I came back to see if my baby was still asleep. As I looked out the window again I saw a huge pile of dust in the arroyo about a quarter of a mile or more from the house. It looked just like the cattle were running in every direction and I could see horsemen running around there and I heard shooting. A man on horseback then galloped up toward the house and instead of riding on the road, he rode right into a three-wire fence. "He's sure crazy," I thought. "What's the matter? The horse is running away with him." I saw an Indian come out of the arroyo and ride toward him. His horse broke right through the fence and they followed him. These Indians had cut the fence before they had come up. I could barely see there was so much dust.

The man kept leaning his body over the side of the horse and I thought, "Maybe he's been shot." I saw that it was Bill Finn and I thought, "Why don't he do something? He always carries a gun and he's supposed to be such a good shot." I screamed at him, "Do something!" An Indian was right on him then, hitting him with a club, but he never stopped. He just kept spurring his horse and riding on. When he got to the barn he jumped another fence. That horse was scared and wanted to get away.

He hollered to me, "Where are your children?"

"I don't know."

"Get them in the house." He rode down to the men's bunkhouse and jumped off his horse. He ran inside and got a rifle. I ran back into the house and got the sheriff's colt revolver and ran out to where the children played all the time. They weren't on their merry-go-round. They weren't anywhere I could see, not one of them, not a chick or a child anywhere.

Just then two Indians rode right down in front of all those houses that we had there.[11] Finn shot at one of them. He was hid down here behind the warehouse and just as he shot at one, Joe Hosteen Yazzi, whose daughter I had raised, took a deliberate shot at me from behind the blacksmith shop. I took a couple shots at him and the Indians reported to me afterwards that I shot his fingers but I didn't know it was him until later. If somebody's going to shoot at me I'll shoot back. Joe Hosteen Yazzi told Des-glena-spah that he really didn't shoot at me, but that I shot to kill him. I did my best to kill him but I was clear over at my house. "I was just trying to scare her into the house," he said. He always thought a lot of me. I never talked to him about it and I never liked him.

Finn rode around in front of the store and as soon as Joe Hosteen Yazzi vanished from behind the barn, I went in the back where Finn was and said, "What in the world has happened?"

"The Indians attacked us."

"Where's Mr. Wetherill?"

"He's down there."

"But why did you leave him down there? Why didn't you stay and fight, too?"

"I didn't have any cartridges. I thought I had two in my chaps pocket and I tried to get them out but I couldn't have done anything for him if I'da stayed there, anyway."

He paused a minute then said, "I hate to tell you, but Mr. Wetherill's dead." I couldn't believe him.

"What could I do?" Finn said. "They shot him with a rifle and he fell right off his horse." Just then the horse came up. He'd ridden my horse and it was wet with lather and shaking all over.

"I'm going down there," I said.

"No, you can't go down there, you mustn't go down there."

I tried to get on the horse, anyway. "Don't you go down there, you can't do any good. He's dead."

I asked the men in the store, the Gabaldons, to hitch up a wagon. "We shouldn't move him because he's been murdered," they said. "There's a law that says if you move a dead body you're responsible for having done the deed."

"I don't care, I'd just as soon be responsible. I'm not going to leave my husband down there for the coyotes to eat. I'll go get him myself. If somebody will come and help me lift him in I'll go get him but I won't leave him there." They begged me not to go. They said they'd put a man down there to build a fire and watch him, but I stood my ground.

Finally they put a cot in the wagon. They said, "You mustn't touch his clothes or you'll be held responsible."

I said, "I don't care what I'm responsible for, I'm bringing my husband here and I'll take care of him."[12]

They brought him back and put him on the back porch and we put sheets over him to block out the sun. "Your father has been killed," I told the children. "Chis-chilling-begay shot and killed him. I don't want you to go and look at him because I want you to remember him as he was alive, not now." Elizabeth looked anyway and she's always regretted it. Marion doesn't remember him at all and Bob has a slight memory of him, but Dick remembers him well.

The Navajos came and made a circle around Mr. Wetherill's body and sang and danced. I asked them what they were doing, and they said they asked the Great Spirit to forgive them for what they had done. They thought that they would scare somebody, but they didn't intend to kill Mr. Wetherill. The Navajos were just as frightened as children who set a house on fire. They went over to Joe Hosteen Yazzi's house and talked all night about what they could do.

After Chis-chilling-begay killed Mr. Wetherill the Indians told him, "Look at the trouble you got us all into, now. You get away from us, we don't want to have anything to do with you." He rode back down to Blake's and announced that he killed Mr. Wetherill. Of course Blake was horrified.

"Help me, what can I do?" he said.

"You better go see your agent."[13] He told me later he tried to go to sleep but he couldn't and he couldn't eat and so he rode into Shiprock to see Shelton during the night. When he got there, Shelton's first question was, "Who have you told about this besides George Blake?"

"Nobody."

"Any white man see you do it?"

"Nobody but Finn."

He didn't lock him up or anything, he just let him stay around the post there, so I've been told.

Then Talle came off the mesa. "If you'll give me a good horse, I'll be in Gallup by morning. I'll send the authorities here and we'll see what can be done about this."[14] Shelton countermanded the order, said the Indians were not on the warpath, and then he told the Indians not to go near Chaco Canyon.

Tom O'Fallon and Lee Ivy came down from the mesa and said that the Indians had tied them up there, and then afterward they came up and untied them. O'Fallon's sworn statement never mentioned it. He tried to cover up his own inefficiencies.[15]

Mr. Six came the next day with three or four policemen and wanted to know what happened. "I guess you know without my telling you," I said. "Stacher and Shelton have murdered my husband."

He opened his eyes, and said, "Why do you say that?"

"They're responsible for these Indians in the first place and the awful things that they told the Indians that caused them to do this because Stacher was absolutely determined to build a school here in Chaco Canyon. If I were allowed to talk to the Indians I could get a hundred of them within twenty-four hours to testify, but they're afraid, just as you are. You're afraid of losing your job, too."

"Mrs. Wetherill, I've known you a long time and I never knew you felt like that."

"How else should I feel? This was planned."

"Where's Mr. Wetherill. Have you buried him?"

"No, he's on the back porch. Would you like to look at the work you government men have done?" He went back there, and stood there without removing his hat. "Look, you scum of the earth," I said. "Get out of my house and off my premises and don't let me catch you here. I'll shoot you if I ever see you again. Any man that will look at a man that you've known as you have Mr. Wetherill and hasn't got sense enough to remove his hat, is no associate of mine or my family." I ran him off the place and the next time I saw him was in court. He gave valued evidence of what a rage I was in. I wasn't in a rage, I was just telling the truth. He was lucky to get off alive. I could have killed him right there on the porch where Mr. Wetherill was. I've always regretted that I didn't, such a cur as that. That's the kind of man that the government sent out to train the Indians to be white people.[16]

The Indians were frightened. They thought the soldiers would come and kill them and all the traders were sure the Navajos were going to kill them. I was not afraid there'd be more attacks that first night. I was Diné, you know.

The Navajos left their horses tied up on the fence posts in front of the store. That night they never came for them. The next morning I approached the horses speaking in Navajo and pulled off the bridles, and turned the horses loose. I put the bridles on the fence posts, and they stayed there for a long time afterwards.

But I tell you, I lost my mind. I didn't know what to do. I had to be guided by other people. Somebody decided that we'd have to have the coroner there. This was June and it was hot. "We can't keep Mr. Wetherill here long. If they don't come soon I shall go ahead and bury him myself. He's my husband."

Finally the coroner came and they made the coffin and fixed it up and buried him where he always told me he wanted to be buried. "Anybody's liable to die any time," he always said in a laughing way. "I want to be buried right up there next to that big, round rock near the cliff."

"I'll be buried there, too," I said.

"We'll be buried there together then, won't we?" There's now as many as twenty graves because so many of the Indians have wanted to be buried near him. For so long I couldn't look up in that direction where he was buried because I felt he was there. Then I got so I could. [17]

The Indians were told not to come to my house, but we were friends. I'd saved their lives and saved their babies, I'd taken care of them, given them medicine. I fed them when they were poor and helped them in every way we could. They'd come at night and tap on my window and I'd open it and they'd sit outside and talk to me. They asked me if I was all right, if the children were all right and if we had meat to eat or if they could do anything. While Mr. Wetherill was still laying on the porch there they came and talked to me. They didn't obey Shelton or Stacher either one.

One Navajo said, "You're not afraid of us, are you?"

"No, I'm not afraid of you, but how did you know that I'm not afraid of you?"

"Every time we come to your window, you're wide awake and sitting up. If you were afraid you'd cover your head. We know you don't sleep."

We agreed to meet in the arroyo to talk. They could go clear up and down the canyon for miles without ever coming out where anybody would see them. I would go down to the arroyo and see what they wanted. "You've gotten very poor," they said. "You don't eat, you cry too much." I guess those things have to be. It was in my life anyway.

I was confused mentally. I couldn't sleep. After his death, I moved into his little bedroom which had one window, quite a tall, good window, and a fireplace in the corner. One night something wakened me, I can't tell you what it was, and I sat straight up in bed. He hadn't been buried yet, he was still on the back porch. I saw him standing in the doorway just like he used to do. If he'd been away and came home late at night, I'd hear him come into his room and I'd say, "You got back earlier than you thought." He would always come and put his hands up on each side of the door frame into my room and tell me where he'd been or what he'd seen. It must have been a dream or something that I imagined, but he stood there right in that doorway with his hands up as he always did. He shook his head and he looked sad. "I'm so sorry to leave you like this," he said. "I'm so sorry to leave you with all these children and when you know how things are you'll know why I'm feeling so sorry. I won't see you anymore."

I knew afterwards why he talked that way. Fred Hyde had insisted on him insuring his life for twenty-thousand dollars. I didn't know he had bought a policy. Fred Hyde wrote from Paris and said he knew I'd be all right because of the insurance. When I wrote the company about it, they told me he had borrowed on it.

Al Wetherill came right over and stayed with us for several days. Mr. Wetherill never told me about our financial condition, never said anything to me about it at all. Everything seemed to be as normal as it had always been. When we investigated, we found there wasn't any money.[18]

Al gave me a twenty-dollar gold piece. He was the only person that ever gave me a dollar. I never needed it before and wouldn't take it afterwards, too proud. I sold things. Legally I should never have sold anything, but the rugs in the house belonged to me. I sold many of the horses that belonged to Mr. Wetherill and me with the quarter-circle star brand, and the cattle with the triangle bar triangle brand. The Hyde Exploring Expedition stock was branded HEE, so it was easy to determine what was mine to sell and they tried to get me into trouble about that but they never made it. I had to go and prove it in court that it was mine.

One of Welo's daughters brought in some sheep and goats, and the children got on their Shetland ponies with Lee Ivy and gathered up a few others. We only gathered about a hundred fifty sheep out of eight thousand. We never did find a single cow, and we had lots of cattle. We had the Durhams and Jerseys that we kept right in the canyon, milk cows, and I guess we gathered fifty out of several hundred horses we owned. The white people stole the stock, not the Indians. The Indians were too frightened. They didn't know these people that came in and said they were after the Wetherill stock. Shelton told them not to have anything to do with me.

Clayton Wetherill came to Chaco Canyon a couple weeks after Mr. Wetherill's death and told me to get a lawyer.[19] When he left [to attend the arraignments in Farmington] he shook hands with me. "You're not big enough to stand it, I don't believe."

"Stand what?"

"You are in trouble now. Your husband has been killed and everybody will torture you all they can. You'll be gossiped about. They'll accuse you of things. Do you know that you're a very attractive woman?"

"Do you know I've given birth to seven children?"

"That hasn't spoiled you any. You are the chatelaine of Chaco.[20] You'll get along some way, somehow. You'll find your level somewhere and you know your level's pretty high up. You've always lived well. I've met your mother and father and they're fine, educated people. You'll probably meet a lot of commonness before you get through with it but I guess you'll know how to brush it off." With that he said goodbye.

We stayed at Pueblo Bonito through September and I made three trips to court in Aztec between June and September.[21] The trips took three days each and they were a hard and hot three days sleeping on the ground with all the children. There was no one at Pueblo Bonito to take care of them, so they had to come along, and we had to bring a goat along in the wagon to feed Ruth because I didn't have any more milk. She was only six weeks old. On another trip I left the baby with Lee and went with Finn.

Every freighter that came through told my son, Dick, that if they were him, they'd go out and shoot a few Indians. My son had too much good sense, but I had a daughter who would have loved to have done it. I had to get them out of there. They had to go to school, and I couldn't afford a tutor. I decided to move to Farmington for the winter since I had to go there so often. Ivy's mother rented me a nice little home they had just built in Farmington.

I boxed up all my books and we put them in the ruin and nailed it up. I packed some furniture and dishes and silver. We had three wagons loaded with plunder, plus the surrey, two horses for each wagon, two cowboys, and five children. Finn and Ivy brought up the horses, sheep, goats, and cows, and kept them in the barn.

We got established at the house. House chores and children were below Mr. Finn, so Lee helped with the house and the children and Finn took care of the stock out on the pastures. I never went out of the house except to go to court.

Dick was only thirteen and he smoked when I wasn't looking. I found a tobacco pouch once and asked him who it belonged to. He just took it from me without denying or admitting it. He always carried matches and a bottle of strychnine for poisoning coyotes. Made money that way.

We had to get lawyers, of course, but if I'd known what I know now I wouldn't have got any lawyers. Ranahan and Davies were big lawyers in Santa Fe and they took the case for twenty-five hundred dollars. I had to sell everything I could get my hands on to pay them and then Mr. Ranahan only came when the Indian was tried the last time.[22] I spent everything I had to convict that Indian.

Chis-chilling-begay's trial was put off and put off.[23] I thought I would lose my mind. I wanted to kill him myself. I couldn't take much more. Finally the trial came and he was represented by a lawyer from Washington by the name of Clark.[24] I met Clark's train, because I wanted to know what he looked like. He looked like a bulldog. Just as soon as he lit, Shelton began to tell him about the case. "We don't have much chance to win this case. That's Dick Wetherill's wife, she's a fox." I'd heard that said about me before.

The trial drug on in the heat and the poor Indian came in with a breechcloth and G-string on, the perspiration running off him. One by one they cleared the audience who kept egging him on. They questioned Chis-chilling hour after hour, and he wouldn't say anything. The interpreter didn't tell the truth either, to protect the Navajo. Every once in a while I caught up on him and he'd have to correct himself.

I sat next to Mr. Davies while he questioned Chis-chilling. Mr. Davies was getting worried because the Indian hadn't yet admitted to the murder. They were all saying they didn't know who actually shot him. "Ask him if he had a gun," I said to Mr. Davies. Chis-chilling said yes, he had a gun. "Ask him if he pointed it at Mr. Wetherill," I said. Yes, he pointed it. "Did he pull the trigger?" Yes, he pulled the trigger. "Then what happened to Mr. Wetherill when he pulled the trigger?" He fell off the horse dead. He admitted it without intending to. I knew how to approach him, being a Navajo myself. There's the fox in me.

They convicted him for [voluntary] manslaughter and he was to go to the pen in Santa Fe for five to ten years.[25] When Chis-chilling-begay sat in jail in Aztec he asked my forgiveness. "When I was a little boy I went with my father to the San Juan river to catch some horses of ours that had run away," he said. "We saw where the horses went into the river. Father told me to hide in a bush while he swam across to get them. I stood there and hung onto my father's hand and began to cry. I didn't want to be left there alone. A cowboy came down a hill on the other side of the river. We were standing there right on the bank and that cowboy shot and killed my father. That's why I killed Mr. Wetherill. He was a white man."[26]

But how could I forgive Chis-chilling-begay for killing my husband?

Stacher had it all planned to be in Oklahoma while it happened. He didn't fool me a bit and I told him so, too. Shelton, the big man who employed so many people and spent so much government money in the San Juan, would be at home and he'd handle everything. It was just as plain to me that it was planned as though it had been written down on paper and presented to me. Shelton and Stacher did everything in this world they could think of to clear their petticoats. They tried to make it look like Finn had killed Mr. Wetherill but they couldn't do it, because that Indian confessed to George Blake. Blake told me himself that Shelton offered him five thousand dollars to leave the country.[27]

Shelton lost his job, but Stacher cleared his coats with his lies and he just died last year. He's had a long time to suffer over that murder. I hoped he'd live two hundred years so he'd have a longer time to think about it when he was trying to sleep at night but he didn't live long enough as far as I was concerned.

After school was out in May, we went back to Pueblo Bonito. We didn't have much stock left. Indians would find one or two and drive them in right up the canyon. They dared to come see me. They would butcher a cow and bring me meat. They got tired of following Shelton and Stacher's orders to stay away. But no one ever took those bridles off the posts. Before I left I put the bridles on the counter where the store once was. When anyone came in, I'd say, "This was yours, wasn't it?" They'd say, no, they didn't think it belonged to them. But if I stepped out they'd slip it under their blanket and go out with it.

Just as I was leaving Pueblo Bonito, Hosteen Bí'al, my adopted father, came up to me and said, "I'm going with you."

"No, you can't go with me. I'm very poor and I can't take care of you any more. You're getting to be an old man, you don't want to live far away from your people. You are their medicine man."

"You don't care about me," he said.

"I care for you very much. I think of you as my own father. I know some people in Gallup that have a nice store and I think that might be a nice place for you to stay. Anasazi asked them if you could live there and make sand paintings. You can ask him."

"I can't ask him. He's not here."

"You say you can talk to people in the spirit world. Surely he's there."

He looked at me and said, "You don't believe that." But he did move to Gallup and he made sand paintings for them until he died.

NOTES

[1]Richard evicted the Stachers, and they moved to Crownpoint, just southeast of Chaco Canyon, March 7, 1910, where Stacher eventually built his school for the Navajos. Among other things, Stacher was sure Richard was selling liquor to the Indians and that Bill Finn stole horses from the Navajo and marked them with his own brand. After he sold his store, Richard boosted his debts collecting efforts and is said to have rounded up some three hundred horses to offset debts. McNitt said Stacher told Navajos who traded heavily at the store that if Anasazi were to leave Chaco Canyon, their debts would be forgotten.

[2]In November 1909, Talle leased 11,520 acres of railroad land, and Stacher granted him permission to cross Indian lands to reach the acreage he leased as long as he did not camp on the reservation or use Navajo water sources. But Stacher was sure such permission would be taken advantage of, and it was his wish to control leasing as much as possible to protect range land for the Navajos. On May 5, 1910, he begrudgingly recommended that Talle be granted a lease on railroad sections on two townships south and southeast of Seven Lakes, according to Brugge. Grass was good there, but the lakes were rapidly going dry, which may be the reason why he rented pasture from Richard.

[3]Brugge said there were highly variable accounts concerning the ownership of the horse and how it came to be at the hogan of Hosteen Nez Begay, or Hastiin Neez Biye', also known as Antonio Padilla. One story says Richard had given the purebred to his daughter, Elizabeth. Nez Begay stole the horse, and witnesses saw him whipping it as he rode. The Navajos, on the other hand, said either the horse belonged to Nez Begay and he wanted to sell it to Richard, or he had already sold it to Richard, and the horse ran back to Nez Begay's hogan.

In a note to the CIA dated January 31, 1910, Stacher lists Hosteen Nezbega as a policeman who worked for him to keep Spanish-American sheepherders based in Albuquerque and San Rafael from trespassing on the reservation. This interesting bit of trivia seems to have been overlooked by the historians. (See Brugge.)

[4]In her recollections, Marietta confuses Chis-chilling-begay with Nez-Begay as being the one who was confronted by Finn. I made the corrections in the text.

[5]The Navajo version to this story is that Finn accosted Nez Begay at the door of the hogan.

[6]The Navajo version to the story is that Chis-chilling-begay, Nez Begay's brother-in-law, was working in a nearby cornfield when his sister called him to aid her in helping her wounded husband. They dragged him into the shade and concluded he was dead. The problem with this story is that the Navajos probably would not have touched the man if they thought he was dead.

[7]Brugge said Chis-chilling-begay thought Nez Begay was dead and he bought ammunition from Blake, telling him he planned to avenge his brother-in-law's death. Blake then rode the three miles to Nez Begay's hogan were he found him alive but in need of medical attention.

[8]Brugge says Chis-chilling-begay hid his rifle in the rocks then joined a number of Navajos gambling in the arroyo near Pueblo Bonito. Chis-Chilling's testimony said the Navajos were at the Mexican's house near Pueblo Del Arroyo. Their horses were tied nearby, and Welo had a rifle in a scabbard on the horse. There is no mention in the record of black paint.

[9]This is not the conversation that entered the record later on. Apparently, Richard saw the gun and pulled it from Welo's scabbard or hands, emptied the ammunition on the ground, and shattered the stock against a fence post. The Navajos said that Richard cursed and challenged Chis-chilling-begay, although the reason why he did so was never explained. Chis-chilling-begay then asked Richard if he wanted to kill him, and Richard said, "I want your head," which the Navajos took as an allusion to the Anasazi skulls Richard collected. Brugge says that although Chis-chilling-begay had been dissuaded from killing Finn, he was now rearoused enough to get his rifle he had hidden in the bushes. Speculation on whether Richard threw the barrel on the ground or kept it with him as he rode on influenced the outcome of the trial.

[10]Finn said he heard two shots, one that just missed his own head and the other that found its mark in Richard's hand and chest. He saw that Richard was dead, and he fled as the Navajos continued shooting. John Arrington, in his autobiography, and McNitt, described this as an ambush, but the Navajo version resembles a classic western shoot-out. The testimony Shelton gave, which Chis-chilling-begay used as his defense, was that the Navajo got his gun and started back to Pueblo Bonito when he saw Finn and Wetherill galloping toward him with their guns drawn. Wetherill pointed the broken gun barrel at Chis-chilling-begay and fired. The Navajo jumped off his horse and they began shooting at each other. He shot at Wetherill six times until he fell off his horse, then twice at Finn as he ran. He then went to Wetherill lying on the ground and asked him if he was still on the warpath and shot him again in the head at point blank

range. Ten or twelve Navajos were involved at the first encounter, but Finn could name only Tomás Padilla, Billy Williams, Besh Ligai (or Pesh-li-ki), and Tomacito as conspirators in this stage of the episode.

[11]The first Navajo to follow Finn out of Rincon del Camino was Tomás Padilla, and the two who attacked at the house were Tsoh Bik'is (or Tso-Bakis) and Joe Hosteen Yazzi. Brugge said the Navajos near the trading post, assuming he meant Tsoh Bik'is and Joe Hosteen Yazzi, heard the shots and tried to stop Finn during his retreat to the Wetherill home, believing that he had been involved in something. McNitt said these two heard the shots and when they went to investigate, saw Finn and, thinking he was returning for more ammunition, tried to stop him. They said Tsoh Bik'is was not armed, but he may have had a quirt. He was the one who allegedly clubbed Finn. Finn shot Tsoh Bik'is in the side and was later arrested for intention to murder because he verbally threatened the Navajo, but this charge was dropped. The Navajos charged with complicity in one way or another were Hastiin Bik'is, Tomacito, Billy Williams, Tomás Padilla, Besh Ligai, Hosteen Nez Begay, Joe Hosteen Yazzi, and Tsoh Bik'is. McNitt added Juan Ettcity to the list, but he was the only one who was not charged.

[12]The tutor, Eleanor Quick, testified that Talle had come down from the mesa, reported the location of the body and gave orders to move it. She said that when no one volunteered for the chore, she was the one who finally "shamed some Mexican ranchhands into taking her to the body."

[13]Chis-chilling-begay indeed confessed to Blake, and Blake sent him to Shelton at Shiprock with a note Blake wrote stating honestly what the Navajo had done.

[14]Talle rode to Thoreau to send a telegram to Fort Wingate for troops. Everyone concerned believed the Navajos had planned a massacre and would attack the people at Pueblo Bonito. McNitt reported that Talle reached Thoreau, and alerted B.P. Six and Charles Pinkney, and went on to Gallup. As a result of Talle's alarms, riders set out for Pueblo Bonito from three directions. A friend to the Wetherills, George Ransome, was the first to arrive from Gallup at midnight on the twenty-third, and he brought word that Al Wetherill and Sheriff Talle would arrive in the morning. Stacher's clerk, Six, and his stockman, Pinkney (who had replaced Jones), and twelve Indian policemen, arrived from Thoreau sometime during the night but waited until daybreak before storming the ranchhouse. Stacher himself returned from Oklahoma and arrived later that same day (June 23). Twenty-four hours after Richard's death, Justice of the Peace James T. Fay started out at sunset with deputized John and

Paul Arrington. He met Sheriff William F. Dufer of Aztec at Simpson's store in Gallegos Canyon and continued on to Joe Hosteen Yazzi's hogan where they found seven frightened members of the so-called war party. They told Judge Fay that Anasazi had been killed by Chis-chilling-begay, that Bill Finn had been shot, and were wondering when the soldiers would be sent to shoot them. Al Wetherill and Sheriff Talle arrived at Pueblo Bonito expecting three railroad cars full of militia to arrive momentarily, although this order was canceled, perhaps by Shelton, as Marietta suspected.

[15]Apparently Tom O'Fallon slipped away the next morning, and no mention of being tied up appears in the record.

[16]Stacher's clerk, B.P. Six was indicted for carrying a revolver when he went to investigate Richard's death.

[17]Eleanor Quick said she chose the gravesite and attended to the burial.

[18]Marietta was appointed administrator of the estate in August 1910, and discovered a balance of $74.23 in their Albuquerque bank account. George Blake was appointed property appraiser in July and reported the sum value of five thousand dollars for the buildings and material assets. The Navajos owed Richard eight thousand dollars, and the Anglos and Spanish Americans owed about three thousand dollars more. Marietta held notes from Indians amounting to $1,519. She was able to collect about ninety-three dollars and fifty cents. George's younger brother, Albert Blake, collected $785 in cash and goods that amounted to $2695 in trade. Tomacito was hired as a police escort for Blake at $2.50 a day to pay off his four- or five-hundred-dollar debt to the estate. Marietta filed suit against Stacher for eight thousand dollars for interfering with the collection of debts and got an injunction against him to restrain him from further interference. The injunction was lifted as a result of a hearing, and Stacher considered suing her for libel and charging her with perjury. She continued to complain about the disappearance of her stock, and he was unable to offer any information on it other than Tomás Padilla seemed to have some of her stock, but he denied it. She was unable to give him any proof of who had her stock on what shares. Stacher tried to get money from her to pay what the estate owed the Indians. In the meantime, Shelton criticized Stacher for allowing Blake to use overtly coercive collecting methods, and Finn was accused of stealing more horses. (See Brugge and McNitt.)

[19]According to McNitt, on June 27 a Navajo brought word of Richard's death to Clayton and John Wetherill, who were excavating with Dr. Prudden at Marsh Pass in Arizona two hundred miles west of Chaco Canyon.

They dropped their work and drove night and day to the Wetherill ranch. At Pueblo Bonito they found Marietta and Miss Quick attending to the ranch affairs, with a couple "slow-witted" cowboys and three children searching for the lost stock. Six and Pinkney were harassing their every move. Al and Talle had returned to Gallup, and Finn was facing arraignment in Farmington for shooting Tsoh Bik'is. In Farmington they heard that Shelton was spreading slanderous stories about Richard. "The object of Pinkney and Six, it appears, was to put a decisive end to any communication or cooperation between the Chaco Navajos and Richard Wetherill's widow," McNitt wrote. "If this also brought ruin upon the ranch, Shelton's desire that 'this nest should be cleaned out' would be realized." Gallup police ringed the ranch and the Navajos were ordered to stay away from the canyon, to stop digging wells for the Wetherill's stock, or herding their stock spread out over many miles. McNitt says the Navajos were also told they didn't have to pay off their debts.

[20]Actually it was Dr. Prudden who called her the chatelaine of Chaco.

[21]Several preliminary trials were held in the summer of 1910 and the grand jury proceedings were held in November in Aztec, New Mexico. Chis-chilling-begay was indicted for first-degree murder and placed under Shelton's custody until trial. Charges against Joe Hosteen Yazzi, Tomacito, Hastiin Tsoh Bik'is, and Billy Williams were dropped. Tomás Padilla and Pesh-la-ki were charged with assault with intent to kill and were released on five-hundred-dollars bond each. As well as the charge of assault on Hastiin Tsoh Biye', Finn was charged for assaulting Hosteen Nez Begay and for stealing Hastiin Tsoh Biye's calf. Too late, he filed a charge against Nez Begay for stealing and killing the Wetherill horse, but that was dismissed.

[22]Counsel for the prosecution included attorneys Edwards and Martin of Farmington, District Attorney Alexander Reed of Santa Fe, and Assistant District Attorney E.P. Davies. Marietta hired Reed and Davies.

[23]Chis-chilling-begay's trial in Farmington began in June 1912, nearly two years after Richard's death. Tsoh Biye' died in March 1912, so those charges against Finn were dropped. Finn was to stand trial for his assault against Nez Begay in Santa Fe in October, but Paul Arrington took the Navajo on a horse-buying trip, so the trial was not held until December. Finn received a suspended jail term and was assessed court costs. The remaining Navajos still under indictment were tried and found innocent. (Brugge said the three Navajos indicted and released on bond until found innocent were Joe Hosteen Yazzi, Hastiin Tsoh Biye' and Tomás Padilla, conflicting with McNitt's report.)

[24]The defendant's lawyer was Charles Johnson of Durango. Shelton also secured William A. Palmer and U.S. District Attorney H.W. Clark of Las Vegas.

[25]He was paroled June 11, 1915, and died at his home near Chaco Canyon in 1950, at about age eighty.

[26]On September 19, 1890, Indian Agent Vandever reported to the CIA the murder of Thez-chilla who Brugge thinks was Chishci'ili, Curly Hair. Thez-chilla went off the reservation north of Farmington with his wife and son and two other Navajo couples to hunt deer. A white man named John Cox and four companions stole a blanket from Thez-chilla and when tracked by the Indians, refused to give it up. The cowboys drove the Navajos off, and as they retreated, one of the horses stumbled, and a Navajo's rifle accidentally discharged. The whites immediately opened fire, and Cox killed Thez-chilla. Although Vandever wished to present the Navajo's argument to a jury, Cox was never tried because of "skillful manipulation of court dates." The Navajo expected equal treatment in this case, because they'd heard that another Navajo had been sentenced to twenty-five years for killing a white man in Arizona.

Chis-chilling-begay included in his statement of August 1910, two months after the murder, some incriminating accusations about Richard that were either fabricated for his self-defense plea or should have been used as motive for premeditated murder. He said Richard shot any Indian horse or burro that strayed into his pasture, then cut them open and put poison in them to kill coyotes. He had been subject to some of Richard's extreme methods of debt collecting, and in one case he was handcuffed and threatened to be taken to Aztec if he did not pay up. Chis-chilling gave him some sheep and a blanket. Another time, Richard threatened to kill him with a butcher-knife if he did not make payment, and again he gave him some sheep.

[27]Brugge says Marietta was the only one to cite overt land conflict as a factor in Richard's murder, and in fact, "Her account is full of such striking disagreements with contemporary sources that it is probably one the of the least reliable that exists, in spite of its detail." He goes on to say, "The several versions of the event present so much conflicting detail that a completely unbiased narrative cannot easily be constructed today." Marietta's conspiracy theory may be correct, however, because McNitt said Shelton first tried to have Finn charged for murdering Wetherill over his love for Marietta. On the other hand, Finn actually believed Chis-chilling-begay meant to kill him. Finn told John Arrington that the first bullet was meant

for him, and Chis-chilling-begay had to resight in order to kill Richard because the Indian stood between them.

Nevertheless, the agents worked feverishly to cover something up. Mc-Nitt found a copy of a letter Dr. Prudden wrote to the Commissioner of Indian Affairs demanding an investigation of the murder, citing, point by point, the evidence of conspiracy and slander committed by Shelton and Stacher. One point of evidence was an article in the *Farmington Enterprise* stating that Shelton admitted the murder was premeditated. Shelton later corrected the remark, and the editor of the *Enterprise* was forced to print a retraction in which he apologized for publishing Shelton's confidential statement but did not admit to misquoting him. The CIA investigated without Prudden's knowledge and compiled a thousand-page document of affidavits given to agent Maj. James McLaughlin stating that Richard was a brutal tyrant. Most of the material was provided by Shelton or people loyal to the Indian agency, McNitt said. Some of these affidavits have been published in Brugge's report on the Chaco Navajos and the dates for most of the information postdated Richard's murder. The document did not include Prudden's letter, which was said to have been "lost."

Shelton became involved in a few more controversial matters not related to the Wetherill case resulting in protests by Navajos. His resignation was accepted in 1916.

Epilogue

I Was a Gypsy the Rest of My Life

I WAS A GYPSY the rest of my life. Less than a year after Mr. Wetherill died I moved from Pueblo Bonito to the Jemez Mountains above Cuba on a piece of land I bought from Epimenio Miera of Cuba.[1] He and his wife came out to Pueblo Bonito in the winter to ask me to come and see it. In the spring we rode up there and there was snow on the northern hillsides that bogged down my mare. Ponderosa pines lined both sides of the wide valley and trout jumped in three streams running through the land.

"I'll take it," I told the man.

"Poco, poco," he said. Make haste slowly. There was no house on the hundred sixty acres.

We rode back down to Cuba and Mr. Miera and I agreed he would take all the mules of mine my cowboys could find, plus some rugs, in trade for the land. Mr. Miera was a wealthy man.

We were able to find ten mules, and I wrote Mr. Miera asking him if that was enough. He said eight would pay for the ranch and the two others would buy whatever groceries and supplies I needed.

I packed up all our plunder, locked the doors, and set out once more to Cuba. Six miles from Cuba we turned right into Señorita Canyon which goes over the mountains into Jemez Springs and sometimes washes out. We camped at an old corral and had a big bonfire. It was so cool and lovely after so much misery down in Chaco. We started early the next morning and almost reached Rio Las Vacas, which I always called Mountain Lion Hill. The hills were getting steeper all the time. The surrey wouldn't go up one hill so I waited behind in it with the children while the cowboys drove the other wagons up the hill, even though the horses balked. Marion and Ruth were restless so I let them out and then went on up to help drive the wheel team. Those horses just flew up the hill and I had to run to keep up with them while trying to stay out of their way. At the top of the hill I heard those kids screaming. They'd followed me up the hill through a spring and they were muddy and bawling.

We got to the place we were going to live on the third day. A stream, fifteen feet wide, ran by the house we built. Ferns grew everywhere and the wild raspberries and strawberries were in bloom. There wasn't a day I didn't see at least five deer come down to that spring and drink and they paid no more attention to us than if we weren't there.

Finn and Ivy started gathering Mr. Miera's cattle, and my children started taking care of the horses. Elizabeth could ride anything on four legs. I boarded Mr. Miera's men, too, and that gave me my groceries, and I had Maria and Antonio there doing the cooking. I didn't have much to do but be happy and take care of my babies.

I saw some of the most marvelous sights there. I stood on that porch, that open room with the one open side, when we'd have those terrific lightning storms and the thunder sounded like it was tearing the earth in two. I would see it strike those big pine trees and make kindling of them. I saw a lightening bolt hit a big tree right in the top and run right down the tree into the ground. The crack of that thunder sounded like a pistol shot. I never knew how terrific nature was until I sat there with my children and watched those storms. I had forgotten how beautiful trees were and how lovely it was to have the water right there at the door and that beautiful spring with those deer coming down. I'd walk outside the door and they'd stand there and look at me with those big, brown eyes, and go on ahead and drink and walk away.

The house was on a prominent point fifty feet above a creek. After I got over worrying about the children getting lost I let them go down there. They dammed up the stream and one of them went upstream to drive down the fish while the other one stayed at the dam and grabbed them as they came by. They weren't large trout, about eight inches long. Elizabeth was quick, she acted like she was going to catch a fly the way she poised herself waiting to flip the fish out. Maria fried them crisp and nice.

The house was always full of flowers, wild white and blue iris lilies. Later on in the summer the berries got ripe and it was nothing for those children to pick a three-pound lard bucketful. I put some up. One time Elizabeth came up to the house and told me a very big man was picking the raspberries, too. She'd seen his tracks.

My children learned to track from the day they could walk. The tracks turned out to belong to a grizzly.

Ruth was a big, healthy baby, about a year old in June when one day she came and put her face in my lap while I was sewing. She just slumped to the floor. I picked her up and saw she was having a convulsion. That was the first indication of illness I'd ever seen her have. I took her into the kitchen and told Maria to get some hot water quick, and some cold. We put her into a hot bath with mustard in it and wrapped cold towels around her head. After a few minutes she came out of it.

I immediately sent for the doctor down in Jemez. The old man said babies had convulsions when they were teething and maybe she was teething. She seemed to be all right, but she had a funny little cough, although she didn't have a cold. The doctor didn't know what was wrong. I'd take her out doors and the cough would go away, but as soon as I brought her back into the house, the cough would come back. We moved our beds to the porch and slept out there in the open. I thought she could have been like those people who couldn't be around wool or feathers.

She seemed to be fine in the next two weeks although she still couldn't go into the house. One evening I was feeding her and Marion. The sun hadn't set yet but the clouds sank down the mountains like they were going to smother me. It made me feel kind of oppressed and the air seemed rare. Bob and Elizabeth were on the river fishing. Marion and Ruth sat in their high chairs and all of a sudden Ruth just straightened out and she was dead.

Maria and I did everything in the world we could. We put her in hot water and we massaged her. In half an hour she turned kind of a bluish-black on one side. She was paralyzed and had a stroke. It was her heart and she needed more oxygen, that's why she stayed outside. She died June 22, 1911, exactly a year after Mr. Wetherill had died.

I thought I couldn't take it, it was just too much. But I did. I had my other children. Everything comes to me kind of the hard way, don't it? There were so many violets, white and blue, all over the mountain, and the children went out and fixed her a nice little coffin and put her in it and covered her with violets. We buried her in the mountain, and I wouldn't mind resting there myself.

I didn't talk about her to the children for twenty years. You see, I'm very selfish. I only think of myself. Everyone told me to get away, but I had to make a living and help gather Mr. Miera's cattle.

Mr. Miera came and told me I wouldn't be able to stay there in the winter. "You'll have to come down to the valley with your horses," he said. "They'll know when it's time and just come down by themselves. You won't need to worry."

We moved down to Cuba and there weren't many public schools at the time. I put Robert with the brothers and Elizabeth with the sisters in Jemez. Robert tended to the altar and swept out the church for his room and board. The schools enrolled mainly children from Jemez Pueblo. Richard went to school in Cuba. The teachers didn't speak English, so he became a Spanish scholar.

Ivy and Finn spent the winter gathering cattle. Miera sold his ranch to a senator in Santa Fe. Finn came back and asked me how much money I had and I said I had a little. "Now that I've got all of the Miera cattle out of the mountains, all the Mexicans are trying to sell me their brands. I think it would a good thing to invest in cattle and buy those brands up." With my permission, Finn traded my interest in land at Chaco Canyon that held that section of coal for a hundred cows and a hundred calves. I didn't mind. I knew that land wouldn't be worth anything for another hundred years and I knew I wasn't going to live that long.[2] Mr. Wetherill wouldn't have minded, either. All he wanted was protection for the ruins.

Juan Sandoval, a young friend of mine, advised me to take up a small holding of one hundred fifty-nine acres of land anywhere that belonged to the government. It was the government's plan to encourage people to establish farms and ranches in that country. I already knew of a place on the Rio Puerco about a mile above Gonzalitos that took in the river on both sides. It was right in a little rincon bordered by a white and yellow sandstone cliff. Not far from there I discovered the place where the Spanish had smelted the gold from some mine. I found hundreds of adobe crucibles they used for molds.

I built an L-shaped house there up in the pines out of ten-foot piñon poles covered with mud and straw. Elizabeth and I were expert mudders. Bob and I chopped down the logs and drug them with a team and leveled the ground. I worked like a man all the time. We finished the house in the fall of 1912.

I don't remember just how long I lived there. Finn and Ivy stayed with me all those years. They called me Mother because I always mended and washed and ironed their clothes. Finn worked on the herd and he bought brands, too. He'd sit in barrooms and talk to the old men who used to run cattle but were too old now to ride the range. He'd buy their brands for ten dollars in my name and gather up the strays that wore the brands. That's how he increased the stock. The herd grew so large that there were just too many to keep in the Rio Puerco Valley and the grass wasn't too good. The cowboys told me we would have to find a new headquarters. We moved to Luciana's Lake on the other side of Mesa Portales, twenty miles from Cuba.

People said Epimenio Miera was an old rascal and a thief and pretty severe with the people who worked for him, but that wasn't the way I knew him. Epimenio moved to Cuba with his brother Wencesalo when they were young. Wencesalo became engaged to a beautiful woman and while he was away buying her trousseau, Epimenio moved in and married her. Wencesalo married her sister and became a wealthy man. Epimenio built his wealth with his big store in Cuba. But his wife fell off a horse and became a cripple, so Epimenio took a mistress in Gonzalitos, and Wencesalo became a drunk.

Well, I had to have friends. Anyway, Epimenio advised me to go to Luciano's Lake and build an adobe house as big as I wanted on the sandy hill, which I did. I never could reconcile Mr. Wetherill's or Ruth's death but these moves didn't bother me one particle. It had grama grass about two feet high, God's own country for cows and horses. I rented two townships of land there and fenced it, and it took us all summer to build the house. We took our doors and windows from the old house, and I sent to Albuquerque for big, double windows. The floors were just like the ones I saw in the pueblos. We mixed mud with salt, ashes, and beef blood we saved after butchering. We spread the mixture a few inches at a time and I'd smooth it over with a wet sheepskin while I knelt on sheepskin-covered boards. We planted fruit trees, and wheat that we flooded from the lake, and oats that grew as high as my head, and there was one time I had five hundred ducks.

Fred Hyde came from France and lived in one of the bedrooms where the cowboys slept when they were home, but they were rarely home. The beef we ate, we'd dry great chunks of it. I could always trade beef for beans and I had corn. I never paid for anything, but traded a horse here and there to Mr. Miera for my groceries. I never went into debt to the people who were good to me.

Chaco Canyon still haunted me even then. Sheriff Dufer came out and arrested me on a bench warrant, dead or alive, on account that I hadn't appeared in court. The postmistress of Cuba saw this registered letter come in and she didn't know what to do with it, so she just put it up in a pigeonhole and never delivered it to me.

The snow then was deep and it was a terrible time of year for me to make the trip. "I don't see the necessity," I said to Sheriff Dufer.

"The court isn't satisfied with the way you're paying the debts," he said.

"How can I pay the debts when the white people have stolen everything that I wasn't sitting on? I sold everything I owned to pay the lawyers and I had no more money to pay the debts. I didn't know I owed money."

"Why are you hiding out here, then?"

"I didn't know that I was hiding." I had a nice four-bedroom house with a living room and dining room. I had my piano and all my lovely rugs.

"You'll have to talk to the judge about it."

The sheriff didn't want to wait until I got someone from Cuba to take care of the children. We left as soon as I could get ready. My cowboys wanted to kill him, burn his wagon, kill his horse, and bury him where nobody could ever find them. I told them they were crazy. Finn went with me and Sheriff Dufer had two deputies and they were all afraid of Finn's marksmanship. We stopped at Hatch on the first night and Mrs. Hatcher found a rock to heat to keep at my feet on the trip. The next day the snow was deeper and the wind was blowing and it was cold. I saw signal fires and I mentioned them to the deputy next to me.

Dufer jumped up, "Where?"

"Don't you see on those points down the canyon there? There's one over here and there's one over there and I saw two further back."

"Do you suppose the Indians are on the warpath?"

"I wouldn't know. I wouldn't think they are." He sure drove after that. The further we went the more signal fires we found and to this day I don't know what that was. Dufer kept telling Finn to ride ahead and break the trail. He didn't like Finn behind him.

We got to Aztec and went to court. The judge asked why I hadn't come and I said I hadn't been notified. "I sent a registered letter notifying you to come."

"I doubt very much I would have come this time of year," I said. "It's a terrible trip for a woman to take and I'm leaving a little girl with one little old cowboy."

"I held court to discharge you from being administrator of the estate and put Mr. Pierce, the banker, in charge."

"Good, I'm certainly glad you've done that because I didn't ever want to be administrator of the estate because there wasn't any." I told him the whole story about Stacher and Shelton ordering the Indians to turn loose the thousands of sheep out on shares.

"Well, Mrs. Wetherill, they're treating you kind of rough, aren't they?"

"I'm getting used to rough treatment. I've had several years of it and I'm getting awfully tired of it."

The judge discontinued the hearing and never resumed it. Sheriff Dufer had to take me back and how I enjoyed that. He brought along his two deputies to protect himself against Finn, not me. I could protect myself. I carried a gun and they never knew what moment me or Finn would shoot him.

Finn died in 1918 in Kansas City of pneumonia. He had taken a carload of steers there for me and ten carloads for another man. McNitt told me the people over on the San Juan said that Finn was in love with me and that I was fond of him, which I was, but not in that way. I needed him to help run the cattle and horses. That was the only way to make a living and to send my children to school. So I hung on to him and he was always nice to me though he got kind of mad at me occasionally with some of my ideas. He told me what was what, too, and I'd see he was right. But they said he was in love with me; if he was I never knew. He never declared it to me. He went with girls all the time. Women were crazy over him. Some-body would tell me they heard I married Bill Finn. I'd say, "For the relief of all you people, whenever I marry, I'll wear a placard on my back stating the date and name of the man I married."

I liked Mr. Hyde very much and he knew how to be nice to a lady but as far as marrying him, that was a different matter. You can respect a man and like his company without marrying him. The same way with a man, he don't want to marry. I never dreamed Mr. Hyde wanted to marry me, but I found out later that he did and I didn't have sense enough to know it at the time.

I want to live long enough to see the world give Mr. Wetherill credit for what he did. I don't care about myself, I just want someone to get it down about what he did and the sort of person he was. I will tell you this: if we could put the time back and I was a girl again there is no man I would want to marry but Mr. Wetherill.

I wanted to learn all about the Indians. I came pretty close to doing it. I lived among them most of my whole life, and the more I learn about them the more I know that I don't know all about them. I've learned they're my superiors.

Marietta Palmer Wetherill said she lived like a gypsy the rest of her life, but she did not refer to much of it in her taped recollections. She moved from New Mexico to operate a small ranch and trading post at Chambers, Arizona, and worked in stores in Utah. She moved to a little house on Peach Avenue in Albuquerque, New Mexico, during her later years. She died in her sleep there at age 77 on July 11, 1954. Her ashes were buried in Richard's grave along the cliff near Pueblo Bonito.

NOTES

[1]On another tape she called the land Piños Negros and implied that she already owned it and that it was signed by President McKinley personally. William McKinley served as president between 1897 and 1901. On yet another tape she wasn't sure if Richard had bought her that land as a respite from the hot summers of Chaco Canyon or if she bought the land from Epimenio Miera after Richard's death.

[2]Marietta deeded the Chaco section to which they had title to Epimenio A. Miera in August 1911, although the sale had been made in April 1911. The patent to Richard's homestead claim was granted November 4, 1912, two and one-half years after his death, according to McNitt. Brugge says that on October 5, 1912, 12.98 acres of the Wetherill homestead went to Roger, Marietta's son. She had sons Richard and Robert, but no Roger. Marietta mentions several times that the land was sold for taxes. She believed Professor Edgar Hewett finagled it for the university. She is probably referring to the University of New Mexico, with which Hewett became associated a decade or two later and which entered into joint archaeological projects with the National Park Service until the 1970s. It now houses the archives for whatever Chaco material did not go to the Smithsonian Institution. On June 27, 1912, Charles F. Spader was appointed postmaster and weatherman at Putnam (Pueblo Bonito) to succeed Richard and reportedly lived in the ruins and began trading there.

|| ▲ ||

Bibliography and Sources

Published Works

Austin, Martha and Regina Lynch. *Saad Ahaah Sinil, Dual Language, A Navajo-English Dictionary*. Rough Rock, Arizona: Navajo Curriculum Center, Rough Rock Demonstration School, 1983.

Bahti, Tom. *Southwestern Indian Ceremonials*. Las Vegas, Nevada: K.C. Publications, 1970. Revised by Mark Bahti, 1982.

Bailey, L.R. *Bosque Redondo: An American Concentration Camp*. Pasadena: Socio-Technical Books, 1970.

Bailey, L.R. *The Long Walk: A History of the Navajo Wars, 1846-68*. Los Angeles: Westernlore Press, 1964.

Brugge, David M. *A History of the Chaco Navajos*. Albuquerque: Division of Chaco Research, National Park Service, U.S. Department of the Interior, 1980.

Cather, Willa. *The Professor's House*. New York: Alfred A. Knopf, 1925.

Fletcher, Maurine S., ed. *The Wetherills of the Mesa Verde: the Autobiography of Benjamin Alfred Wetherill*. London: Associated University Presses, 1977.

Frazier, Kendrick. *People of Chaco: A Canyon and Its Culture*. New York: W.W. Norton & Company, Inc., 1986.

Gabriel, Kathryn. *Roads to Center Place: A Cultural Atlas of Chaco Canyon and the Anasazi*. Boulder: Johnson Books, 1991.

Hrdlička, Aleš. *Physiological and Medical Observations Among the Indians of Southwestern United States and Northern Mexico*. Bureau of American Ethnology Bulletin 34. Washington, D.C.: Smithsonian Institution, 1908.

Iverson, Peter. *The Navajo Nation*. Albuquerque: University of New Mexico Press, 1981.

Judd, Neil M. "Everyday Life in Pueblo Bonito." *The National Geographic* 48:3 (1925) 227–262.

Judd, Neil M. "Intramural Burials." In Neil M. Judd, *The Material Culture of Pueblo Bonito*. Washington: Smithsonian Institution, 1954.

Lamar, Howard Roberts. *The Far Southwest, 1846-1912: A Territorial History*. New York: W.W. Norton & Company, Inc. 1970.

Lekson, Stephen H. "The Idea of Kiva in Anasazi Archaeology." *The Kiva* 53:3 (1988) 213–234.

Lister, Robert H., and Florence C. Lister. *Chaco Canyon: Archaeology and Archaeologists*. Albuquerque: University of New Mexico Press, 1981.

MacDonald, Eleanor D., and John B. Arrington. *The San Juan Basin: My Kingdom was a County*. Denver: Green Mountain Press, 1970.

Matthews, Washington. *Navajo Legends*. Boston: American Folklore Society, 1987.

Matthews, Washington. "The Night Chant: a Navaho Ceremony." *Memoirs of the American Museum of Natural History* 6. New York: Knickerbocker Press, 1902.

Matthews, Washington. "Noqoìlpi, The Gambler: A Navajo Myth." *The Journal of American Folklore*, 2:5 (1889) 89–94.

McNitt, Frank. *Richard Wetherill: Anasazi, Pioneer Explorer of Southwestern Ruins*, Revised edition. Albuquerque: The University of New Mexico Press, 1966.

Niederman, Sharon. *A Quilt of Words: Women's Diaries, Letters, & Original Accounts of Life in the Southwest (1860-1960)*. Boulder: Johnson Books, 1988.

Pepper, George H. *Pueblo Bonito. Anthropological Papers of the American Museum of Natural History* 27. New York: American Museum of Natural History, 1920.

Prescott, William H. *The Conquest of Mexico and The Conquest of Peru*. New York: The Modern Library, 1843.

Prudden, T. Mitchell. "An Elder Brother to the Cliff Dwellers." *Harper's New Monthly Magazine* (June 1897) 56–62.

Reichard, Gladys A. *Navajo Religion*. Tucson: The University of Arizona Press, 1983. Originally published by Princeton University Press, 1974.

Schmedding, Joseph. *Cowboy and Indian Trader*. Caldwell: Caxton, 1951.

Simpson, James H. "Journal of a Military Reconnaissance from Santa Fe, New Mexico, to the Navajo Country." Reports of the Secretary of War, Sen. Exec. Doc. 64, 31st Congress, 1st Session, Washington, D.C., 1850. Reprinted by the University of Oklahoma Press, 1964.

Stephens, John Lloyd. *Incidents of Travel in Central America, Chiaps and Yucatán*. New York: Dover Publications, Inc., 1969. Originally published in 1842.

Stephens, John Lloyd. *Incidents of Travel in Yucatán* 2. Norman: University of Oklahoma Press, 1962. Originally published in 1843.

Terkel, Studs. Interview by Tony Hillerman on *Second Century*. Kathryn Gabriel, producer. Albuquerque: KNME-TV, December 1989.

Tozzer, Alfred Marston. "Notes on Religious Ceremonials of the Navaho." In *Putnam Anniversary Volume, Anthropological Essays Presented to Frederick Ward Putnam in Honor of his Seventieth Birthday, April 16, 1909*. New York: G.E. Stechert & Co. Publishers, 1909.

Underhill, Ruth. *Here Come the Navaho!* Bureau of Indian Affairs. Lawrence Kansas: Haskell Indian Institute, 1953. Reprinted by Treasure Chest Publications, n.d.

Wetherill, Marietta. "Adventure in Anthropology," as told to Mabel C. Wright, *New Mexico Magazine* (July 1954) 22, 41, 56.

Wetherill, Marietta. "Death of a Medicine Man," as told to Grace French Evans. *Scribner's Magazine* (May 1932) 304–308.

Wetherill, Marietta. "My Friend Geronimo," as told to Mabel C. Wright. *Sun Trails Magazine* (February 1953) 22–23.

Wetherill, Marietta. "When My Trail Crossed Geronimo's," as told to Mabel C. Wright. *Sun Trails Magazine* (May 1952) 6–7.

Young, Robert W., and William Morgan. *The Navajo Language: A Grammar and Colloquial Dictionary*. Albuquerque: University of New Mexico Press, 1980.

Unpublished Works

Dinwiddie, Douglas M. "Louis Blachly and the Pioneers Foundation: An Early Oral History Project in Southwestern New Mexico." Paper presented at the annual conference of the Historical Society of New Mexico, April 19, 1985. Copy on file at the Center for Southwest Research at the University of New Mexico General Library.

McNitt, Frank. "Interviews with Mrs. Richard Wetherill April 24, 1952, and September 15, 1952." Frank McNitt Collection, Wetherill Papers, Holsinger Box II, State Records Center and Archives, Santa Fe, New Mexico.

Vivian, Gordon. Memorandum to Superintendent McNeil, Chaco Canyon National Monument. Subject: Interview with Mrs. Marietta Wetherill, October 29, 1948. Manuscript at Chaco Culture National Historic Park.

Wetherill, Marietta. Oral History. Audio tapes by Lou Blachly. Center for Southwest Research, University of New Mexico General Library, Albuquerque, New Mexico.

The following is an approximate breakdown of the specific Marietta Wetherill tapes used in each chapter of this book as referred to by their number assigned by the Center for Southwest Research at the University of New Mexico General Library. Because of the intricate editing of her tapes, it is impossible to list every tape that was used, but it is hoped the list will be of some service to scholars and researchers. Please keep in mind Marietta's words were not printed verbatim in this book.

Chapter One: 423, 427, 433, 467
Chapter Two: 424, 426, 427, 428, 430, 432, 435
Chapter Three: 426, 428, 440, 441, 457, 497
Chapter Four: 423, 433, 435, 438, 442, 443, 448, 462, 468
Chapter Five: 438, 439, 441, 454, 455, 463, 471, 497
Chapter Six: 438, 498
Chapter Seven: 423, 439, 442, 446, 447, 448, 449, 455, 457, 463, 467, 470
Chapter Eight: 423, 443, 448, 454
Chapter Nine: 423, 450, 450, 451, 461, 471
Chapter Ten: 451, 453, 454, 473, 447, 470
Chapter Eleven: 464, 473, 483
Chapter Twelve: 426, 443, 449, 454
Chapter Thirteen: 423, 434, 449, 448, 453, 455, 457, 470
Chapter Fourteen: 458, 459, 463, 491
Chapter Fifteen: 460, 461, 462, 463, 464, 465, 466, 494, 495
Chapter Sixteen: 433, 441, 443, 453, 478, 496
Chapter Seventeen: 435, 476, 477, 478, 479, 480
Chapter Eighteen: 448, 449, 451, 452, 453, 468, 470, 471
Chapter Nineteen: 426, 461, 470, 471, 472, 481, 483, 485, 490
Chapter Twenty: 483, 484, 485, 486
Epilogue: 472, 473, 485, 486, 487, 488, 490

Acknowledgments

SPECIAL THANKS TO SHARON NIEDERMAN for bringing the oral history of Marietta Wetherill to my attention in her book, *A Quilt of Words: Women's Diaries, Letters and Original Accounts of Life in the Southwest, 1860-1960*. Much appreciation to photo archivist Ronald Xavier Montoya of the State Records Center and Archives in Santa Fe, New Mexico, for helping me find the photographs for this book, most of which were previously unpublished; and Judy Murphy, Kathleen Ferris, Kathy Gienger, John Grassham, Terry Bugliotta, Stella De Sa Rego, Rose Diaz, and B. Michael Miller at the Center for Southwest Research at the University of New Mexico General Library for endlessly exhuming the dusty transciptions of Marietta Wetherill's tapes from the basement. And to Barbara Johnson Mussil, Michael McNierney, and Richard Croog, for believing so wholeheartedly in this project.